ACCLAIM FOR *THE DECISION SERIES* ™

Acclaim for *The Second Decision*

A classic entrepreneurial and leadership self-awareness journey!

Verne Harnish

Founder, Entrepreneurs' Organization and Gazelles; Author of Scaling Up, Mastering the Rockefeller Habits, *and* The Greatest Business Decisions of All Time

I love this book and I will be giving copies to every business client I coach. It is well written, incredibly well researched, and pulls no punches. As you read this book you get the feeling that Randy is reading your mind. This book is written the way you, as an entrepreneur, relate to and think. The end result is a clear path to grow in your role as a leader and entrepreneur, as it challenges you to look inside yourself by answering tough questions throughout. Read it, grow from it, and share it with every entrepreneur you know.

Rich Russakoff

"Coach To The Best"; Author, Make Banks Compete to Lend Your Money

The Second Decision is a must read for every entrepreneurial leader— male or female—regardless of the industry you operate in … the information applies to all and all should apply it!"

M. Louise Jurkowski

Entrepreneur, Chair of Leadership North Carolina; Founder of BJAC (now EYP), one of the largest woman-owned architectural firms in the southeast

I encourage you to use Randy's Entrepreneurial Qual Card very objectively, which may mean letting others help you assess the answers. Far too often I observe that for many entrepreneurial leaders commitment means "I know I should," or "I really want to," or "I'm going to really try." That's not what will get the job done to become a qualified entrepreneur.

Bill Buxton

Master Chair, Vistage International; thirteen-time Chair Excellence Award; Global CEO Peer Advisory Group

Reading Randy's book and completing his Qual Card will go a long way in assisting the entrepreneur with that all-important second decision to launch and leave or launch and lead—and win! After thirty years of naval service, ten years of senior executive corporate leadership, and now five years in higher education, I passionately believe that *The Second Decision* is a must read for entrepreneurs at all stages of the corporate life cycle, and for every potential senior-level executive/leader!

R. E. "Benny" Suggs

Rear Admiral, US Navy (retired); Associate Vice Chancellor, NC State University

Great read for bootstrappers and venture capital–backed entrepreneurs alike. Every founder must decide what they want to do when they grow up. But whoever thought such a hard decision is best made right as your company starts to hit it big? Make the right decision and you'll turn your current rocket ship into a repeatable process that is more valuable than any single exit.

Aaron W. Houghton

Serial Entrepreneur, Co-Founder at iContact.com, Co-Founder and CEO at BoostSuite.com; #4 Most Influential CEOs under 30 —Small business website Under30CEO, 2011

Acclaim for *The Third Decision*

Over my fifty-year business career, there are few thought leaders who bring forth a business idea that is profound and will reshape the way we think. Peter Drucker, Dale Carnegie, Napoleon Hill, Jim Collins, Michael Gerber, Patrick Lencioni, Malcom Gladwell, and Simon Sinek come to mind. I believe Randy Nelson's concepts of *The Third Decision* and The Decision Series for Entrepreneurs® are in this illustrious list.

Tony Hutti
CEO/Owner, Renaissance Executive Forums™

A thought-provoking and insightful new book from Randy Nelson picking up from where his first book, *The Second Decision*, leaves off, flipping the table to the personal side. Using his own brand of storytelling and exercises, Randy challenges leaders to identify their own list of nonnegotiables, those areas of their personal life where they are not willing to compromise ... as well as provoking us to ask the difficult question, "Are we setting ourselves up for regret personally, when we focus on our business, to the exclusion of all else?"...

Cheryl Beth Kuchler
Founder and President, CEO Think Tank®

The Third Decision reads both like a detailed guide and a conversation with a wise and trusted mentor. Randy Nelson clearly knows entrepreneurs ...

Dan Sullivan
Founder, The Strategic Coach, Inc.

The Third Decision will be the most important book Randy will write … It is possible to build and run successful businesses while enjoying a magical family life and Randy Nelson has nailed it here in *The Third Decision*. Don't just read it, share it with your life partner!

Jack Daly

Expert Sales Speaker, Trainer, CEO Coach and Thought Leader

… Randy has created a manifesto for how to both survive and thrive in this new world of endless acceleration. A must read for the new breed of enlightened entrepreneurs!

John Ratliff

Managing Director, Align 5 Advisors

… Randy is right. I hope you will read this book and commit to making the Third Decision. *The Second Decision* made you fully accountable to your business; now accept full accountability for your family life …

Barbara H. Mulkey, PE

Director, Shelton Leadership Center at NC State University

… *The Third Decision* helps me realize how much better life can be outside of the business for myself and those I love … This may be one of the most significant life application books on my business shelf!

Todd Hopkins

Founder and CEO, Office Pride

Acclaim for *The Fourth Decision*

In *The Fourth Decision*, Randy Nelson provides an invaluable framework for the Entrepreneur's Life Stages. In addition, the concepts of "What's next?!" and "Your future core purpose" definitely resonated with me ... all of the entrepreneurs I have known would have benefited from this information early on. This book gives every entrepreneurial leader a road map, no matter what stage of life they currently occupy.

Sam Reese

CEO, Vistage Worldwide, Inc.

There are loads of business books out there—Randy's are business doctrines with practical, informative, compelling, and actionable guidelines on how to maximize literally any organization. Randy has the unique ability to help you slow down, look in the mirror, and make more informed decisions, much faster and with discipline and incredible confidence. Simple concepts and clearly outlined—no doubt this book will stand the test of time. I'd encourage any leader who is looking to scale their organization to read it—and share it.

Ann Jacoby

CEO, Six Sails Market Research / BCC Research, LLC / Futuresource Consulting, Ltd.

As with his other books, Randy's *The Fourth Decision* lays out a blueprint for the serial entrepreneur to follow as we continue our journey. Randy has an uncanny way of looking at the bigger picture and dividing that picture into obtainable steps. I have followed Randy's methodology for over fifteen years and look up to him as a strong business partner, mentor, and very good friend. Whether you are just starting out or making that exit decision, *The Fourth Decision* asks you all the right questions.

Darrell McDaniel
CEO, NSTAR Global Services

Randy had me at "The Entrepreneur's Life Stages." His winsome narrative and innovations of how to live well in both business and family came at the perfect time and is a must read for the entrepreneur or anyone who needs a strategy to do the same. Read this book and learn from one of the clearest voices in leadership and strategic planning. *The Fourth Decision* was a game changer and will forever remain on my go-to resource shelf.

Wendy K. Clark
President, EO Raleigh Durham Chapter, Serial Entrepreneur, Community Developer, and Nonprofit Strategist

Every time I crack open a Randy H. Nelson book, I know I'm in for a masterclass in setting up our fast-growing global business for further success. In reality, this isn't a book, *it's a toolbox* and Randy has given you the tools to build up your strategy to maximize the impact of your company in the marketplace. In addition, *The Fourth Decision* forces you to evaluate your own as well as your organization's leadership skills, and provides you with the practical tools needed to identify and complement your strengths and weaknesses. It's up to you to make the choice to incorporate the right systems and start making better-calculated decisions, but Randy has laid out the path and *The Fourth Decision* will give you enhanced confidence to take the next right steps now!

Michael Wiuff Andersen
CCO, Arcane Tinmen ApS—Denmark

Each of the Decision Series books from Randy is an evolution to the next level of Entrepreneurship. *The Fourth Decision* is interestingly and appropriately about **Maximized Entrepreneurship,** and certainly promises to help us all to continue in the journey of entrepreneurship and leadership learning.

Vishal Kumar

Portfolio Leader, ARM Group

Randy has written a masterpiece with *The Fourth Decision*. The book brilliantly guides the way to both accelerate and grow your business successfully, as well as to—surprisingly—have more than enough time to spend quality time with your loved ones!

I have read many books about accelerating growth and how to become a better leader, but none of these books provided such wise, practical, and proven approaches like Randy Nelson nailed with his book *The Fourth Decision*. Every entrepreneurial leader should read this book!

Antoine Jansen

CEO, Marval—United Kingdom

Randy's coaching superpower is motivating and inspiring entrepreneurs to consistently ask the right questions—about themselves, their leadership teams, their organizations' full potential, and ultimately the decision of *"What's Next?!" The Fourth Decision* is a must read for every self-aware business and entrepreneurial leader.

Kevin Isaacson

Serial Entrepreneur, Intrapreneur, CEO, Southern Hobby

Our company had the good fortune of having a set of exceptional leaders that took us from $0 to $10 million in revenue. We reached a plateau and realized that we couldn't base our future on the good fortune of running into an endless supply of available, exceptional leaders.

Randy Nelson's Decision Series helped us turn strong leaders into exceptional ones. The Decision Tools and Full Potential Growth Model have helped us establish exceptional growth as the norm at our eight-thousand-plus-employee company, and he has managed to turn the art of leadership into a teachable science.

Bridgett Hurley

Chief Development Officer, Global Growth

A great book for teams to make better, data-backed decisions and meet their maximum potential.

In this book, Randy does a great job of helping leaders understand how to audit their current reality and ask hard questions. He then provides clear tools to create a growth strategy that not only leads to success but maximized potential.

Alex Faust

Director, The Growth Institute

(site of The Decision Series Workshops)

This book provides practical tools you can use to improve your life and your business. It's a *must read* full of insight and opportunity, especially for portfolio entrepreneurs looking to reach full potential with the multiple businesses they own. Apply yourself within, have your leaders apply themselves, and then go win!

Brian C. Allen

President and CEO, Precision Walls, Inc.

What Randy Nelson has done to improve our business can truly not be understated! The knowledge he's shared and that we've received from his books have moved our company's way of thinking to another level. We've had some real "aha" moments by simply practicing what Randy teaches. Wherever you are personally and/or with your business, Randy's insights will move you to the next level of success. I consider Randy a friend and a true asset to our company!

Jeromy Murray
President, Beckett Collectibles

As a fellow military veteran and one of the most successful entrepreneurs I have had the privilege to work for, and collaborate with, over the last sixteen years, Randy takes leadership and business growth to the next level in *The Fourth Decision*. Your personal and entrepreneurial life often follows a pattern that Randy has identified through his research and work with thousands of high-growth companies. Having the self-awareness to understand these patterns and leverage the tools Randy provides will help you ensure you reach your full potential and live the rest of your life without regrets.

Dean Bundshu
Founder, Bunker Labs, Raleigh-Durham, Serial Entrepreneur

Once again, Randy has blended his successful military and entrepreneurial careers and brought the best of both worlds to *The Fourth Decision*. If you are willing to do the hard work that Randy challenges you to do, then full potential is within your grasp ... and more importantly, while also enjoying your entrepreneurial journey!

Cheryl Beth Kuchler
Founder and President, CEO Think Tank®

The Fourth Decision delivers the Leadership Decision System needed for us to make significantly better *Diamond Level Decisions* in our personal and professional lives! In our exponential growth journey, we have been the direct beneficiary of Randy's coaching and mentoring and I would highly encourage leaders everywhere to implement his tools for self-awareness and decision-making!

Ajay Sharma
CFO, Entrust Global Group—India

I have admired all the books in The Decision Series™ for their practical application and for directly helping us to successfully build our business and our leadership skills over the past four-plus years. However, I have special appreciation for this book. We have fully adopted the Three+ Business Model Tool, choosing to build Farragut with the Full Potential Growth Model, as well as the Revenue Lever Strategy tool, Qual Cards, and many other tools. The tools have created more clarity for the entire organization—not just the CEO. Using the standard processes and tools created by Randy, we now have more people/leaders get and stay involved in strategy creation and, using these tools, we have seen them significantly increase their ownership of its execution. Not only do Randy's tools work, but they guide you toward your full potential if you are willing to do the hard work to get there!

Shail Jain
CEO, Farragut

Throughout the Decision Series Randy has written THE GUIDE for every entrepreneurial leader to follow, from Individual Leadership (*The Second Decision*) to Personal Life Leadership (*The Third*

Decision), and now in *The Fourth Decision*, it's all about Organizational Leadership and reaching your full potential. Make no mistake, Randy will challenge you to grow your leadership skills at every turn of the page, so get ready to stay outside your comfort zone, where true growth happens. And if I were you, I would take every opportunity to learn from this top thought leader … through his books, his workshops at The Decision Center™ and his inspiring public speaking (yes, he remains one of my finest students!).

Mikki Williams

Professional Speakers Hall of Fame, TEDx speaker, Executive Speech Coach, Highly Acclaimed Vistage Leadership Chair

THE
FOURTH
DECISION

What's Next?!

Randy H. Nelson

THE

FOURTH

DECISION

What's Next?!

The Maximized Entrepreneur

ORGANIZATIONAL LEADERSHIP

ForbesBooks

Published by ForbesBooks, Charleston, South Carolina.
Member of Advantage Media Group.

ForbesBooks is a registered trademark, and the ForbesBooks colophon is a trademark of Forbes Media, LLC.

Printed in the United States of America.

10 9 8 7 6 5 4 3 2 1

ISBN: 978-1-950863-78-5
LCCN: 2021925885

This custom publication is intended to provide accurate information and the opinions of the author in regard to the subject matter covered. It is sold with the understanding that the publisher, Advantage|ForbesBooks, is not engaged in rendering legal, financial, or professional services of any kind. If legal advice or other expert assistance is required, the reader is advised to seek the services of a competent professional.

Advantage Media Group is proud to be a part of the Tree Neutral® program. Tree Neutral offsets the number of trees consumed in the production and printing of this book by taking proactive steps such as planting trees in direct proportion to the number of trees used to print books. To learn more about Tree Neutral, please visit **www.treeneutral.com**.

Since 1917, Forbes has remained steadfast in its mission to serve as the defining voice of entrepreneurial capitalism. ForbesBooks, launched in 2016 through a partnership with Advantage Media Group, furthers that aim by helping business and thought leaders bring their stories, passion, and knowledge to the forefront in custom books. Opinions expressed by ForbesBooks authors are their own. To be considered for publication, please visit **www.forbesbooks.com**.

Dedicated to my wife, Kristi, for your unwavering support of my entrepreneurial and leadership dreams.

And to Ellen Wojahn—my writing partner in The Decision Series— you are simply the best at what you do.

And to my clients—without you, none of this would have been possible.

CONTENTS

SECTION TWO: LEADERSHIP

A Wayfinder for the Maximizer: Where Have We Been? What's Next?!

Our Coaching Partnership— Growth from $10 Million to $500+ Million in the Past Seven Years

I met Randy Nelson in 2014. At that point in my career, I was the president of Beckett Media, which has been the voice of the collectibles industry from the time Dr. James Beckett published his first *Sport Americana Baseball Card Price Guide* in 1979 to the launch of the first issue of *Beckett Baseball* magazine five years later. In the thirty-plus years since that rather simplistic first issue of *Beckett Baseball*, the magazine—and the company itself—has grown in significant proportions, similar to the very field it covers.

And I grew significantly, thanks to Randy, as an entrepreneurial leader, from running a $10 million company to leading a successful global portfolio of companies and leaders.

Randy began coaching me individually in 2014 and continued to coach me for the next seven years. He has been a trusted coach, mentor, teacher, and advisor to me, but as you will soon see, the depth and breadth of his coaching extended far into our portfolio of companies in the Entrust Global Group.

When I wrote this foreword, Entrust had just acquired our fourteenth company since my initial meeting with Randy, and the portfolio of companies that I led globally as the founder and group CEO of Entrust Global Group had grown to over $500 million in revenue, and to over one thousand global employees in eight countries, spread over four continents.

When I look back at our explosive and highly successful growth, I realize that the growth story coincided with the publication of Randy's three books:

- *The Second Decision: The Qualified Entrepreneur*, published in 2015

- *The Third Decision: The Intentional Entrepreneur*, published in 2019

- *The Fourth Decision: The Maximized Entrepreneur*, published in 2022

As the leader of a growing portfolio of companies, one of the best decisions I ever made was to commit to a learning culture at Entrust, and to continue that commitment regardless of the economic conditions throughout the world and our respective countries that we operate in—learning is not meant to be an on-and-off switch but rather a continuous stream of repetition and new learnings. Our six Core Values below made it very easy for us to make this commitment:

- Invest in people—our employees and our customers.

- Hire the best, expect the best, and insist on accountability.

- Keep climbing, never stop learning, and always innovate.

- Never compromise our integrity, character, or ethics.

- Be workmanlike and steadfast. No job is too small at any level.

- Think globally.

So as I was writing this foreword, I thought the best way to share my experience in working with Randy was to share our growth story, as that speaks volumes for the content of the Decision Series books, especially *The Fourth Decision*, which you are about to read, as well as the services that Randy provides to growing organizations such as Entrust.

Here are the lessons learned over the past seven years while working with Randy, lessons that I would pass on to any prospective entrepreneurial leader who we could inspire to take a similar growth journey of their own:

- Commit to becoming and staying a learning organization—forever. Along with this commitment, we were successful because we also embraced discipline, accountability, and qualification.

- Commit to growing your own leadership skills first—if I was not committed fully, then it was not fair to ask my leadership teams to make the same commitment.

- Focus on leadership development—always. Randy now works with multiple layers of our leadership team and throughout our portfolio companies globally.

- Don't just promote people to leadership—verify their potential first through qualification.

- Commit to the five challenges of Randy's Decision Series:

  1. To grow our leadership skills as fast as Entrust is growing, because the growth of Entrust is limited by the growth of our leaders, starting with myself.

  2. To grow our self-awareness, because the lack of self-awareness is the fatal flaw of a leader at Entrust.

3. To double our personal capacity every two to three years, and to always be qualifying for our next level of leadership. You will learn about "qual cards" in *The Fourth Decision*. Commit to them, as they are indeed *game changers* when done well.

4. To become more intentional with our decisions and to set nonnegotiables, living and leading our lives with a work-life blending focus, regardless of how large our growth goals continue to be.

5. To grow our financial leadership skills, mining for gold and diamonds with our data, for the purpose of *making better-calculated decisions faster and with more confidence*, at all levels of Entrust. Randy's tools in the second section of this book are proven and priceless—but they take work and commitment. Do both. Embrace the truth and trends and revenue levers!

- Be willing to be challenged, always—learn to like living outside your comfort zone. That is where growth happens.

- Progress, not perfection.

- We built a global language of business that can be repeated across organizations within our portfolio and integrated every global business and new acquisition with this language and Randy's trainings through the Decision Series, most recently with the advanced Fourth Decision content, as this book is dedicated to building organizational leadership, whereas *The Second Decision* focuses on individual leadership and *The Third Decision* on personal life leadership.

- Be willing to change. The world does. Your competitors do—and so must you.

- Be willing to say, "I don't know what I don't know"—then the learning begins.

- Be coachable and learn how to listen with the intent to understand.

- Randy's coaching and content applies to leaders everywhere, not just entrepreneurs. It is also built to be collaborative with other learning systems, not competitive. He built the Decision Series so that 1 + 1 can = 5+ with your learning systems.

We went all in with Randy and have remained that way for seven years, and I anticipate for the next seven years, and the next seven years after that.

Why?

Randy has built his own companies, and they were built to last, now thirty-two years, twenty years, and nine years old, and all industry leaders. They have produced over a billion in sales to date. He developed strong leaders who eventually took the CEO position of his first two companies—he walks the talk and is willing to share his invaluable experiences, along with his peers' experiences, both successes and failures to help others learn, avoid making the same mistakes, and accelerate successes.

Randy is a proven coach of entrepreneurs, intrapreneurs—and leaders everywhere. With his What's Next?! philosophy, there is never a time when he will not

> We went all in with Randy and have remained that way for seven years, and I anticipate for the next seven years, and the next seven years after that.

provide value if we maintain a growth mindset ourselves. Whether you are a $5 million, $500 million, or $5 billion company, the Decision Series content will help you move to the next level, both personally and professionally. What's next? Once you decide, then go forward with a sense of urgency!

Randy is a committed learner himself, spending the past twenty-five years in groups such as Entrepreneurs' Organization and Vistage and learning from the very best thought leaders in the entrepreneurial and leadership spaces.

Randy is a proven "leader of leaders." He spent six and a half years as a Navy submarine officer in the 1980s, and for his entire life he has been called into leadership roles at very high levels.

Randy is a respected thought leader and public speaker in the entrepreneurial leadership space, most notably with his best-selling Decision Series books and challenging growth workshops.

As I look forward, I truly believe that we are just getting started, and with our partnership we have with Randy, that our future growth will be challenging, rewarding, and fulfilling, both personally and professionally—because we are as committed as Randy to growth and aligned to the content of *The Fourth Decision*, his next best-selling book in his Decision Series, which guides the way to reach full potential in your organization by transforming the individual, qualifying the team, and scaling leadership across the organization.

If you believe you have that same commitment and are willing to operate outside your comfort zone to grow your entrepreneurial leadership skills, buckle in and enjoy *The Fourth Decision*, and then go back and read *The Second Decision* and *The Third Decision*.

If you truly desire to reach your full potential, then engage Randy and his Decision Center coaches. They are long-term coaches, mentors, teachers, and advisors for leadership development and business growth who will indeed keep you outside your comfort zone!

—Sandeep Dua, Founder and CEO, Entrust Global Group, 2014–2021

PREFACE

The book you hold in your hands represents the zenith of the Decision Series for Entrepreneurs, a now three-volume set of books written for those who are determined to top out as the successful and fulfilled architects of their own entrepreneurial lives.

Getting to this point has been a step-by-step progression for both me and my readers.

In *The Second Decision*, I urged my readers to become *qualified* entrepreneurs (QEs), committed to self-awareness and lifelong learning. It was a book exploring *individual leadership* in the entrepreneurial realm.

In *The Third Decision*, we expanded beyond the workplace, considering what it takes to become *intentional*—namely, to fit an entrepreneurial career into a life lived well and without regrets. Here, *personal life leadership* was the focus.

In this book, *The Fourth Decision*, we seek to become *maximized*. Having done the work and reaped significant rewards as entrepreneurs over the past decade or so, we now turn to what's next for our companies and our own lives, using decision-making tools I've developed over my ten years of coaching, mentoring, advising, teaching, and writing. My aim here is to show how each of us can achieve a level of true *entrepreneurial leadership*, however we choose to define it, by expanding our focus to include *organizational leadership*.

After *The Fourth Decision*, just one book remains to be written in the Decision Series—"The First Decision." Once the series has looked at all the requirements and challenges of an entrepreneurial career, it will be time to go back to the beginning and share all of the knowledge compiled in my books with a most important cohort of new readers: those considering an entrepreneurial career or at the beginning stages of starting a company. We who have become *qualified, intentional,* and, after this book, *maximized* will be in the ideal position to ensure that the world's next crop of entrepreneurs has an easier, more satisfying, and more productive path than we did. Our economies depend on reducing the all-too-common problem of entrepreneurial burnout and improving on the rate of failure in entrepreneurial companies—which remains stuck at about 70 percent.

One of the key things I have learned in writing these books is that the very best entrepreneurs among us are those who continue improving our skills year after year. In this way, we are like professionals in sports, music, education—any field, really. Indeed, for me, the very inspiration for this series stemmed from the continuous improvement ethic I learned on a Navy nuclear submarine. It was the "qual card" I had to fill out at each level of my career that first formed the question in my mind: Shouldn't there be some sort of qualification process for entrepreneurs? Why didn't such a thing exist?

Like the other books in the Decision Series for Entrepreneurs, *The Fourth Decision* is a compilation and a distillation of all of my experiences with all of my influencers. I'm grateful for the opportunity to share what I've learned.

In the first half of the book, you'll find that the focus is on you and your life as a *maximized* entrepreneur, or ME for short. I think you'll find a lot of angles and insights with which to judge where you are both in business and in life, and what the indicators say about phases ahead of you. The second half of the book provides you with some tools that can be useful as you seek to *maximize* your company (or companies), while also scaling your *entrepreneurial leadership* within the organization. These are the tools you'll use to decide how you'll cap off your journey as an entrepreneurial leader.

The hardest question I'll put in front of you, and I'll do it again and again, is that crazy-simple one: "*What's next?!*" This is the question that drives us, step by step, to an understanding of how we want the rest of our career to play out. Once a path is chosen, it's that same question that prods us to keep moving. Notice the exclamation point I added to the question. It's there to convey the urgency we need to bring to our decisions, big and small, if we're serious about getting where we're going. You'll be seeing that "*What's next?!*" question at the end of each chapter's maximized entrepreneurial qual card (MEQC).

I'm relying on you to engage honestly and vigorously with the self-audit opportunities I present throughout the book. Do this, and I can promise you, you will come away personally and professionally healthier and more capable of extending your entrepreneurial longevity. Of course, if you recognize that you need more hands-on assistance than the self-audit can accomplish, then seek out a coach or peer group to help you move forward.

With that, all that's left to say is *"Welcome to your next self-awareness journey!"* Get ready for another encounter with knowing yourself, improving yourself, and complementing yourself—plus a couple of new "thyselfs" that pertain particularly well to highly successful entrepreneurs like you, ones who

> # Welcome to your next self-awareness journey!

seek to *maximize*. Simply by being here, you're proving once again that you're ready to learn, think, decide, and implement. And when you're ready to make the Fourth Decision at the back of this book, you'll have graduated from the Decision Series for Entrepreneurs. But like any graduation, it's also a commencement—a new beginning. You'll be starting the next chapter of your life as a *maximized* entrepreneur, one who seeks to adopt an "annual checkup" regimen to ensure that both you and your company (or companies) reach full potential.

What Is the Fourth Decision? What Does It Mean to Be Maximized?

I learned to always take on things I'd never done before. Growth and comfort do not coexist.
—GINNI ROMETTY, FORMER CHAIRMAN, PRESIDENT, AND CEO OF IBM

Maximized entrepreneurship—that's the goal of the book you hold in your hand. But what does that mean? Who's ready to be *maximized*?

Well, think of it as a job description. These are the qualifications for those ready to become a *maximized entrepreneur*, or ME as I'll refer to it throughout the book.

The Maximized Entrepreneur's Qualifications

- **Significant *successful* experience**. Has ten years, give or take, in an entrepreneurial career—with an outstanding record of achievement.

- **Energy.** Not tired or bored or suffering from inertia, no matter their age or entrepreneurial track record.

- **Curiosity.** Always wondering what's coming and how they might play a part in it. Uncertainty is considered exciting, because it brings opportunity.

- **Self-knowledge.** Possesses a clear sense, born of experience, of their own skills and deficits. Clearly understands that the fatal flaw of any entrepreneurial leader is always a lack of self-awareness.

- **An innate drive toward self-improvement.** An insatiable desire for skills development is what lays the groundwork for maximization. When you think *"maximized,"* think lifelong learning. Then, think *lifelong implementation* of your learning.

- **A focus that has widened beyond "entrepreneur" and toward "entrepreneurial leadership."** Accepts that mature or maturing companies need to be led by more than just the entrepreneur who's at the helm. The drive within the organization must be toward true entrepreneurial leadership—whether that's within a typical pyramid, or shared between partners, or built as a structure across the breadth of the company. It's about maximizing value for employees as well.

- **A bias toward creative discipline.** Organizations headed by maximizers are motivated to build for ongoing innovation.

- **A sense of limits or preferred parameters.** Seeks their lane and takes steps to stay in it. This isn't a restriction to a specific industry or type of business; it's more a skill set, a way of operating a business, or a strong personal interest in a product or service. A maximizer stops to consider what might be his or her best, most *maximized* role.

- **A commitment to an entrepreneurial "calling."** With ten years under your belt (or five, or more than ten; your mileage may vary), the recognition is clear: living an entrepreneurial life is what you were put on earth to do, so what better time than now to consider what you've learned, decide what you still need to learn, and choose for yourself how to *maximize* this choice of yours for life?

That's quite a list of candidacy requirements, but I suspect that most of my readers easily qualify. If you've picked up this book, you're probably ready not only to *maximize* yourself as an entrepreneurial leader but to move well beyond mere entrepreneurial success into *an entrepreneurship-centered life that is maximized in all respects.*

I'm positioning this book for people who are well past any need to prove their entrepreneurial credentials; they simply want to further enhance their skills for the betterment of the organizations they lead, and for their own fulfillment. An entrepreneur who is ready to *maximize* has already made the transition from the self-confident (potentially arrogant) start-up entrepreneur whose main goal was to make a mark in the world. They want to look back on their entrepreneurial careers someday with pride and satisfaction, knowing that they did their best to ensure that both they and their companies succeeded in reaching full potential. An entrepreneur who is ready to *maximize* has reached a high level of success and begun thinking about "*What's next?!*" Such entrepreneurs recognize that they didn't get where they are on their own and—most importantly—that there are still high levels of long-term success they can reach for and conquer.

Now, if this book is going to help you recognize which mountains remain to be climbed in your *maximized* entrepreneurial life, then let's ask the next question: *What is the fourth decision?*

Simple: It's the one you'll make to map your route. It may not lead you to any new pinnacles, but then again, it's highly possible it will. The one thing I'm certain of is this: it'll take you where you truly want to be. The possibilities for a highly successful entrepreneur like you include the following:

- **Single company-focused entrepreneur.** Perhaps you'll home in on building your current company to its full potential, using this book to find new ways to bust through plateaus and status quos.

- **Start-up/buildup entrepreneur.** Maybe you'll be contemplating or planning a near-term exit via resignation (perhaps to allow for succession), through a sale or a merger, or as a means to speed your retirement from this phase of your ME career.

- **Exited entrepreneur.** You may be actively or not-so-actively looking for new business or leadership opportunities, trying to identify that next step in your entrepreneurial career/life.

- **Intrapreneur.** You're working within a company you founded and sold, or joined (1) to enhance your skills, (2) to gain industry experience, or (3) to tackle specific consulting projects. Some experienced entrepreneurs will be very happy in such a role, especially at certain stages of life. Others will soon consider the launch of a new start-up.

> It may not lead you to any new pinnacles, but then again, it's highly possible it will.

- **Serial entrepreneur.** Having already built and exited two or more companies, you may be looking to add another notch or two to your belt.

- **Habitual entrepreneur.** This describes you if you're always working on something entrepreneurial, and often several things at a time. You might see yourself in other categories on this list, but this is also a category of its own. As many of us consider ourselves natural-born entrepreneurship addicts, continually playing with possible business plans is just part of our pattern.

- **Portfolio entrepreneur.** This is somebody who enjoys having fingers in lots of pies. This kind of entrepreneur somewhat resembles an entrepreneurial investor but seeks more managerial involvement or influence than a typical investor might.

While I'm writing entirely through the lens of my thirty years as an entrepreneur (and coach, advisor, and teacher/mentor too), I know that the lessons and perspectives I offer in these pages will have broad relevance for anyone who may be considering their next steps, whatever the profession may be.

The basic fact informing this book is that the very best among us—no matter the precise stripe of our career—aren't easily satisfied with what we've already done. It's born in us to want to excel, to want to do more things or different things. I recognize these traits in myself. I've also seen them time and again in my EO (Entrepreneurs' Organization) and Vistage peer networking groups. And these are certainly the themes that run through and between many of the books written by the entrepreneurial thought leaders I count as mentors.

Whether they were my own businesses or somebody else's, I've now had the pleasure of helping grow hundreds of companies to scale—discovering what works and identifying what doesn't. As part of my work, I've spent *thousands of hours* talking to entrepreneurs about their hopes, dreams, passions, and frustrations. I've got data to share in this book, lots of experiential data, and it starkly reveals the ways in which business builders can think they're doing the right thing—when they're actually not. In short, I've done the legwork to figure out what's missing when entrepreneurs try and fail to install true entrepreneurial leadership in their organizations.

Again, this isn't a book for brand-new entrepreneurs. It is for the people who've been entrepreneurs long enough to pack a few key attributes:

Grit. Work ethic. Maturity. Integrity. Loyalty. Energy. Leadership. Curiosity. Technical skill. Broad and deep business experience.

Not every entrepreneur starts out with a list like this. In fact, I didn't. When I left the Navy, I had seven years of submarine leadership under my belt, but I didn't have experience in business. For some employers, that was a deal breaker. To them, I was no more interesting as a job candidate than if I'd come to them straight out of college. But to others—the wiser employers who better understood the intangibles that make a great hire—my fellow military veterans and I were in heavy demand. Aside from the missing business experience, I had those key attributes I just named, most of

> I've got data to share in this book, lots of experiential data, and it starkly reveals the ways in which business builders can think they're doing the right thing—when they're actually not.

which is stuff that no amount of industry experience alone can guarantee. It's the kind of stuff that's either born in you or bred into you over time.

But I know that my readers have a longer list of attributes, including the ones you've gained by reading the Decision Series. Add these:

Self-awareness. An understanding of what role you're qualified for, courtesy of The Second Decision. *A set of personal nonnegotiables that ensure you'll live a regret-free entrepreneurial life, courtesy of* The Third Decision.

Add to these the Fourth Decision, which is simply, yet challengingly, this:

Maximized entrepreneurs are those who make a conscious choice to commit proactively to a lifetime career as an ME. They become fully ready to embrace their drive toward full potential, for both themselves and their companies. They are fully ready to achieve true entrepreneurial leadership with both strategic and tactical alignment—through a new or enhanced application of discipline, both in their professional and personal lives. They commit to undertaking the preparation necessary for making the Fourth Decision.

Oops, there's the D-word: "discipline." Does this mean you can look forward to a future of working harder and better? Yes, it may. But it's at least as likely that becoming *maximized* will mean establishing leadership (yours or someone else's), imposing a discipline, and then delegating the implementation and accountability to other individuals or a team. The maximized leadership focus is much more organizational than individual, and it's what separates this book from the others in the Decision Series. Let me remind you of the path we've been on together:

- *The Second Decision: The Qualified Entrepreneur* (QE). (Key watchword: "build.") This book assumes that the idea on the napkin worked, and you're off to the races building your company. The QE decides what role they will take in the company in the next three to five years and commits to becoming qualified through the Entrepreneurial Qual Card (EQC), either by continuing to lead the company as a QE or by selecting someone else to get qualified, so they can lead the company in the years ahead. The goal? Doing what's best for the business you're building.

- *The Third Decision: The Intentional Entrepreneur* (IE). (Key watchword: "blend.") Life and work. Work and life. The IE decides which personal life nonnegotiables to commit to over the next twelve months—areas that aren't up for discussion or compromise. The IE commits to these nonnegotiables while clearly understanding the consequences of the decisions they are making. The aim is to live a regret-free entrepreneurial life, without alibis.

- *The Fourth Decision: The Maximized Entrepreneur* (ME). (Key watchword: *align*.) My goal in this book is to continue inspiring entrepreneurs like you to keep improving yourselves, even when you're already a demonstrated success, and to align all aspects of your personal and professional lives to productively live the life of an ME throughout your career. The mission now expands to ensure that the lessons don't stop at the top, but spread throughout the company and become self-perpetuating, whether you're at the helm or not.

Ideally, the two books that preceded this one have helped you get where you are today. You're a winner by anybody's measure. You're feeling at the top of your game skills-wise. You've come to understand that leadership is necessary, whether you're doing the leading or letting others take that role. Our businesses would have never launched without us; this we know for certain. But they can remain successful long after we've moved on, once we've instilled a thriving culture of entrepreneurship, leadership, and discipline. That last word is one we may tend to shy away from, but it's important for *maximized* entrepreneurs to embrace it anew.

> The very best learn that entrepreneurship and discipline are not polar opposites, but rather they are complementary and much-needed skills in every organization.

Let's also look at that phrase "entrepreneurial leadership," for it, too, has a new or enhanced definition. At this stage of your career, you very well might be moving forward every day in your current role, just as you have for a long time. Or maybe your company is doing well enough that you're beginning to wonder how much you still have to contribute, or whether the nature of your contribution should change somehow. To me, this isn't a question to avoid or postpone; it's exactly the right time to take it up again.

This book will help you engage with the *"What's next?!"* question in a more detailed, granular way. The effort begins, of course, with self-awareness. And as a loyal reader of the Decision Series, you know by now that my favorite motto for increasing self-awareness is this: *Know thyself. Improve thyself. Complement thyself.*

Allow me to dig into these a bit, looking at them from a Fourth Decision perspective.

Know thyself. You may feel you're pretty clear on who you are and who you're not, so the "know thyself" explorations I've built into this book are designed merely to ensure that the future will still find you enjoying the life of an entrepreneur or entrepreneurial leader. By the time you reach the "Reset" chapter, you'll be in full command of whether there's a new you ready to be born—or not!

Improve thyself. Throughout the books in my series, I've consistently challenged you to do four things. I've called them my Four Pillars. Here, I've revised them to my Four Challenges:

1. Grow your self-awareness, because a lack of self-awareness is the fatal flaw of a leader.

2. Grow your leadership skills as fast as your company is growing, because the growth of a company is limited by the growth of its leaders.

3. Double your personal capacity, every two to three years, to become qualified for what's next.

4. Be intentional, committing to your nonnegotiables over the next twelve months.

The Fourth Decision will be no different. True MEs continue to learn and improve themselves, and they expect the same of their organizations and the employees within them. To fully implement what they learn, *maximized* entrepreneurs look to surround themselves with *qualified* individuals who are ready to extend the entrepreneurial leader's influence throughout the organization.

But this book also introduces a new challenge to build on:

5. **Enhance your financial leadership skills.** This fifth challenge, which I'm backing up with an entire section of tools in this book, only sounds simple. What I'm talking about is deepening and enhancing your ability to gather data and metrics you can rely on while also combining them with your ME intuition. This fifth challenge is key to helping you *make significantly better-calculated decisions faster and with more confidence.* That means doing so routinely, of course, but also prospectively, as a hedge against the times when the worst happens. Nobody gets to this point in an entrepreneurial career without experiencing downturns, disruptions, recessions, and even the economic near-stoppage caused by the 2020 coronavirus pandemic. Contingency and crisis planning requires more from us than

mere goal setting and revenue projecting. This, my friends, is what makes *The Fourth Decision* a commencement instead of a graduation: *maximized* entrepreneurs learn to continually evaluate the gap between their current skills and their full potential—and then develop the forward-going techniques necessary for holding themselves accountable. How else can we hope to ensure that our companies reach full potential, with or without our entrepreneurial leadership?

Complement thyself: Congratulations to you for self-confidently believing in yourself and your abilities, because this has been a critical success factor for you. But we experienced entrepreneurs have learned that a growth company can't be a one-man or one-woman show. Having reached the stage of becoming *maximized*, we know that hiring great people is just the beginning of "complement thyself." In this book we'll also talk about how to get out of the way and let each of these great hires embark on their own self-awareness journeys. That's important for helping our companies reach full potential. But it also plays a critical role in our own happiness—or lack of it—as we commit to lifelong entrepreneurial leadership.

Here's another bit of review:

Learn. Think. Decide. Implement.

This is the familiar, step-by-step method by which we create change, whether it's in our lives or in our companies. As we all know from rugged experience, the first three of these can flash by pretty quickly, maybe even instantaneously, as we confront a problem. We also know that if there's going to be a time lag in the process, we can rely on it falling between "decide" and "implement."

Of course, the kinds of decisions we face have morphed over the years of our entrepreneurial career. The time frame we look at in our decision-making has also changed. Consider the following:

- "The First Decision" (book yet to come). Short-term decisions are the name of the game for start-up entrepreneurs. Daily and weekly actions and reactions are par for the course here, as we remember all too well. Monthly and quarterly decisions are within our best intentions, but often we feel that start-up life is moving too quickly to slow down for these. (Hint: This is because we haven't learned how to *slow down to speed up* yet.)

- *The Second Decision.* The *qualified* entrepreneur looks out three years to make a very key decision: what role he or she wants to play in their company's near-term future (leader, role-player, or creator). The self-awareness journey required to make the decision helps determine which seat is going to be the right one, and what kinds of tasks will be required to self-qualify for the job.

- *The Third Decision.* The *intentional* entrepreneur commits to establishing a list of nonnegotiables for the next twelve months, and then reevaluates these priorities on a yearly basis going forward. The aim, you'll recall, is to strive for a blend—not a balance—between our personal lives and our business-building drive.

- Now, in *The Fourth Decision, our decision-making time frame is five to twenty-five-plus years*, during which you will consider both the future of your company (or companies) and your own onward career path.

There are many possibilities for how to answer your questions about the future. If you want to retire, or just keep doing what you're doing, these are absolutely valid choices, no shame at all. I'm certain you'll at least consider whether to sell your company—though whether it actually happens is another question that only you can answer. By reading this book, you'll come to see that a decision to exit is far more than a yes-no, go or no-go, proposition—in fact, it's a multistage process that includes preplanning and postsale aftereffects, many of them surprisingly psychological and emotional in nature. But we're entrepreneurship addicts, right? I'm confident that, sooner or later, many of you who choose an exit—many of *us*—will be right back to First Decision territory, happily struggling to get a new company off the ground.

There'll be one very important difference, however: next time around, you'll be operating with the mindset and knowledge you've gained through becoming a *qualified*, *intentional*, and newly *maximized* entrepreneur.

The Maximized Entrepreneurial Qual Card (MEQC) — *What's Next?!*

Learn. Think. Decide. Implement.

Initials

1. Review the maximized entrepreneur's quali-
    fications list and put a check mark next to all
    that apply to your career.

    - Significant *successful* experience   _____

    - Energy   _____

    - Curiosity   _____

    - Self-knowledge   _____

    - An innate drive toward self-improvement   _____

    - A focus widened beyond "entrepreneur"
      and toward "entrepreneurial leadership"   _____

    - A bias toward creative discipline   _____

    - A sense of limits or preferred parameters   _____

    - A commitment to an entrepreneurial "calling" _____

2. Commit to making the Fourth Decision, adopting
    a mindset that allows you to begin thinking
    ahead to the next five to twenty-five years.
    Maximized entrepreneurs learn to continually
    evaluate the gap between their current skills and
    their full potential, and then develop the forward-
    going techniques necessary to hold themselves
    accountable for closing the gap.   _____

3. Commit to moving forward as an ME, ready to learn new ways of combining entrepreneurial leadership and discipline. _____

4. Commit to the Five Challenges (Pillars) of the Decision Series—growing your self-aware-ness, growing your leadership skills, doubling your personal capacity, setting or resetting your nonnegotiables, and enhancing your financial leadership skills. _____

Signature: _____

Date: _____

A Wayfinder for the Maximized Life of an Entrepreneur: Where Have You Been? What's Next?!

This section focuses on the various life stages of the entrepreneur, challenging you to look at your choice to become an entrepreneur under a different lens, from that of a career maximized entrepreneur, and providing additional resources to help you consider what changes you need to make to reach your full potential and enjoy the ride throughout your entrepreneurial life.

Align. The Fourth Decision is focused on alignment at all levels for the entrepreneur, from work to life, from entrepreneurship to leadership, from vision to execution, etc.

Unconscious competence. You know how to do something, and it is second nature—*you rock at it*. For the maximized entrepreneur, this extends to both the entrepreneur and their organization(s), and when done well, everyone rocks at what they do, consistently.

The ME Equation identifies the components of self-awareness needed for the entrepreneur to successfully make the journey to a maximized entrepreneur.

The Self-Awareness Decision Tool is a practical development tool for the entrepreneur, built from the ME Equation and designed to get the right people in the right seats doing the rights things, starting with the entrepreneur themselves.

Entrepreneurial Life Stages is a provocative new look at your entrepreneurial life, from youth to the elderly, designed to challenge your thinking from the shorter term to building out an entrepreneurial life that you can thoroughly enjoy as a career, and at every stage of it.

The ME transition phase tool describes what every single entrepreneur will go through in their career: the exiting of their company and the transition to their next stage in their entrepreneurial career. It is not a question of if, but when this will happen, to all of us.

These concepts and tools work together, overlap, and build on one another to give you a guide to thinking about your entrepreneurial journey over your entire lifetime.

Let's get started with the ME Equation and the Self-Awareness Decision Tool.

CHAPTER 1

The ME Equation and the Self-Awareness Decision Tool

Discipline is the habit of taking consistent action until
one can perform with unconscious competence.
Discipline weighs ounces but regret weighs tons.
—JHOON RHEE, MARTIAL ARTIST

I don't know what I don't know.

I know what I don't know.

I know what I know.

These simple phrases are invaluable to understanding the growth that occurs when one moves from being an entrepreneur to becoming a *qualified* and *intentional* entrepreneur. As many of you know, I have used these three phrases as touchstones throughout the Decision Series for Entrepreneurs. Here they are again, standing at center stage as you begin your third self-awareness journey, at the end of which you'll achieve the highest rank of entrepreneurial leadership. You'll be *maximized*.

What you and I are aiming for in this book is a level well beyond the three sentences above, something that has been referred to as

unconscious competence. As you can see in the illustration, getting to this level requires you to develop complete self-awareness and make use of it—until it's no longer necessary. Once you reach unconscious competence, you're essentially so good at what you do that it's effortless. It doesn't require any thought at all.[1]

UNCONSCIOUS COMPETENCE
... THE MAXIMIZED ENTREPRENEUR

Unconscious Incompetence	Conscious Incompetence	Conscious Competence	Unconscious Competence
You don't know that you don't know how to do something.	You know that you don't know how to do something and it bothers you.	You know that you know how to do something and it takes effort.	You know how to do something and it is second nature; you rock at it.

Let me walk you through this.

When we began our careers as start-up entrepreneurs, it was necessary to believe we could accomplish anything that we set our minds to (and then directed our considerable efforts toward). How else could we take the leap necessary to start and run our companies?

At this earliest stage, we might have very mistakenly believed we were operating in the zone of **unconscious competence**—but that would have been our ultra-self-confidence talking. In reality, we began the journey operating in the zones that are familiar to any somewhat self-aware beginner: those of **unconscious incompetence**

---

1   The Cottontown Chorus of Bolton. Retrieved from www.cottontownchorus.co.uk.

and **conscious competence**. **Unconscious competence** comes much later. At the end of this book, in fact.

Yes, we skipped over something in the illustration—conscious incompetence. Hang on, it's coming. But first I want to get us on the same page with regard to the other two—number 3 and number 1.

The entrepreneur—conscious competence—"I know what I know." This is the strong self-belief that helps us select what sort of entrepreneurial business to start. The start-up entrepreneur sees a need in the market, combines it with a personal skill set in which they have great confidence, and begins. While most of us also acted because we were tired of working for somebody else, the self-confidence factor was uppermost. It had to be to get our companies off the ground. Still, ignorance was bliss. Equipped as we thought we were to build our growth companies, we soon learned we weren't.

The entrepreneur—unconscious incompetence—"I don't know what I don't know." Thank goodness for that ignorance. The guts that allowed us to launch our start-ups came as much from what we didn't know as what we did. Not knowing what mistakes we could make, because we didn't acknowledge any limits to our capabilities, caused us to goof up repeatedly. But a few things saved us. That self-confidence. That trust in our own skills and luck. That stubborn willingness to work circles around anybody else to fix our mistakes and find success. If you're reading this book, you know what it's like to be among the winners of this very unforgiving game.

If you haven't read the introduction to this book, I encourage you to do so, for it contains some important points about the previous books in my Decision Series for Entrepreneurs. Briefly, as many of you know, by writing *The Second Decision: The Qualified Entrepreneur*, I chose to start there—instead of with the as-yet-unwritten "The First Decision" to start a company—because I'd lived through all of the typical entrepreneurial mistakes and saw how much time I'd wasted making them. The resulting book is aimed squarely at all who, like me, have learned how much our companies rely on us to improve our skills—or to make room for those more skilled.

My ultimate goal in writing that book was to drive growth-stage entrepreneurs to take important, productive steps to *build* into their organization more discipline and better long-term leadership. This means setting up the company with a qualified entrepreneurial leader suited to its next phase of growth—whether that's the same entrepreneur with improved skills or someone else. In the context of the previous illustration, growth entrepreneurs take a self-awareness journey aimed at achieving *conscious incompetence*. In other words, to reach a point of "I know what I don't know."

In *The Second Decision*, you progressed from **unconscious incompetence** to **conscious incompetence** and became *qualified* through the Entrepreneurial Qual Card, which was modeled after my Navy "qual card." In the Navy, you're always training for your next position. You can't move up until somebody checks you out on every task and bit of knowledge and signs your qual card. Note that only *after* my qual card had been signed could I begin then racking up experience. For example, I became qualified to lead the submarine in the captain's absence before I actually tried my hand at the wheel. I had the requisite knowledge to begin working in the role. But the experience part was just beginning.

For entrepreneurs it's often the opposite: We do the job, and then, if we ever become qualified, it happens *after* we've racked up the experience—much of it painful. Getting qualified in this way is the Navy equivalent of being a junior military officer, a rank not even close to becoming a commanding officer. You're trained, but everybody knows you're not fully equipped. Entrepreneurs who have become *qualified* have gained the requisite knowledge to continue leading the businesses they've built. It's the *individual knowledge* that will either help them lead their companies into the future or show them that other people, with other skills, should take over the leadership role.

A quick disclaimer: I'm not saying an entrepreneur has to wait any particular length of time to start or grow a company, or to call themselves the CEO. Many younger and/or much more inexperienced entrepreneurs have had significant success building very large and valuable companies. But even they often acknowledge that more self-awareness, training, and discipline would have made the job easier and perhaps more successful quicker.

> We do the job, and then, if we ever become qualified, it happens *after* we've racked up the experience—much of it painful.

My next book, *The Third Decision: The Intentional Entrepreneur*, met entrepreneurs at the often uncomfortable junction between succeeding in business and trying to succeed in life. In that book, I invited us all to consider how we might better *blend* our chosen entrepreneurial life with whatever we want outside of the business. Just as we negotiate a roller coaster of highs and lows in starting and growing a company, we do the same if we opt for more from life, such as creating a family. Both things take work. And both things benefit from increased self-awareness. The *intentional* entrepreneur commits to blending work and life by developing a list of nonnegotiables. These act as restrictor plates in our decision-making, ensuring that we achieve the work-life *blend*—not balance, mind you—which we seek in our entrepreneurial lives. Our nonnegotiables help us enjoy the payoff of not just business success but something much bigger: living a life without regrets or alibis.

Whether in business or life, it often takes a heaping helping of **unconscious incompetence** to gets things off the ground. But it's not enough. Over time it takes a growing sense of our own **conscious incompetence** to keep the business healthy and the goals of our personal life on track.

Growing from "I don't know what I don't know" to "I know what I don't know" takes true introspection. Again, the journey is better when it's not solo. We need the experience and perspective of others. We become *qualified* by allowing our peers, other entrepreneurs, to teach us. We are reminded that our spouses and close family members often have a far better understanding than we do of how well we're functioning—both as businesspeople *and* human beings.

As entrepreneurs, we *start*. Then, we *build*. Then, we seek to *blend*. What comes next?

Our challenge here in *The Fourth Decision* is to *align everywhere*—to do the work necessary to ensure that there is not just individual knowledge in place to help our companies reach full potential but organizational knowledge as well, and that we have alignment all around, including with our personal lives.

We need to cultivate

- self-confidence *and* self-awareness,

- creativity *and* discipline, and

- entrepreneurship *and* leadership.

"And" is a critical word for the *maximized* entrepreneur. It reflects our need to continuously improve, to add new dimensions to what we can already do. An entrepreneur starting a company can get away with being undisciplined, but an ME cannot if he or she wants to maximize both the potential of the organization and their own career as an entrepreneur. A start-up entrepreneur can be a pure risk-taker, as he or she creates, but an ME understands the necessity of becoming disciplined enough to accept not just risk but to embrace the benefits of controlled risk. An entrepreneur is all about entrepreneurship, forever and always, but an ME also embraces leadership in a way that rises to a new level—that of true *entrepreneurial leadership*.

Start. Build. Blend. Align.

It will take me the rest of this book to describe just how each of us can enhance the "start, build, and blend" foundation we've built to fully "align" ourselves and our entrepreneurial lives. But I can offer you a basic structure for the self-awareness journey that lies ahead. It's a trio of sayings: **Know thyself. Improve thyself. Complement thyself.** I've written and spoken about these slogans for years. My clients who have used the principles of the Decision Series for Entrepreneurs to build their organizations often feature them prominently. These slogans are engraved in steel plates and posted on the walls of the "cabins" (meeting rooms) of the Entrust Global Group in Delhi, India.

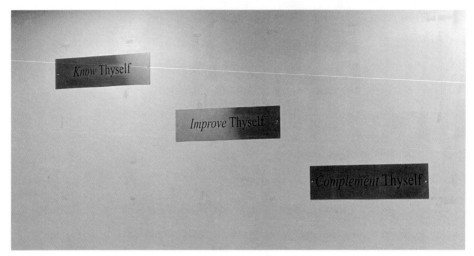

Posted on the walls of the "cabins" (meeting rooms)
of the Entrust Global Group in Delhi, India

"Know thyself" is where all self-awareness begins. After many years as an entrepreneur, I assume you've had your ups and downs, some more severe than others, offering you plenty of opportunity to gain the data and the insight to truly know yourself, knowing what you love and what you dislike.

You're also to this point because you've shown your willingness to "improve thyself." You've learned what you're capable of, and you probably have a pretty good idea where your time and energies are best spent.

Being willing to improve carries with it at least the possibility that you'll "complement thyself" to ensure the continued growth of your business.

Taken together, this trio of statements represents the achievement of *individual leadership*, and the jumping-off point for the *organizational leadership* themes and goals you'll find in this book. Working through them will also help you determine what aspects of "improve thyself" and "complement thyself" still require some attention as you seek to become a *maximized entrepreneur*. That's a mouthful of a term that just happens to have the initials M and E. From this point forward, I'm going to (mostly) stop using the full term "maximized entrepreneur" in favor of "ME." If you read "me" every time you see it, so much the better!

The ME Equation

To know thyself *and* improve thyself *and* complement thyself is great. But it only takes us so far. To truly maximize, we need more. So let me introduce you to a new equation, containing elements of approval and acceptance. Without these, a self-awareness journey like the one I have charted for you can become more an Achilles' heel than a competitive advantage.

Know thyself

… *Approve thyself*

Improve thyself

… *Approve others*

Complement thyself

Why add these elements of approval? Why insert the idea of acceptance? Instead of answering directly, let me provide an anecdote.

Over the past three decades, Farragut has grown to become one of the leading providers of workers compensation and property tax solutions in the United States. Over the past five years that I have counted Farragut among my clients, the leadership team and I have spent many days working

> Without these, a self-awareness journey like the one I have charted for you can become more of an Achilles' heel than a competitive advantage.

together at the Decision Center. As part of our effort, we conducted assessments on the leadership team, including the CliftonStrengths 34 (https://www.gallupstrengthscenter.com/Purchase/en-US/Product), the Kolbe A (www.kolbe.com), and the Culture Index (https://www. cindexinc.com/). I highly endorse all three of these assessments, in addition to many others that are in the marketplace, including the DiSC, Myers-Briggs, Enneagram, Leadership Circle, and Personality Research Form (PRF). Find what works best for you!

Ed Parker, a product specialist for Farragut, took the assessments to heart. He listened to all the feedback tapes available from the various assessments, and he thoroughly reviewed his report. After all was said and done, Ed came to a highly interesting conclusion. For him to move forward, he needed to tell himself it was okay to be *himself*.

Wow. Sit back and think about that for a second. Ed felt the need to approve himself.

When you're willing to become vulnerable, to take assessments that include 360-degree reviews in which you get straight-talk input from the people in your organization, you can't help but come to "know thyself." But Ed was the first person to show me that to "know thyself" is not enough. If it were, we would all walk away too painfully aware of our weaknesses. We might even let them overshadow the very important things we've learned about our strengths. Ed showed me that to meet our full potential, we need to see the whole picture, to *approve* who we are. Seeing ourselves in full, being okay with it, yet seeing how to move forward with resolve and optimism—Ed got the importance of this quickly and easily. So much so, in fact, that he invited his wife and children to take some of the same assessments. It was "a life-changing experience for the entire family," he said.

APPROVE THYSELF

We entrepreneurs think we know ourselves very well. We're risk-takers with self-confidence galore, right? But as we grow alongside our companies, we either learn the necessity of "improve thyself" or we become less and less equipped to lead. Similarly, when we come up against the limits of our skill set (or interests), we come to understand why it's important to "complement thyself."

I love what Verne Harnish said in his best-selling book *Scaling Up*:

"To get to 10 employees, founders must delegate activities in which they are weak. To get to 50 employees, they have to delegate functions in which they are strong!"

What "approve thyself" really is, then, is a permission structure for getting out of your head and into your heart. It allows you to worry less about what you think you should be doing, or should be able to do, and key into what you really want to do. You don't need to brood over the skills you lack. You can free yourself from a role that may not fully fit you. You can take a clear-eyed look at what your company needs, feel good about identifying it and doing something about it, and then move on.

I'm not saying that any entrepreneur should stick to doing what he or she knows how to do. I'm saying that once you've moved beyond "know thyself" and "approve thyself," it becomes easier and far more productive to find what you care about most—

> What "approve thyself" really is, then, is a permission structure for getting out of your head and into your heart.

and do the work to *maximize* your abilities in these areas. The only areas that need to be jettisoned are the ones where you know you'll always be weak. Why not let your defeat become someone else's opportunity for victory?

This brings us to the second addition I'm making to the "know thyself, improve thyself, complement thyself" equation.

APPROVE OTHERS

In our heads, we know that the true measure of a leader is not how much we ourselves can do, or how many roles we can handle at the same time. True leadership is measured by how well we develop people, processes, and infrastructure strong enough to function without the entrepreneur's hand on the wheel. Normally, this means offering access to training and other forms of personal development. But at a more fundamental level, this means seeding and growing self-confidence within your organization.

> **True leadership is measured by how well we develop people, processes, and infrastructure strong enough to function without the entrepreneur's hand on the wheel.**

Self-confidence is a superpower for any entrepreneur. But without self-awareness, the entrepreneur stays stuck at "I know what I know" and doesn't take the journey to "I know what I don't know." This is a critical failure, not just for an individual entrepreneur's growth but for the entire organization's growth. Without knowing what we don't know and accepting it—which involves adopting an "approve thyself" attitude—we lack both the motivation and the self-acceptance required to look beyond ourselves for solutions. We become blind to the complementary skill sets that may be nearby, perhaps already on our payrolls.

So the new twist I'm adding with "approve others" is simply the next step. Once we've found the complementary skill sets that we ourselves lack, we shouldn't chip away at these people by telling ourselves—and them—every tiny detail of how or why they're still less than perfect. When we find people who can do what we can't, we shouldn't focus critically on whatever skills they're still developing. It's like looking a gift horse in the mouth.

Know Thyself + Approve Thyself + Improve Thyself + Approve Others + Complement Thyself = Unconscious Competence

You now have the full equation that sums up the road to ME. This is the progression that brings us to the ultimate goal of **unconscious competence**. Best of all, it brings our entire organization along with us. MEs who make the proactive decision to approve others, and to complement themselves with people with better skills than theirs, while also committing to delegating opportunity and authority to them—*these* will be the companies and organizations that will achieve long-term success and reach their full potential.

What's more, reaching **unconscious competence** pays as many dividends for the entrepreneur as it does for the organization. From a personal perspective, it's a lot like reaching *self-actualization* and *transcendence* on Maslow's hierarchy of human needs pyramid. By getting to the peak of the pyramid, you know exactly who you are and what you bring to the world. And this gives you the wherewithal to get out of yourself and do the work the world most needs you to do.

Understanding Unconscious Competence

Take a look at any athlete anywhere. Talent begins the career and carries the athlete to ever-higher levels of competition. But as that career progresses, the goal becomes playing not necessarily harder but smarter. Why? Because they've figured out that to win and stay at the top, these athletes need to surround themselves with great teammates *and become a better teammate themselves*. Talent, a strong will, and tremendous effort just aren't enough. Without strategy, discipline, and team spirit, even the best among them ends up just another player who failed to achieve his or her potential.

Whether we're athletes or entrepreneurs, there are pivotal moments when we have to slow our forward movement so we can gather what we need for a next-phase push. This is the slow-down-to-speed-up advice I've been talking about throughout the Decision Series for Entrepreneurs. It's much like an athlete coming to the recognition that it's not all about him or her, that the team matters too. It's similar for entrepreneurs when we learn it's actually not all about us. It's about ensuring that the company reaches its potential, which starts with providing it the best possible, most *qualified* leadership.

Slow down to speed up involves establishing a new baseline for yourself. Having already reached a point where your company isn't just about "me" anymore, it's time for you to prepare for a transition to ME—*maximized* entrepreneurship. This represents true *entrepreneurial leadership*, the equivalent of a mountaineer's push for the peak. You're standing just below that peak now, within reach of securing the **unconscious competence**, which not only ensures that you can do anything you want (and do it very well), but that your efforts and activities will make a difference. The untapped opportunities and undeveloped markets of the world await your skills. The future's start-up entrepreneurs and wannabe entrepreneurial leaders of society are looking for all the wisdom you can gather to offer them. And our economy desperately needs you. Whether in times of economic growth or severe disruption, the world will always need successful, experienced, entrepreneurial leaders—both to create jobs and help society reduce the still-dismal failure rate of young, growing companies.

Know Thyself *and Approve Thyself*

+ Improve Thyself

+ Approve Others and Complement Thyself

= Unconscious Competence

= the ME Equation

I often talk about a list I derived by asking clients and speech attendees to tell me the first word that came to mind when I said "entrepreneur" and "CEO." Across a decade of asking the question, the list has remained pretty much the same. The entrepreneur always comes across as the creator and the risk-taker, and the CEO as the leader and the disciplined communicator.

But what if we combined the lists?

Entrepreneur	*and*	CEO
Crazy/Fearless	*and*	Disciplined
Risk-Taker	*and*	Responsible/Steady
Creative/Innovative	*and*	Organized
Energetic/Driven	*and*	Communication/People Skills
Maverick/Independent	*and*	Communicator
Intelligent	*and*	Visionary

To me, the "ands" make it ME—a *maximized* entrepreneur. It's the whole package, and at this stage of our career, I think it's what we're shooting for when we seek to make the Fourth Decision.

Just for fun, consider a few more combinations—ones I mentioned at the beginning of the chapter, ones that ought to describe us at the height of our careers:

Self-Confident	*and*	Self-Aware
Right Answers	*and*	Right Questions
Entrepreneurship	*and*	Leadership

The ME seeks to operate their organization and career in a state of unconscious competence. No longer merely *qualified,* and functioning in states of conscious incompetence and conscious competence, the ME is moving on in hopes of taking the next big step. By getting this far, you've shown that you not only know how to do something, but that you rock at it. You've also displayed the self-awareness necessary to determine what you're not good at and find others who can rock it. It's having made the effort to improve, but when that wasn't sufficient for your organization's needs, finding the complementary personalities and skill sets to get the whole organization rocking. And all along the way, it's about approving each step, accepting what is now, and welcoming what will be in the future.

There. You now understand the meaning of becoming an ME—a *maximized* entrepreneur. While I'm not aiming to help you decide whether to start another business, or retire, or find a way to "give back," I do believe that this effort to *maximize* yourself as an entrepreneurial leader will inevitably involve such considerations. If you come away with a clearer sense of where you want to go, all the better. But my main goal is to take you to the pinnacle of your powers—and the tip top of that Maslow's pyramid, where self-actualization and transcendence live.

The journey of *The Fourth Decision* will be similar to *The Second Decision* (and when it's written, "The First Decision"). At the end of each chapter, you'll be filling out a "qual card" inspired by the ones I did for skills acquisition in the Navy. Your MEQC will be a checklist aimed at keeping you on task and providing food for thought. Unlike most organizations, the Navy doesn't rely on writing a good job description, or simply hiring for qualifications and hoping for on-the-job training. The Navy relies instead on establishing knowledge requirements and a process for checking to see that the requirements have been met. There, knowledge takes priority over experience. As I've mentioned, it also allows for experience, because nobody's going to let you drive the submarine until you can prove you know how.

It's been my longstanding belief that we entrepreneurs can and do benefit from a similar approach. I'm not arguing for giving knowledge complete priority over experience when it comes to starting and running a company; how could that work? But I do believe that our companies and our economies would benefit if the two could better coexist.

The Self-Awareness Decision Tool

To get us off to a fast start, I have an exercise for you, and it's centered on this chapter's topic: self-awareness. In fact, it takes the theoretical content of this chapter and turns it into something challenging and real. We start with a favorite question: it's the "You have been fired" question.

Imagine that you have been fired, and in the year since it happened, your successor has been wildly successful. Referring to the upper portion of the chart, enter the top three changes he or she made—things you either chose not to do, did not know how to do, or did not know what to do. Then move on to the next section, where you'll input the results of the assessments that you have taken. In this example, the leader has taken the Culture Index, Kolbe A, and CliftonStrengths 34.

TOOL: SELF-AWARENESS DECISIONS

NAME/DATE	Baseline - "The Truth and the Trends"		
	1	**2**	**3**
You have been fired Your successor has been wildly successful over the past 12 months. What did they do that (1) you didn't want to do, (2) you didn't know what to do, and (3) you didn't know how to do it?			

Assessments/Date Completed	"The growth of a company is limited by the growth of its leaders" "Double your personal capacity in the next 12 months" "The fatal flaw of a leader is their lack of self-awareness"		
Culture Index			

Kolbe A	Fact Finder	Follow Through	Quick Start	Implementor

CliftonStrengths 34	1	2	3	4	5
Top 5 Strengths					
	30	31	32	33	34
Bottom 5 Strengths					

Self-Awareness (Top 3 in Each)		1	2	3
Know Thyself	**What** are your greatest strengths/ your areas of Genius/Excellence? *Don't include strengths that you are just competent at (Genius/Excellence/ Competence/Incompetence)*			
Accept Thyself	**What** are your greatest weaknesses - that if you don't improve upon or delegate to others - the company will underperform? *Which strengths are also weaknesses?*			
Improve Thyself	**What** specifically do you need to commit to improving in the next 12 months to double your personal capacity?			
Accept Others	**What** do you need to delegate in order to set the organization up to reach its full potential? *BY WHEN?*			
Comple- ment Thyself	**Who** do you need to complement yourself with so that the organization is set up to reach its full potential? *BY WHEN?*			

The Decision Series™

Now let's get to the crux of this exercise. The next five blocks will move you from the theory of this chapter to actually putting it into practice.

The first question asks you to define your areas of genius and excellence. It's important to note what the question is *not* looking for in the areas in which you're merely competent, or worse, incompetent. It's really asking for your unique abilities, so think hard and set the bar high. Above all, don't just check the blocks, don't just fill in the answers you think you should. Remember, a lack of self-awareness is a leader's fatal flaw, so let's confront the brutal truth!

The second question is the opposite of the first—it asks about your weaknesses. But note the clarifying aspect of the question: Where will the company underperform if you choose to remain active in your areas of weakness? Which strengths of yours have become a weakness over time?

The third question is all about you and doubling your personal capacity every two to three years. In what specific areas do you need to improve? No one-word answers here, please. Put some real thought into your responses here and throughout the exercise.

The last two blocks are looking for specifics. What do you need to delegate and to whom?

This exercise—which will be enhanced as a tool later in the book—is great for encouraging your own self-awareness, but it also can help you develop it in leaders of all types and at all levels of your organization. At a very minimum, you should be filling this out annually and looking for opportunities to share it with your current and emerging leaders at the same interval. But as the growth and complexity of your business increases, it could become a quarterly requirement.

Done right, this exercise allows you to clear the starting gate and begin your ME journey through this book.

Here is your qual card for the "ME Equation" chapter:

MEQC—What's Next?!

Learn. Think. Decide. Implement.

Initials

1. The ME commits to growing his or her self-awareness by taking at least three assessments, such as Kolbe A, CliftonStrengths Finder, Culture Index, Enneagram, Leadership Circle, DiSC, Myers-Briggs, and PRF. In order to be qualified, the assessments have to be reviewed by a professional who is trained in the assessment and then the ME reviews the results with a coach, a peer group, etc. _____

2. The ME defines and explains the ME Equation, detailing how full potential is reached through all the different components of the equation. _____

3. The ME completes the Self-Awareness Decision Tool, filling out all blocks completely—repeating this on at least an annual basis, and explaining in detail the answers to all blocks in the tool. _____

4. The ME commits to doubling his or her personal capacity every two to three years. This "improve thyself" task should be undertaken only after completing the baselining in number 1 and number 3 of this chapter's qual card and reaching the strengths and weaknesses awareness that is required to "accept thyself." _____

5. The ME commits to the Unconscious Competence level as the standard for the remainder of his or her ME career, both for himself/herself and for the organization. _____

6. The ME reads or rereads their notes from
    The Second Decision and *The Third Decision*
    books, prior to moving on in this book, to get
    maximum value from *The Fourth Decision*. The
    ME discusses in depth *The Second Decision*
    and *The Third Decision* notes during the
    checkout—with a coach, peer group, etc. _____

7. The ME commits to and can fully explain the
    "and" philosophy, giving at least ten examples
    of how the *"and"* applies in his or her entrepre-
    neurial career. _____

Signature: _____

Date: _____

CHAPTER 2

The Entrepreneur's Life Stages, Part I

The only person you are destined to be
is the person you decide to be.
—RALPH WALDO EMERSON

Where we are, and where we're going. Let's start this chapter by taking a look at the difference between who we are as entrepreneurs compared to the MEs we hope to become:

Entrepreneurs are driven by autonomy. We want to make our own decisions and be our own boss.

Maximized entrepreneurs are driven by autonomy too, but MEs are also willing to hold themselves accountable for the decisions they make. They are aware that there are consequences to their decisions, and they accept those consequences.

✳

Entrepreneurs are idea people. We are constantly thinking about the next thing, sometimes to the detriment of what's best for the business. We will never retire!

Maximized entrepreneurs learn to say yes to the right things and no to most things, especially as they age. They don't retire, by and large—they just learn to work differently.

Entrepreneurs want to be relevant. We want to change the world, and we have the self-confidence and sheer willpower to make it happen!

Maximized entrepreneurs want to change the world throughout their career, but they are fully aware that to remain relevant, they must continue to improve. They do this by knowing and accepting themselves and complementing themselves by accepting others.

*

To begin getting a closer look at the typical ME's life, let's start by revisiting a few questions and considerations, for entrepreneurship is a lifestyle choice that can and does morph over time. *Imagine yourself at age sixty-eight.* What do you want life to look like near the end of a normal career? More specifically, what would you want people to say about you in the following areas?

- Your business

  _____

  _____

  _____

- Your family

  _____

  _____

  _____

- Your significant other

_____

_____

_____

- Your health

_____

_____

_____

- Your friends

_____

_____

_____

Homing in on the above answers, think about the key issues that will affect the next and possibly last stage of your career. You may recognize this line of questioning from other books in the series, but here, I'm inviting you to reengage with some of these questions and considerations, for entrepreneurship is a lifestyle choice that can and does morph over time.

Do you want to be actively working at sixty-eight? Or do you want to be fully or partially retired?

_____

_____

_____

Do you think you'll still be striving to be relevant in the business world at age sixty-eight? Or do you think you'd happily move into a life of leisure or alternate pursuits?

_____

_____

_____

Now, consider your answers from a younger perspective, maybe ten years older than you are today (or five years, if that works better). Are there any differences between your answers for age sixty-eight and those you'd fill in for a younger you?

_____

_____

_____

What do your answers tell you about what you're doing and why?

_____

_____

_____

What is your Core Purpose?

_____

_____

_____

Finally, think for a moment of where you're trying to go and how you're doing on getting there. In which areas of your life are you setting yourself up for regrets?

_____

_____

_____

After taking these assessments, tempting as it may be to think that starting and running companies is a young person's game, it's really not. Let's look at some statistics:

Forty years old. According to studies out of Duke University, the Ewing Marion Kauffman Foundation, the Founder Institute, and Northwestern University, the average entrepreneur is actually forty years old when launching his or her first start-up. The average age of those leading fast-growth start-ups is forty-five years old.[2]

Forty-three years old. This is the average age of the ten-thousand-plus-member Global Entrepreneur's Organization. Recent data shows the age range as follows:

- 11 percent are under thirty-five

- 32.5 percent are ages thirty-five to forty-two

- 30.8 percent are ages forty-three to forty-nine

- 19.5 percent are ages fifty to fifty-six

- 6.1 percent are age fifty-seven and over

69.9 percent married. Entrepreneurs tend not to be single when they launch their first business, with nearly 70 percent married and an additional 5.2 percent divorced, separated, or widowed.

59.7 percent involved in parenting. Survey respondents indicated they had at least one child when they launched their first business, and 43.5 percent had two or more children.

2.3 companies on average. Most of the entrepreneurs in the sample were serial entrepreneurs (SEs), with more than two start-ups to their credit.[3]

---

2   "What Is the Average Age of Successful Entrepreneurs?" *Business World,* February 13, 2019, https://www.businessworldit.com/startups-funding/what-is-the-average-age-of-successful-entrepreneurs/.

3   Dharmesh Shah, "12 Facts about Entrepreneurs That Will Likely Surprise You," *Venture Beat,* September 25, 2009, https://venturebeat.com/2009/09/25/12-facts-about-entrepreneurs-that-may-surprise-you/.

To summarize the results of these various studies:

- The average entrepreneur was forty when he or she launched a first start-up.

- High-growth start-ups were launched by people over age fifty-five more than twice as often as people under thirty-five.

- Age did not drive entrepreneurial success as much as previous start-up and industry experience.[4]

Here are a few more data points to add to the mix :[5]

PERCENTAGE OF PEOPLE WHO MARRIED, BY AGE

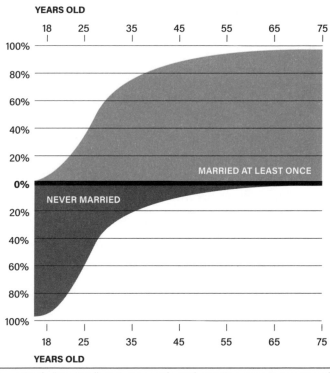

4 George Deeb, "Age Really Is Just a Number When It Comes to Entrepreneurial Success," *Entrepreneur*, July 14, 2014, https://www.entrepreneur.com/article/235357.

5 Nathan Yau, "Percentage of People Who Married, Given Your Age," FlowingData, https://flowingdata.com/2017/11/01/who-is-married-by-now/.

PERCENTAGE OF CHILDLESS WOMEN IN THE UNITED STATES IN 2018, BY AGE

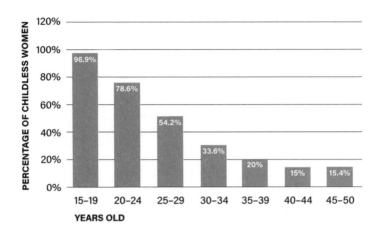

So the average entrepreneur starts his or her first business at age forty, the average age of the leader of high-growth start-ups is forty-five, 80 percent of people will be married by the age of forty, and over 80 percent of women will have had a child by age forty.

Since we're picking up at a point when you've been in your entrepreneurial career for about ten years, it's fair to assume you're nearing, currently in, or just past the thick of everything—and by that I mean entrepreneurial growth management, marriage, and children. It's the time of life when it's almost groan-worthy when you hear that old "You get one life, so make the most of it" advice. Yet we should be actively and periodically looking at doing just that, whatever the phrase may mean for each of us as individuals. Happy people do better at everything. At all ages and stages of our career, we need to be sure we're loving the job *and* the life.

I want to take a few pages now to remind you of how thoroughly entrepreneurship and life intersect and intertwine. I'm going to touch on eight impacts on an entrepreneurial life.

1. The four stages of your life

2. Raising kids and the *aha* moment

3. The U-curve (or U-bend) of happiness

4. Recessions

5. Your fluid and crystallized intelligence

6. Physical and mental health

7. Midlife for maximized entrepreneurs

8. Working energetically until you are well into old age

TOOL: ENTREPRENEURIAL LIFE STAGES

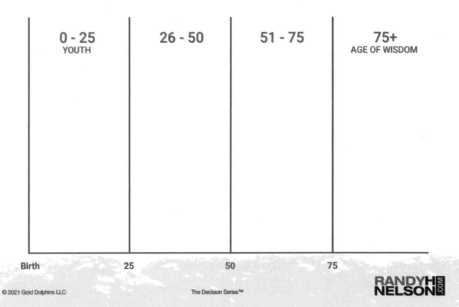

Recognize this illustration of life phases? We've referred to it in previous books, but this time we'll focus entirely on the middle phases, leaving out youth (zero to twenty-five) and the over-seventy-five age group, which many of us would consider old age.

Obviously, I'm going with averages for the purpose of simplifying things here. There are plenty of parents at age twenty, and that fact makes forty-five-year-old grandparents easily possible. The critical learning is simply that life has phases, and we each need to think about how the phases of our life differ and why. What we want and need in one phase may be quite different in the next, right?

Now that you've seen the whole life span, let's narrow the window in a way that is most relevant to MEs, people with ten years of entrepreneurship under their belts. Instead of looking at a career that spans ages twenty-five to seventy-five, let's focus attention on thirty-five to sixty-eight. This recognizes that some of you may have launched your first start-up at age twenty-five and, well, you'll soon understand why I chose sixty-eight. If thirty-five to sixty-eight represents a typical ME's career span, then ages thirty-five to fifty-one might be considered one's early career, and fifty-one to sixty-eight would be a late phase of that career. If you're older than sixty-eight as you read this, congratulations and thank you—you've got more wisdom to bring to the table for yourself and the rest of us!

Why did I divide the ME career in two? To recognize two very distinct phases in life that impact these halves of a career. Between ages thirty-five and fifty-one, most of us are hip deep both in building a business and growing a family. Between ages fifty-one and sixty-eight, we're entering the empty-nest phase, when business growth continues but no longer in hot competition with the hectic pace of family activities during child-rearing.

Another disclaimer: Not everybody raises kids, not everybody finds the cruise control in running a business, and not everybody reading this book has turned thirty-five yet. Acknowledged. I still hope what you read in this chapter will give you some insight into the phases you've seen or may yet see in your life.

Let me show you some research on life phases, based on Hindu teachings. Each phase is called an Ashrama, but specific phases get their own names.[6]

TOOL: ENTREPRENEURIAL LIFE STAGES

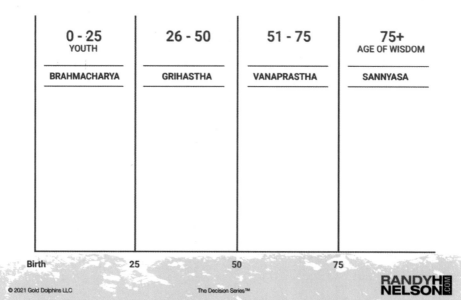

0 - 25 YOUTH	26 - 50	51 - 75	75+ AGE OF WISDOM
BRAHMACHARYA	GRIHASTHA	VANAPRASTHA	SANNYASA

Birth　　25　　50　　75

© 2021 Gold Dolphins LLC　　The Decision Series™　　RANDYH NELSON

The first stage is **_Brahmacharya_**, the period of youth and young adulthood. It's dedicated to learning.

The second stage is **_Grihastha_**, when a person builds a career, accumulates wealth, and creates a family. In this second stage, the philosophers identify one of life's most common traps: people become attached to earthly rewards—money, power, sex, prestige—and thus try to make one or more of these a lifetime pursuit.

6　"Hinduism," Wikipedia, accessed November 3, 2021, https://en.wikipedia.org/wiki/Hinduism.

The third stage is the antidote to these worldly temptations, called *Vanaprastha.* The name comes from two Sanskrit words meaning "retiring" and "into the forest." This stage, starting at around age fifty, is one in which we purposely focus less on professional ambition and become more devoted to spirituality, service, and wisdom. It is the stage for study and training for the last stage in life, *Sannyasa.*

Sannyasa is the ultimate stage of life. It is dedicated to enjoying the fruits of enlightenment. Doing so requires us to resist the conventional lures of success in order to focus more widely, encompassing things that may be more important and longer lasting. This is sometimes referred to as self-transcendence, which is best known as the apex of Maslow's hierarchy of needs, a life-stage tool I've referenced throughout the Decision Series. At the bottom of Maslow's pyramid are survival needs such as food and shelter. When these are satisfied, our psychological selves reach for higher goals such as love. The highest achievements are the ones that make us most fully ourselves (self-actualization) and take us beyond ourselves, satisfying needs that contribute to the world and its future (self-transcendence).

The Hindu philosophy of Ashramas is similar to the wisdom we find in many philosophical traditions: it suggests that we should be prepared to walk away from the rewards of success well before we feel ready to do so. It tells us that even though we're enjoying the heights of our professional prestige and accomplishments, it's then that we should begin scaling back our career ambitions—that is, if we hope to scale up our metaphysical ones.

Retire into the forest? Not MEs! How can we do that at age fifty if we didn't even start our businesses until age forty, on average? Good point. For us, it appears the Vanaprastha stage either has to be delayed or it has to look different. Most likely, our building phase extends into the Vanaprastha stage, and into the Sannyasa phase as well—though any building we're doing at these points is likely to be of a much different type or form than it was in our thirties and forties.

Don't take this to mean that "entrepreneurs don't age." We do, just like everybody else. And it's my belief that how we age—as an entrepreneur or as an ME—will go a long way toward determining how happy we'll be. Let me remind you of the happiness curve we discussed in *The Third Decision*.

THE U-CURVE
Self-reported well-being, on a scale of 1–10

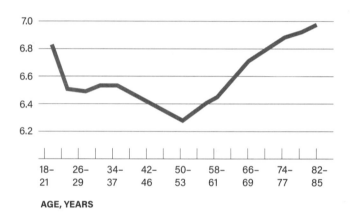

Source: Adapted from PNAS paper: "A snapshot of the age distribution of physchological well-being in the United States" by Arthur Stone

As the graph shows, people self-report their level of happiness as being high in their youth, then sagging through their twenties, thirties, and much of their forties.

The U-curve (or U-bend) shows that four main factors affect our level of happiness at any given age:

Gender. Women are, by and large, slightly happier than men. But they are also more susceptible to depression. A fifth to a quarter of women experience depression at some point in their lives, compared to a tenth of men. (For more information on mental health and entrepreneurs, refer to chapter 11 in *The Third Decision*.)

Personality. Neurotic people—those who are prone to guilt, anger, and anxiety—tend to be unhappy. Extroverts tend to be happier than introverts—which means that those who enjoy working in teams and look forward to parties tend to be happier than those who work with the door closed during the day and hole up at home nights and weekends.

External circumstances. Married people tend to be happier than single people. Employed individuals are happier than the unemployed. People with children in the house report being less happy than those without. More-educated people are happier, but that effect disappears when controlled for level of income. (See also chapter 7 in *The Third Decision*.)

Age. Worry peaks in middle age, then falls sharply. Anger declines throughout life. Sadness rises slightly in middle age and declines thereafter. What this tells us, of course, is that the losses and health problems of age do come with a silver lining of greater happiness.

TOOL: ENTREPRENEURIAL LIFE STAGES

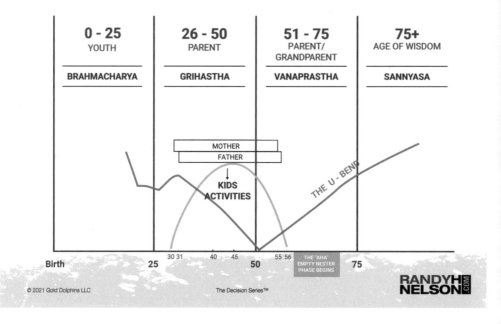

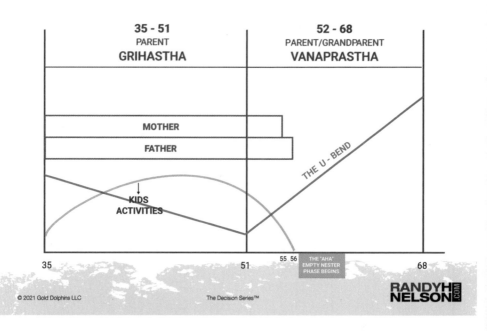

What all of this tells us is that the first half of the ME phase (thirty-five to fifty-one) is a period where feelings of happiness tend to be declining markedly. However, the second half (fifty-one to sixty-eight) is, for most of us, a time of consistently increasing happiness.

As you've seen, what you're doing besides being an entrepreneur has a substantial impact on first-half happiness. Some of those include what you might call (drum roll) the parenting factor.

Parenting spans roughly twenty-five years, allowing us time to raise one to two children on average. Around the world, humans are procreating later, with the median age of first-time mothers now at thirty, up from age twenty-one in 1972. For fathers, it's a first child at thirty-one, up from twenty-seven.[7] No doubt many of you who are reading this book are in the extremely challenging phase that includes both raising kids and growing a company.

For most of us, active parenting ends in our early to midfifties (age thirty or thirty-one plus twenty-five years). I know, there are many second marriages and second families started later in life. But if this describes you, rest assured I'm going to give you the chance to create your own customized chart. Doing so will ensure that this exercise will be fully applicable to your life.

The next element to add to the curve are the kids' activities during your active parenting years. As parents of six, my wife, Kristi, and I were running nonstop, but the same is true for families of one to three children. No kids? Chart your nonbusiness activities instead. We entrepreneurs often overextend ourselves as we are building our careers, saying yes to everything, and only gradually learning to say no. During this phase of our life we are most definitely in a hurry

---

7   Quoctrung Bui and Claire Cain Miller, "The Age That Women Have Babies: How a Gap Divides America," *The New York Times*, August 4, 2018, https://www.nytimes.com/interactive/2018/08/04/upshot/up-birth-age-gap.html.

from the moment we wake up until the time our heads hit the pillow … too many things to do and businesses to build!

As those of us who are already empty nesters know, there comes a day when you suddenly realize that all the high-stress, nonstop activity of raising children is ending. As much as we knew it was coming and as eagerly as we were looking forward to it, it's usually a bit of a shock. Things get very quiet while you wait for the grandparenting phase to begin!

Doesn't it sound fabulous? The kids have moved on into their lives. The house is quiet. Household schedules are suddenly much more manageable. It's just you and your spouse, for the rest of your lives.

Okay, now how fabulous does it sound?

During the coronavirus crisis of 2020, the divorce rate went up, most likely due to the fact that couples were quarantined together every day, without a break. Relationships that were rocky quickly found some footing or became irrevocably worse. As you read this, are you feeling some apprehension? Some regrets, perhaps? Well, stick a pin in this line of thinking too. We'll be back to it.

TOOL: ENTREPRENEURIAL LIFE STAGES

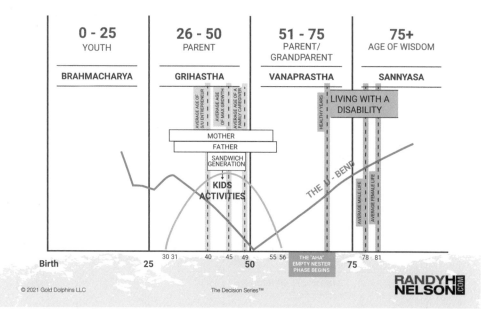

Interesting, isn't it? The trend lines are inverted. And if it looks complicated now, just think, we don't even have our business lives yet.

The graph here includes some additional data, this time on life span:

- The average female lives to age eighty-one. The average male lives to age seventy-eight.

- The average entrepreneur starts his or her business at forty, you'll recall, and if it survives, it will be a fast-growth start-up by the time the entrepreneur is forty-five.

- The average American lives sixty-eight healthy years. The remaining ten to thirteen years are lived with a disability.

59

- The average age of a family caregiver—often someone caring for both kids and aging parents, part of what's been called "the sandwich generation"—is typically age forty to fifty-nine.[8]

Here's our life stages diagram so far.

TOOL: ENTREPRENEURIAL LIFE STAGES

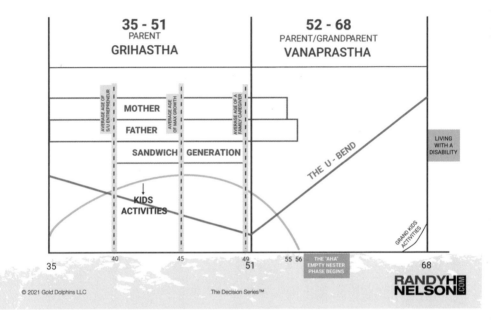

Looking at the curve against the passage of time, it's clear that the time available to generate wealth and enjoy the fruits of one's labor is really quite short—especially if we end up at all limited by health in our later years. Times are different, of course, and medical care has improved greatly. Still, I'm willing to bet that many of you have seen the same pattern I've seen in my family: healthy into their midsixties,

---

8   Claire Samuels, "What Is the Sandwich Generation? Unique Stress and Responsibilities for Caregivers between Generations," A Place for Mom, July 7, 2020, https://www.aplaceformom.com/caregiver-resources/articles/what-is-the-sandwich-generation.

but not many could make the same claim in their seventies. The oldest among us may be seeing the pattern beginning to play out in our own lives. We aren't likely to be as vital at seventy-eight or eighty-one as we were at sixty-eight, right?

And here's why this ought to be front and center as each of us considers our future: the window of time available to us is not as big as we might think. We don't live forever. We don't stay the same as we age. We get one ME life, and there are no do-overs.

But let's add a third component to the ME life curve, one related to outside economic factors such as downturns, recessions, and black swan events. As I write this chapter, the world is trying to find its way out of the almost unprecedented double shock of a pandemic and the resulting near-shutdown of the world economy. I hope that by the time you read this, the combination of reliable treatments and available coronavirus vaccines has restored us to a more normal way of life. But while the next disruption is likely to be something smaller, the lesson of economic history is that there will always be another disruption to cause us pain. Disruptions bring entrepreneurial opportunity, of course—consider that Microsoft, Burger King, CNN, IBM, Disney, General Motors,

> **We get one ME life, and there are no do-overs.**

GE, and Tollhouse Cookies were all born in recessions. Success remains available to the nimble too. Apple, with its new digital offerings and eventually its iPhone, managed to rebirth itself following the 2001 recession. But many, many businesses are less fortunate, and almost untold numbers of them fail when economic indicators dip.

Real Gross Domestic Product

(Quarterly)

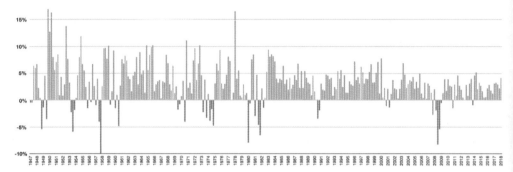

The chart above tells us something important. During our ME careers, we are likely to experience one and probably two to three recessions between the ages of thirty-five and sixty-eight. We can't always predict their exact arrival time or their depth, but we do have the potential to decide how we'll handle the next downturn. Assuming you've already been through a recession during your entrepreneurial career, what do you want to do differently next time? Do you want to be leading the company and pointing it toward success at such a time? Or would you rather that someone else leads the charge? Might you want to sell the company before the next recession arrives, so you don't have to go through such a thing again?

Let's add in another component—our intellectual capacity and how we use it. As you might know, the news on intellectual decline isn't good.

In an article published by *The Atlantic* titled "Your Professional Decline Is Coming (Much) Sooner Than You Think," there are lots of sobering facts about our capabilities as we age:[9]

- On average, success and productivity increase for the first

---

9 Arthur C. Brooks, "Your Professional Decline Is Coming (Much) Sooner Than You Think," *The Atlantic*, July 2019, https://www.theatlantic.com/magazine/archive/2019/07/work-peak-professional-decline/590650/.

twenty years after the inception of a career. The specific timing of the peak and the subsequent decline vary somewhat, depending on the field.

- Entrepreneurs peak and decline earlier, on average. After earning fame and fortune in their twenties, many tech entrepreneurs are in creative decline by age thirty.

- In 2014, *Harvard Business Review* reported that founders of enterprises valued at $1 billion or more by venture capitalists tend to cluster in the twenty to thirty-four age range.

- The most common age for producing a *magnum opus* (think major inventors and Nobel winners) is the late thirties.

- Most successful start-ups have founders under age fifty.

- Authors, meanwhile, were likely to reach the number one spot on the *New York Times* Best Sellers list in their forties and fifties.

The same article provides insight into the psychological impact of our changing abilities. Abundant evidence shows that the higher our accomplishments in life, the more psychologically brutal it is for us to see our abilities waning. While we might hope to take pride (and comfort) in the memory of our accomplishments, it appears that many of us have trouble appreciating anything but what we're able to achieve currently.

In such a mindset, unhappiness grows, fed by a sense that we've become irrelevant with age. The impacts on health and longevity can be real. In one study, senior citizens who "rarely" or "never" felt useful were *nearly three times as likely to develop a mild disability*, compared to those who "frequently" felt useful. The first group was also more than three times as likely to have died during the study.

Unhappy is he who depends on success to be happy.
—ALEX DIAS ROBERTO,
FORMER FORMULA 1 RACE CAR DRIVER

This quotation is not just instructive; it provides reason for optimism. It suggests what we know to be true—that some people manage to beautifully handle the normal decline that is part of aging. What's their secret?

A potential answer lies in the work of the British psychologist Raymond Cattell, who in the 1940s introduced the concepts of fluid and crystallized intelligence.[10]

Fluid intelligence—raw intellectual horsepower. Innovators typically have an abundance of fluid intelligence, and it is at its highest relatively early in adulthood and diminishes starting in one's thirties and forties.

Crystallized intelligence—the ability to use the knowledge gained in the past. Think of it as possessing a vast library and understanding how to use it. It is the essence of wisdom. Because crystallized intelligence relies on an accumulated stock of knowledge, it tends to increase through one's forties and does not diminish until very late in life.

Leaders tend to be older; rare are the CEOs of large companies who are not in their forties or fifties.

Entrepreneurs can and do hit it big with fast growth, exiting early and often with fabulous wealth. But leaders tend to be older; rare are the CEOs of large companies who are not in their forties or fifties. These older leaders have had to learn to

---

10   Paolo Ghisletta and Thierry Lecerf, "Crystallized and Fluid Intelligence," *Oxford Bibliographies*, February 22, 2018, https://doi: 10.1093/OBO/9780199828340-0207.

delegate and build leadership teams—the growth of the company has required it, but so have their own changing capabilities as older leaders. And to my mind, *maximized* entrepreneurs are those who have learned to make magic with their skills and experience. They've learned to play to their strengths, not because the company requires it or their waning skills mandate it, but because they have recognized their crystallized intelligence as true strength. It's an entrepreneurial leader who has self-selected a role that energizes him or her from morning to night.

And to my mind, *maximized* entrepreneurs are those who have learned to make magic with their skills and experience. They've learned to play to their strengths, not because the company requires it or their waning skills mandate it, but because they have recognized their crystallized intelligence as true strength. It's an entrepreneurial leader who has self-selected a role that energizes him or her from morning to night.

Another component for consideration: physical health. Data shows sixty-eight to be the year that a typical person will start living with a disability, one that will persist for the next ten to twelve years of his or her life. None of us wants to be bound or inhibited by age. Ideally, we MEs are positioning ourselves well to make full use of our crystallized intelligence far into the future. But some of us will get in our own way, simply by failing to do everything possible to stay healthy. A Harvard University study found five key factors to healthy aging:[11]

---

11   Monique Tello, "Healthy Lifestyle: 5 Keys to a Longer Life," *Harvard Business Review*, March 25, 2020, https://www.health.harvard.edu/blog/healthy-lifestyle-5-keys-to-a-longer-life-2018070514186.

1. Don't smoke.

2. Have a body mass index between 18.5 and 25.

3. Exercise moderately at least thirty minutes a day.

4. Drink no more than one 150 ml glass of wine a day for women, two for men.

5. Eat a diet that is rich in fruit, vegetables, and whole grains and low in red meat, saturated fats, and sugar.

Men who adhered to all of these health rules saw their life expectancy at age fifty increase from twenty-six more years (to age seventy-six) to thirty-eight more years (age eighty-eight). For fifty-year-old women, the increase in life expectancy is fourteen years—from twenty-nine more years (age seventy-nine) to forty-three more years (age ninety-three). That's an amazing amount of additional time to spend as an ME!

So on to the last two components of our life stages consideration—dealing with the entrepreneurial midlife crisis and finding a way to work energetically into your older age.

Remember the dip in the U-curve (or U-bend) earlier? That's known as the midlife crisis. Wikipedia defines a midlife crisis as follows:

> A transition of identity and self-confidence that can occur in middle-aged individuals, typically 45–65 years old. The phenomenon is described as a psychological crisis brought about by events that highlight a person's growing age, inevitable mortality, and possibly lack of accomplishments in life.[12]

How exactly does a midlife crisis affect an ME in midcareer?

---

12 "Midlife Crisis," Wikipedia, accessed November 3, 2021, https://en.wikipedia.org/wiki/Midlife_crisis.

Looking back at the research on fluid intelligence versus crystallized intelligence, I note that one of the conclusions reached by the researchers is this: the biggest mistake professionally successful people make is attempting to sustain peak accomplishment indefinitely. In other words, they continue trying to make use of their fluid intelligence, which we know begins fading relatively early in life. Better, the study concludes, to enjoy our accomplishments for what they are, in the moment, and then walk away, on our own terms—even if we don't feel completely ready to do so.

We *can* reach and sustain peak accomplishment through our late career and beyond. We *can* adjust our role to ensure not just the health of the company but our own energy for and our enjoyment of what we do. We just have to live into the ME Equation: by knowing, improving, and complementing ourselves, we are able to position ourselves where our energy is highest and our skills are exceptional. Adding to that, we also

Approve thyself

and

Approve others

These additions to the equation are key because they are the attitudes that make it possible to move into our ME phase without feeling like we're giving something up personally, or risking the company's future, by adjusting our role to one we can thrive in for the long term. Remember, while the most profound insights tend to come from those in their early thirties and forties, the best synthesizers and explainers of complicated

> By knowing, improving, and complementing ourselves, we are able to position ourselves where our energy is highest and our skills are exceptional.

ideas—in other words, the best teachers—tend to be in their midsixties or older, some into their eighties. Of course, great coaches, mentors, and teachers can be of any age. But true wisdom really does come with age and experience. In the entrepreneurial community, the facts on the ground validate the research:

- Chairs of Vistage (global CEO peer group) are typically older and provide the wisdom in the room—becoming the "leader of leaders."

- Thought leaders have great wisdom (and some age too). Consider Dan Sullivan of Strategic Coach (in his seventies), Dr. Gerald Bell of Bell Leadership (in his eighties), and Verne Harnish, founder of EO and Gazelles (in his sixties). I'm now in my sixties too, and happily trying to make productive use of my crystallized intelligence via the Decision Series for Entrepreneurs!

Indeed, we live our most fulfilling life—especially after we've reached midlife—by pursuing things that matter and are most meaningful to us. Yet just as there was a gap between being an entrepreneur and becoming both *qualified* and *intentional* in your entrepreneurship, there is most certainly a gap between being both *qualified* and *intentional*—and becoming a *maximized* entrepreneur.

Maximized entrepreneurs are driven by autonomy, like any entrepreneur, but MEs are also willing to hold themselves accountable for the decisions they make, and they are *aware of, and accept that, there are consequences to those decisions. Maximized entrepreneurs learn to say yes to the right things, and to say no to most things, especially as they age. We don't retire; we just work differently as we age.* As an example, MEs learn to slow down and not be in a hurry all the time, as they age, which is the polar opposite of what we do as entrepreneurs to build our careers. Maximized entrepreneurs want to change the world throughout their career, but they are fully aware that *to remain relevant, they must continue to improve by knowing and accepting themselves and complementing themselves by accepting others.* As an ME with years of experience, you do know where your strengths are, and you also know where you need to complement yourself. But there's plenty ahead in the realm of the unknown. As you age, you will have to figure out how you stay relevant, healthy, regret-free, passionate, and energetic while bridging the gaps and using your new self-knowledge to cross into the next phase.

Don't doubt it for a minute: you *can* be successful throughout your life. And yes, of course, you *can* remain relevant. But not necessarily by doing exactly the same thing you're doing right now. That's what's up next: considering the role that's right for your next phase.

> Maximized entrepreneurs learn to say yes to the right things, and to say no to most things, especially as they age. We don't retire; we just work differently as we age.

MEQC—What's Next?!

Learn. Think. Decide. Implement.

Initials

1. Explain the differences between fluid and crystallized intelligence, applying it in a practical way to your entrepreneurial career between ages thirty-five and fifty-one and fifty-two and sixty-eight.

   _____

2. Explain the four Hindu stages of life in detail and apply them to your own life.

   _____

3. Explain in detail your understanding of the U-curve (or U-bend) of happiness, considering how it applies to your life, both now and in the future.

   _____

4. Plot your own life on the ME Entrepreneurial Life Stages chart, noting your child-raising years, their high-activity years, the recessions you've experienced, etc. Identify both known and potential regrets and alibis that may stem from these phases, as well as potential future regrets based on nonnegotiables you haven't set yet.

   _____

5. Set goals and nonnegotiables around your physical and mental health for the next twelve months and also for the foreseeable future.

   _____

6. Describe in detail the two phases of the ME Life Stages in this chapter as they apply to you, during your thirty-five to fifty-one and fifty-two to sixty-eight age ranges. Also capture your own thoughts on a potential or actual midlife crisis and the changes you anticipate making or have already made. _____

Signature: _____

Date: _____

CHAPTER 3

The Entrepreneur's Life Stages, Part II

*The most important days are the day you
were born and the day you know why.*
—MARK TWAIN

MEs are passionate about living this one life to the fullest, but they know that time is not unlimited. So what do you want your time to look like? *Why are you doing what you're doing right now? How might it look the same—or different—in the future?* More directly stated, *What's next?!*

In my coaching practice, this is a consistent and important focus of my work with entrepreneurs—helping them to explore these questions. You will soon see why.

In this chapter, we are going to focus on an additional six components of your customized and future ME life:

1. The four stages of exit for an entrepreneur

2. Your Core Purpose—now

3. Your new baseline—Who am I now?

4. Your roles at the various stages of your ME life

5. What's next?! 5 + 5 = 10 years

6. Your future Core Purpose

To begin, here are the ME Life Stages, reminding us of where we left off.

TOOL: ENTREPRENEURIAL LIFE STAGES

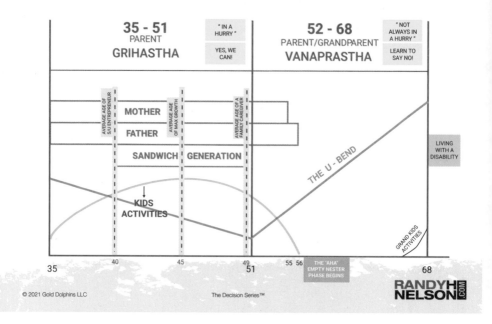

Take a look at the yellow boxes I have added. As MEs, we proactively must learn to say no during our career, as well as to learn how to not be in a hurry all the time … much more on this as the book progresses.

I was forty-five (the age of maximum growth for entrepreneurs) in 2007. We had just sold our business, and we did very well. A very nice liquidity event! I can remember clearly thinking that from that point on in my life, every day would be blue skies and the smile on my face would never fade. I had summited the mountain, and it felt great. My partners and employees, and Kristi and I, had worked hard for this achievement.

But it became clear rather quickly that *I didn't know what I didn't know*. We had been laser-focused on building a valuable business that would attract a buyer. But we hadn't put much thought into what postsale life would look like, except for those forever-blue skies.

Of course, nobody stays at the summit forever. Sooner or later, you have to come down from that mountain peak. For me, it happened quickly. Yes, we had more money in our bank account; financial security improved vastly for us almost overnight. But life, with its flaws and challenges, rolled on. I was already actively building my second business and becoming aware that it would be facing down the Great Recession of 2007–2009. So if I wanted to remind myself that life had actually changed, I'd have to tear myself away from the daily drama and spend a few minutes gazing at the zeroes in my bank account.

I sold that second business and exited at age fifty-two, but only after spending four years with the company that had purchased the business. This transition gave me a second opportunity to learn that *I didn't know what I didn't know*—this time, about selling. But I also learned, that second time around, of the significant struggles that we entrepreneurs can suffer after an exit—especially if there's no set plan for "*What's next?!*"

I learned, intimately and concretely, that when we sell, we sell our "baby," and that with the sale goes our entrepreneurial Core Purpose. That's a biggie, one you can only imagine the shape of until you actually live it in painful detail. When our Core Purpose is no longer there, it's, well, disruptive to say the least.

While building an enterprise, an entrepreneur creates the company's values and purpose, controls the type of people hired, and determines the way time is structured. An entrepreneur, in effect, creates a utopia where one works with the people one wishes to work with, on a purpose of one's choosing, and in the time and manner one chooses. Given the degree of control we all become accustomed to over these large and critical elements of our lives, it shouldn't really come as a surprise that we can be caught totally off guard by the scope of change triggered by the sale of the company.[13]

Every entrepreneur will exit his or her business in some way, shape, or form, at some point on the ME life curve. And that's the point at which you have to ask and answer the question *"What's next?!"*

The Four Stages of Exit

For those who have exited, the words *"What's next?!"* definitely resonate. Those of you who are in the process of exiting also know the truth of the statement. Those of you who are convinced that it's way too soon to think about an exit, or doubt you'll exit without being carried out the door—well, expand your mental comfort zone.

The fact is you don't have as much time as you think you have to design and live the life of an ME—not if you want to enjoy it for the rest of your career. So in this chapter, I want you to switch focus. Look beyond today and, yes, truly begin with the end in mind.

Credit Suisse, in coordination with the Columbia Business School, wrote a whitepaper titled, *"Life after an Exit: How Entrepreneurs Transition to the Next Stage."*[14] The paper discusses the insights

---

13 "Life after an Exit: How Entrepreneurs Transition to the Next Stage," Eugene Lang Entrepreneurship Center at Columbia Business School for Credit Suisse (New York: Credit Suisse Securities USA), 8, accessed November 3, 2021, https://www.credit-suisse.com/media/assets/private-banking/docs/uk/wp-03-life-after-exit-en.pdf.

14 Ibid.

of several authors and includes case studies of various entrepreneurs.

Among the findings in the paper are that the stages of the journey appear to be fourfold, as modeled and prescribed by researcher and leadership coach Frederick Hudson.

THE FIRST STAGE

This stage comes well before the sale or exit. Many entrepreneurs tend not to understand the full intrinsic benefits they are receiving from filling their leadership roles and building their companies—financially, psychologically, and socially. Entrepreneurs in the study consistently stated that *they wished someone had warned them how disorienting a sale would be*, noting that it was their companies that had given them their prime community for relationships, their identity and purpose, and a structure for their time.

If the entrepreneur understands the degree to which the company is supplying meaningful personal relationships, use of time, and sense of purpose, they can take steps to soften the disorienting impact of a sale by preestablishing other social networks, creating other uses of time, and identifying other sources of purpose before the sale is final and the transition begins.

THE SECOND STAGE

This usually encompasses the first year or two after the sale. Even entrepreneurs who had done their preplanning and were more aware of the postsale disorientation likely to hit them reported a difficult or extremely difficult transition. The consistent themes were mourning the lost community and identity, a felt need to find structure, and a search for new and meaningful things to do with one's time. The more the company represented the entrepreneur's identity, the more sadness the entrepreneur felt after the sale. Entrepreneurs who were single without a family, and women who frequently had closer ties with their employees, often had the more difficult time coping with their postexit loss.

However, the first year often goes in one of two directions. One direction is exotic travel or buying and/or renovating homes—both of which tend to leave postexit entrepreneurs unfulfilled and disappointed. A second road leads to a period of overplanning and jumping at all possible opportunities, followed by a period of weeding out activities that proved unfulfilling.

THE THIRD STAGE

Not surprisingly, none of the entrepreneurs interviewed in the Credit Suisse paper ever considered a long-term life of leisure. For them, a "next chapter" necessarily involved work, such as taking an interest, financially or otherwise, in another company or becoming an angel investor in areas of entrepreneurial interest such as woman-owned companies, or those with a particular business model or in a favored industry. The most successful in these categories are those who stick with what they know, limit the size and number of their investments, and give time and wisdom along with money.

Some make poor choices because they didn't spend enough time in the first stage, considering what strengths and attributes had made them successful. Another downfall is overconfidence, a tendency to overcredit skill and underappreciate luck in their previous success. For those entering a new chapter of serial entrepreneurship, success is typically seen in the third or fourth venture—and usually

> The most successful in these categories are those who stick with what they know, limit the size and number of their investments, and give time and wisdom along with money.

when the entrepreneur has recognized that repeatable entrepreneurial success requires not only an understanding of one's skills and talents, but a repeatable business model.

THE FOURTH STAGE

Most postexit entrepreneurs see a new chapter elude them for three years or longer, time filled by "unfulfilling wandering," such as traveling to exotic places, writing books, starting foundations and family offices, mastering complicated investment theories and practices, and launching interesting but failed companies. Each of these activities, however, generally failed a key test: they fell short of being completely absorbing for the exited entrepreneur. However, participants in Hudson's research also reported this to be a time of particular harmony with family and friends. And those who had other identities, as family members or leaders in civic, philanthropic, or other business institutions, appeared to weather the transition more easily.

Todd Yates, a Vistage peer and friend, successful entrepreneur, and the former CEO of Hill Chesson & Woody Employee Benefit Services, told me about a surprising thing in the midst of the 2020 disruption: despite his truly amazing exit, followed by the successful completion of an employment contract with the new owner of his company, he was glad to be living through a pandemic. Without all the enforced time with his family, which brought them closer, he believed he would be feeling very lonely and sad about the change in his status and his daily activities. Todd also readily acknowledged that counseling has been helpful in smoothing out the sense of disruption.

My friend Robbo Newcomb, another highly successful entrepreneur in plumbing and HVAC, offers some additional do's, along with some don'ts, many that seem to confirm the Credit Suisse findings:

1. Plan the transition. Just as the sale itself takes longer than you'd expect, your transition period will also be lengthy—as in, years.

2. Take it slow, "avoid the hard stop." Maybe pull back to three or four days a week in the office postsale. Robbo considers staying involved with the business, albeit in a reduced role, a big plus for him.

3. Stay out of the way of the new CEO and leaders—"They don't need you, and the business needs to move on," Robbo says. By focusing on the organization and its need to succeed, "you won't be as inclined to focus on yourself and feel sorry for yourself."

4. Say no, or at least "not yet" to requests. Give yourself time.

5. View your postsale experience as a multistage process that includes completing business projects, decompressing/unwinding, and reprogramming that hardwired CEO mentality. "Being a CEO can harden you and desensitize you to what is important," he said.

6. Then and only then, enter a phase of self-assessment and exploration. Use your willingness to become self-aware to seek peace in who/what/where you've been and who/what/where you are. Ask a key question: What's important to you? Robbo loves being free of the tyranny of the schedule, the ever-present goals, and the endless to-do lists. Then comes a more-important fill in the blank: Your new circumstances have left you free to do—what?

7. Finally comes a time of "discovery," during which Robbo worked on his personal bucket list, did some reading and learning, and

embarked on inquiries through one-on-one conversations. It was a time of "turning over rocks and testing the waters," of considering what he wanted more of and less of in his life. This discovery period has allowed him to plot a course to "greater significance and purpose, deeper meaning, and fulfillment."

Thanks, Robbo. You've given us the road map we all need. Some of us will work a long time to build one company, and then sell. Some will start multiple companies and sell a few or all of them. Some will be forced to go out of business. Some may determine it's best to turn the business over to a new CEO and take a different role within the company. But no matter the details, *all* of us will have to confront "*What's next?!*" and probably we will do it multiple times in our careers. When we do, we find that our Core Value(s) remain constant, but our singular Core Purpose can, and most likely will, change.

Your Current Core Purpose

To get a notion of where you're going, it helps to know where you are. So ask yourself: *Why am I doing this now? In the context of my current business, what is my Core Purpose?*

For many of us as entrepreneurs, this is one of the most common questions asked of us, and perhaps the most important. When you are a successful entrepreneur, family, friends, and peers will all ask questions aimed at zeroing in on why you do what you do; they want to understand why you're still working like a dog when you don't seem to have to.

The best way to answer such questions is to do some deep thinking about what motivates you. These questions should help by helping you define your Core Purpose.

Why did you start your company?

_____

_____

_____

_____

Why are you doing what you are doing right now?

_____

_____

_____

_____

Why do you want to be an ME in the future?

_____

_____

_____

_____

After considering these questions, my own Core Purpose is crystal clear at this stage of my life and entrepreneurial career: *"To unlock and maximize the inner entrepreneurial leader … by getting the entrepreneur right … first … at every stage of your entrepreneurial career."*

My own personal Core Purpose changed or evolved at different stages of my career, as will yours. My priorities—we've discussed these as "nonnegotiables"—also differed at various stages of my career, as did my role. But the Core Values of my companies (and my personal values) remained consistent.

Take a few minutes to fill in the left column (the "present" blocks) of the next chart. We'll get to the future blocks at the end of the chapter. Note: If you've had multiple roles so far in your career, then be sure to put them all in, and if your nonnegotiables have changed, also indicate how they've shifted.

	PRESENT	FUTURE
Role		
Core Purpose		
Nonnegotiables		
Unique and Exceptional Strengths and Abilities Plus Areas of Genius		
Company Core Values		
Personal Core Values		

Your New Baseline—Who Am I Now?

You've already been introduced to it: **Know thyself. Accept thyself. Improve thyself. Accept others. Complement thyself.**

It's time to begin gathering the self-knowledge that will inform a potential exit, either soon or at some unknown point in the future.

Let's start by setting a new baseline in preparation for determining what might become a new you. This allows you to see who you are today, versus earlier in your entrepreneurial career. List the top ten pieces of advice you would have given your decade-younger self if the two of you were to meet. You might also imagine that you are speaking to a large group of young entrepreneurs, offering advice not only to help them grow their own career but to choose the right role for themselves in the future. Then, after you've written yours, read on to see how your advice compares to that of other entrepreneurs.

THE TOP TEN PIECES OF ADVICE YOUR TODAY SELF WOULD GIVE YOUR DECADE-YOUNGER SELF IF ASKED:

1. _____
   _____
   _____

2. _____
   _____
   _____

3. _____
   _____
   _____

4. _____
   _____
   _____

5. _____
   _____
   _____

6. _____

_____

_____

7. _____

_____

_____

8. _____

_____

_____

9. _____

_____

_____

10. _____

_____

_____

Now, here's a portion of a list published in *Entrepreneur* magazine, titled "An Open Letter to My 24-Year-Old Self."[15] It includes the advice of five billionaires based on the most valuable lessons they've learned:

1. Be ready to run a marathon. You are 20 percent into a 100 percent life. There is no straight path to where you are going. And give something back to the world while you are in your marathon.

2. Have a healthy work-life balance. (Note: I prefer "blend.")

3. Commit. Every true commitment involves time and money. How you use or don't use your time is the best indication of

---

15 Gary Vaynerchuk, "An Open Letter to My 24-Year-Old Self," *Entrepreneur*, November 30, 2017, https://www.entrepreneur.com/article/305386.

where your future is going to take you. Value your time and put a price tag on it.

4. Stay curious.

5. Never stop creating.

6. Enjoy the journey without regret. Stop being so hard on yourself; we are our worst critics. It's going to be okay.

7. Stay open-minded. Ask for feedback. Master your thoughts and emotions. Get an executive coach.

8. Let go of what you are not good at and trust people to do what they do best. Recognize and appreciate peoples' talents. Diversity is vital to the success of a company. Empower empire-builders. Get out of the way.

9. It's not about the money. It's about the purpose.

Gaining a better understanding of who you are will give you a clearer picture of what you want your future to look like.

Your Roles, Now and in the Future

Tempting as it may be to assume that you solved all your identity problems decades ago, there's reason to believe you haven't, especially if you are still evolving from an entrepreneur to an ME. To understand who you are at this point in your life may be the most important qualification step in your drive to become a maximized entrepreneur—it is that important.

Some of this reexamination happens naturally, as we begin thinking about next-phase possibilities, such as the following:

- Building another business

- Renewed focus on expanding your current business

- Considering acquisitions and mergers as new forms of growth and expansion

- Reorganizing management structure and planning for succession

- Considering an exit, be it simply a cash-out of your stake or selling the whole company, and becoming an intrapreneur

- Entertaining the possibility of retirement, be it on time or early

While thinking of all the "whats" and "hows," it's inevitable to also think about the "whys." You're confronted with that biggest of questions:

What's my role now? Why am I doing what I am doing? The latter of these is the Holy Grail for the would-be ME. Maybe your first crack at answering the question leaves you convinced that you're ready to ride that current role of yours off into the sunset. Perhaps you're not seeing any change in how you answered the question early in your career compared to today. If so, I'm here to tell you that you are not looking deep enough. Is it possible that you're looking at the tip of the iceberg, and missing everything underneath and inside of you—the stuff that truly drives you? Role selection is a thread that binds all the books in the Decision Series for Entrepreneurs. In *The Second Decision*, I introduced the idea of choosing an entrepreneurial role for yourself based on self-awareness and assessment. In *The Third Decision*, I zoomed out from a strictly

> To understand who you are at this point in your life may be the most important qualification step in your drive to become a maximized entrepreneur—it is that important.

business focus and invited you to consider how best to balance your entrepreneurial role with the ones that are important in the rest of your life—being a spouse, a parent, even just a self-actualized individual, anyone who wants to have both a successful business *and* a successful life. Here in *The Fourth Decision*, the question is how to take all of the skill and achievement of more than a decade in entrepreneurial business and *maximize* it—however you define that term for yourself.

There are many opportunities out there for proven, successful entrepreneurs who are trying on the possibility of a new career path or role. Listing all the transformations available to you would get pretty lengthy. Instead, let's approach this from a different angle.

What *now* is the highest and best use of everything you bring to the table? To begin figuring out your answer to the question, start by jotting down what turns you on, what gives you a reason to get up in the morning. What gives you energy?

_____

_____

_____

_____

What drains your energy away?

_____

_____

_____

_____

Now think about the aspect of running your business that you feel best at. Or try the question this way: If you could design the perfect business day, what would you be doing?

_____

_____

_____

_____

With the above answers as your foundation, ask yourself this: If your business evaporated somehow, for positive or negative reasons, what sort of new situation might you seek? I'm not asking you to name a business, industry, institution, or nonprofit. I'd rather have you identify whether you want to supervise, invest, market, sell, create new products or services, work with numbers, whatever. To guide your thinking, you might ask yourself what you'd grieve most if somebody gave you your walking papers. Don't say "Everything!" Prioritize. Pick one or two things, and on the qual card at the end of this chapter, note them. They'll be your wayfinders as you do a more detailed consideration of which skills, interests, and activities should feature in any new role you might have in your sights.

Before we move on, let's also consider your boundaries, worries, and fears. Do you have debts and commitments that make it hard to think about doing anything that would put at risk your steady income? Are you a confirmed risk-taker at this point, or would you prefer to migrate to a more controlled risk profile?

Also look at yourself in a more psychological way. Are there personal insecurities and unmet needs you're still working on, ones that might be reduced by sticking around to achieve a couple more wins in your business? Do you doubt that there will be good things ahead for you if you take a leap, either because of market issues or some sense of being underprepared? I'll just say that while your answers to questions like these may not tell you everything you need to know, they may reveal enough for you to see that the timing may not be good for change.

Okay, let's now consider some likely answers. You've considered your interests, skills, and the things that most compel you. You've begun thinking about what sort of situation could fit you in the future. You've also thought about what you'd miss if you weren't in your own company in your current role. In what ways could you continue feeling relevant, useful? Identify the possibilities that suit everything you've learned about yourself:

Being the boss. While others say working with people is the worst part of their job as CEO, there's nothing you like better. Yup, that's where you want to be—standing at the front of a column of people and pointing them in the right direction day after day.

Starting or building things. If you see yourself as a prototypical entrepreneur who still lives for the hustle and the existential challenge of growing an enterprise, this basket is probably where you fit best.

Doing less and/or focusing more. If shouldering the many burdens that come with being CEO is wearing thin, especially when you find other roles both inside and outside your business more attractive, you may be seeking change. You may be happier taking responsibility only for certain segments of a business, be they functions, departments, or special initiatives. But as we'll see, there are lots of possibilities for those with this motivation—the most possibilities, in fact.

Giving back. Want the joy of helping others succeed, using your money, experience, perspective, and insight? The first thing to recognize about goals such as these is that they almost certainly necessitate leaving your current role, if not the business itself.

Bailing out. Looking for time and opportunity to spend your disposable income, travel, hang out with grandkids, or take up a new vocation or hobby? This could be you, and there's absolutely nothing wrong with wanting to take a victory lap. Or early retirement. Or a really long vacation.

Each of these motivations—whether long known about yourself or newly recognized, suggests (or fits with) one or more paths chosen by experienced, successful entrepreneurs like yourself, people seeking ways to *maximize*.

Before I drill down into where the various roles you might consider can take you in your drive to become *a maximized* entrepreneur, I want to address one more motivation, one that hasn't yet been mentioned: *the desire to stop leading and follow for a while.* Indeed, what about those of us who might want to hang up that CEO hat and become somebody's employee? While it's probably a choice more commonly considered among younger entrepreneurs who have experienced dissatisfaction in their entrepreneurial role, or those at any age who have survived a costly business failure, there are other good reasons why someone would consider this shift. Maybe the trade of less responsibility for the same (or more) money sounds good at your current phase of life. Taking a job also can be a nice landing zone between start-ups, or a way to learn a new industry prior to resuming the role of creator. While I won't be spending much time on this goal or interest, I want to acknowledge its legitimacy.

Now let's look at how these various motivations and goals—and the standard Decision Series for Entrepreneur roles that fit them—can play out for experienced entrepreneurs entering a new phase aimed to *maximize*:

Status quo: the appropriate label for anyone who knows that this isn't the right time to make a push toward change that could involve an exit, or perhaps the right opportunities haven't yet come into view.

The dabbler: wants the freedom to pick and choose, but this time you're considering how to fill your days and in what ways to reinvent yourself. Dabblers aren't as disinterested as I once thought. Often, they are simply stuck and not sure what to do next. In my coaching practice, I see this often.

The creator: serial entrepreneurship, social entrepreneurship—the person who is happiest when moving from one start-up to another, no matter the type or product. Let's take a look at the characteristics of the SE, compared to somebody who's more interested in a "one-and-done" approach. Circle all that apply to you:[16]

- Motivated by growth, not just profits.

- Curiosity/desire to keep innovating as a top priority.

- Fierce desire to create businesses / passion for business creation.

- Cut losses / know when to move on, aware that not everything will succeed.

- Failure is an option, but we can't live with regret.

---

16   Neil Patel, "7 Signs You Might Be a Serial Entrepreneur," *American Express*, December 6, 2011, https://www.americanexpress.com/en-us/business/trends-and-insights/articles/7-signs-you-might-be-a-serial-entrepreneur/; Tor Constantino, "5 Traits That Distinguish Serial Entrepreneurs," November 19, 2015, https://www.entrepreneur.com/article/252947Source - 5 traits that distinguish serial entrepreneurs – entrepreneur.com /article/252947; "Serial Entrepreneurs vs. One Time Only Founders—What Are the Key Differences?" *Haggerston Times*, March 29, 2016, https://www.haggerston-times.com/serial-entrepreneurs-vs-one-time-only-founders-what-are-the-key-differences/; Aashish Sharma, "What Is a Serial Entrepreneur?" *Entrepreneur York*, April 14, 2018, https://www.entrepreneuryork.com/entrepreneurship/what-is-a-serial-entrepreneur/.

- Stronger self-confidence and self-reliance than their entrepreneurial selves—they truly back themselves at a much higher level as a serial entrepreneur.

- Understand that money isn't everything. The monetary gain is incidental—it's not the money that drives these leaders, but the challenge of success, the frantic pace of creation, and the excitement of uniting a team.

- Restless professionally (typically after three to four years)—doesn't sit still for long, always another market to enter or untapped problem to solve, very customer-centric.

- Build up company mostly to reach a point of not being needed day to day, at which point a new enterprise can be started. Just want to see the vision through.

- Create a company—mobilize his/her teams, study opportunity to develop a strategy, to the detriment of the operation or daily management function.

- It's not the number of companies created that defines an SE, but instead it's a matter of the SE's mentality and values.

- Plan more for contingency and risk-taking than for their entrepreneurial selves. "Calculated risk-takers."

- Understand that financial losses are the tuition to learn a lesson, master a concept.

Maybe it goes a bit too far, but the message of the quote below is close to target:

*Party with SEs all night long—but partner with
people capable and willing to adopt the discipline
necessary to become a business builder.*
—CHRIS MCGOFF

The role-player: portfolio entrepreneur, investor/venture capitalist, consultant, coach, teacher. Somebody whose entrepreneurial instincts and energies are increasingly turned toward helping other CEOs build their businesses. A portfolio entrepreneur often invests or takes an advisory role with several companies at once. When advice isn't the primary goal, the role-player functions more like an angel or venture capitalist. Some in this slot opt to coach or consult; others may even become business instructors.

The leader: CEO jobs and CEO-like roles. This role offers the possibility of continuing to lead without accepting the financial risk of founding a new company. You can work for another entrepreneur or founder in this role or, as an intrapreneur, head up a particular business segment or new initiative within a corporation. Social entrepreneurship also offers such opportunities. Of course, for those who opt to make an exit by selling their growth company to a larger corporation, intrapreneurship allows a smoother transition than being CEO one day and not CEO the next. It can also offer well-compensated time to consider a next move.

Now, I get asked all the time whether someone can straddle more than one of the above roles. Can a role-player also be a creator or a leader? Or some other combination? Of course! I've done it myself. After selling my second business, I was convinced I would become something of a guide/educate entrepreneur—in other words, a role-player. But then my wife, Kristi, forced me to confront the fact that I was, am, and always will be an entrepreneurship addict. She pointed out that I was going after my book writing and consulting/coaching goals with every bit of the fire in the belly I had exhibited when involved in my start-ups. In other words, I was still a creator.

Today, I'm still that mixture of both roles. But as time goes on, I see myself, more and more, in a new role:

The maximizer: the maximizer focuses on maximizing the organizations they are involved with while blending business and life at a much higher rate, and truly being "present when they are present." Discovering my affinity for this role was the discovery that led me to the theme of this book. How so? Well, for me, heading into my sixties, I simply don't want to devote as many hours each week to my creating and role-playing. I want to do what I want when I want, and I don't want to regret not taking more time off at this stage of my life. I want to flex in and out of my roles and my leisure activities without always having to put them on a calendar. No matter what role I and others like me may choose, the drive is forever forward. MEs, aware of their individual strengths, will always be on the lookout for ways to put them to work in the world.

What's Next?!—5 + 5 = 10

Now we're ready to add a final component to the ME Entrepreneurial Life Stages chart.

What does 5 + 5 = 10 mean? It starts with the one immutable truth: you get just one ME life to live, and there are no do-overs. We've already seen that within any life there are four phases, from youth to older age. We've already committed to living the life of an ME for the rest of our career, and we've begun thinking about what we want and need to live out that life. Finally, we've begun considering how to blend the choices we're making into our ages thirty-five to fifty-one and fifty-two to sixty-eight time frames. All of this furthers my goal, which is to shift you to "I know what I don't know," which is crucial for an ME.

> What does 5 + 5 = 10 mean? It starts with the one immutable truth: you get just one ME life to live, and there are no do-overs.

But now we must refine the career timeline, because for MEs considering an exit, there is a presale timeline of three to five years, and a postsale timeline of three to five years. These time frames need to be recognized and added to your life curve. Taken together you can call it your **ME Exit and Transition Phase.** I'll talk more in-depth about this in the next chapter, but to summarize: If you've lived through a sale, you know that it just doesn't happen in a day. There is preparation for the sale, from getting your paperwork and processes in order; leadership development, so you have a strong team in place to lead the company into the future; and a financial timing decision to make too, based on your revenues and profitability. Finally, there is market timing. Having the world's greatest company doesn't mean anything if the market isn't in the mood to buy it. The coronavirus pandemic of 2020 is a good example, as the world shut down to respond to it. M&A activity plunged and stayed down for several quarters.

My point? You don't just wake up one day and sell your company. It is a process, and it takes time.

Once you are ready to sell, there is due diligence to get through, and then the sale itself. This takes more time. After the papers are signed and the money hits the bank, it's still not over. There's normally an employment agreement requiring you to work one to three years for the company that purchased your organization. And then, finally, comes your transition phase to a new career, which can be fairly short or potentially very long. So combining all of these phases, you're looking at up to five years of your life to go from thinking about selling to starting your new career. And if you choose the route of starting another company, it could easily take five years for you to fully and completely transition from that exit.

5 years (sale of your business) + 5 years (fully transitioned to your new entrepreneurial career) = 10 years of your life in a state of transition as an ME.

You need to factor these ten years into your one-life-as-an-ME career plans. Of course, you can shorten the span significantly by going through the prep without ever actually selling, or by smoothly transitioning into something that you already know. But statistics tell us that everyone sells at some point, and each of us who sells has particular strengths that have the potential to pull us back into the entrepreneurial ring.

Finally, with this understanding, let's look at where you are now with your Core Purpose.

Your New Core Purpose

So why were you born?

_____

When you look at your ME life curve, what is the one word that comes to your mind right now? Write it down:

_____

Based on the content of the past two chapters, what do you need to start, stop, and keep doing, now and in the future?

Start doing:

_____

_____

Stop doing:

_____

_____

Keep doing:

_____

_____

And finally, fill in the Future section of the chart below.

	PRESENT	FUTURE
Role		
Core Purpose		
Nonnegotiables		
Unique and Exceptional Strengths and Abilities Plus Areas of Genius		
Company Core Values		
Personal Core Values		

With this chart filled in, you now have your first draft of *What's Next?! and Why?* for your future. Congrats! You have put some deep thought and reflection into your Core Purpose for the future. You have also spent time thinking about what role you want to play in such a future. Finally, let's take a look at the ME life curve, with all of its components included, both in the ages thirty-five to sixty-eight career phase as well as overall.

Before we move on to the tools section of the book, let's explore more in-depth the prep work involved in the transition to being an ME.

TOOL: ENTREPRENEURIAL LIFE STAGES

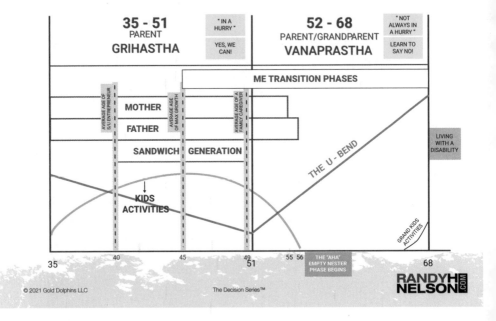

The Decision Series™

RANDYH
NELSON

TOOL: ENTREPRENEURIAL LIFE STAGES

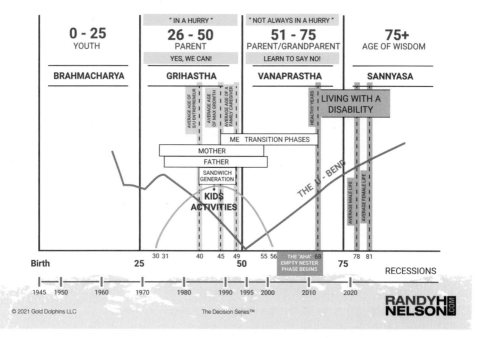

MEQC — What's Next?!

Learn. Think. Decide. Implement.

Initials

1. Discuss your current Core Purpose—Why do you matter as an entrepreneur, and how has this changed (or will this change) across your various entrepreneurial life stages?

   _____

2. Identify the four stages of exit for an entrepreneur. Discuss in detail any experiences in your own career with these stages and your lessons learned. What advice would you give other entrepreneurs?

   _____

3. As part of your checkout, discuss the results of the (minimum three) assessments you have taken during your career. Combine your explanations with an update to the Self-Awareness Decision Tool if you have recently taken new assessments.

   _____

4. Write down the advice you would give a decade-younger version of yourself or an entrepreneurial audience. Explain in detail how the advice applies to you today—in the form of a start, stop, and keep doing list.

   _____

5. Identify and explain which role(s) you would consider for your future. Which roles would you rule out?

   _____

6. Finalize your customized version of the Entrepreneurial Life Stages chart, writing down lessons learned and plans developed for your future.

   _____

7. Discuss why you were born. What does this
   tell you about your personal "What's Next?!"   _____

   Signature: _____

   Date: _____

CHAPTER 4

The ME Exit and Transition Phase

You must find something that you deeply love, and are
passionate about, and are willing to sacrifice a lot to achieve.
—HOWARD SCHULTZ, FOUNDER OF STARBUCKS

A great friend of mine, Aaron Houghton, said something in a podcast that resonated strongly. Aaron sold one of his businesses for over $150 million and, by all *outward* entrepreneurial measurements, the exit was the gold standard, the role model we should all strive for in our exits. But what he said was priceless for preexit entrepreneurs to hear: "I was at a low point in my life two years after the sale, struggling with depression … and being who I didn't want to be. Entrepreneurs are suffering across the board, and when things get hard, we just work harder, and that makes it worse. We work one hundred hours a week just so we don't have to work forty hours a week for someone else."

Nobody describes the issues that successful entrepreneurs face better than Aaron, whose postexit life finds him making a difference in a new way. His organization, Founders First, aims to help entrepreneurs get their mental and emotional struggles out into the open where they can be talked about freely.

The quote at the beginning of the chapter from legendary Howard Schultz of Starbucks strums a chord with all entrepreneurs. We sacrifice a ton to build our businesses, and we do it easily because we love what we do—it suits our personal Core Purpose.

Three other quotes will be guiding us as we move forward.

Success is a lousy teacher. It seduces smart people into thinking they can't lose.
—BILL GATES

How do we live with our success and enjoy the journey in our ME careers, rather than simply letting it drive us toward a destination that guarantees neither success nor joy? How do we avoid losing while we're working so hard to win?

Let your joy be in your journey, not in some distant goal.
—TIM COOK

What will bring us some entrepreneurial peace during the go-go, business-building phase of our entrepreneurial career?

We can never obtain peace in the outer world until we make peace with ourselves.
—DALAI LAMA

Yes, with these questions, I'm suggesting that your current and future entrepreneurial career be adjusted to include words like "joy" and "peace."

What do we get the most energy from? What are we *great at* that we will have a passion for and love to do next? What are we willing to sacrifice now, different than when we were building our first company as an entrepreneur?

Yes, with these questions, I'm suggesting that your current and future entrepreneurial career be adjusted to include words like "joy" and "peace." These should have been part of the goal structure in starting and building a business, but almost certainly they weren't. They should definitely figure strongly in your postexit transition phase.

TOOL: ENTREPRENEURIAL LIFE STAGES

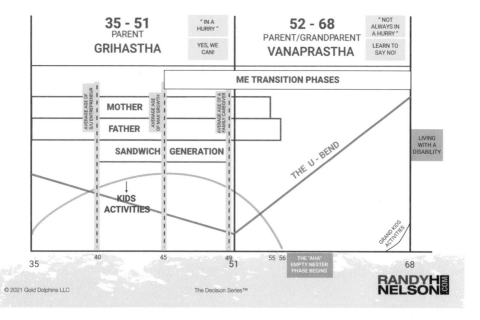

In this chapter we'll focus more closely on what role or roles you may take on in your postexit future—as an entrepreneur, intrapreneur, or nonentrepreneur—and how to prepare for those roles.

We will work through this transition exploration in three sections:

1. Presale—focusing on the prework and due diligence process required for all purchase events.

2. Intrapreneurship—the phase of your entrepreneurial career where you will have a boss, maybe for the first time in your life.

3. Postexit roles—What's next?

Again, this book doesn't pretend to help you through the sale process—there are plenty of other books and consultants out there for that. My goal here is to make you aware of the transitions that may be ahead, and how you can proactively plan for them.

They key ingredient in any transition is the movement from one reality to another. It's the transition from your original Core Purpose to your new Core Purpose, one that's likely in a different entrepreneurial organization or some new context.

> It's the transition from your original Core Purpose to your new Core Purpose, one that's likely in a different entrepreneurial organization or some new context.

Unfortunately, there are certain unpleasant things you need to survive before you can begin working on your future.

Due Diligence

When considering an exit, the very first thing that pops into an entrepreneur's mind is a dollar value, a hoped-for price reflecting the value of the business, perhaps alongside another number for what you'd be willing to accept for this baby of yours.

Instead of mentally counting your winnings in advance, do some dreaming of a different kind. Picture the would-be buyer's inspection team showing up (in person or in your virtual data room) to review the documents you've provided from a due diligence checklist.

According to BizBuySell, due diligence is this:

The process of verifying [that] the information about the business, as provided by the seller, is correct and accurate. Due diligence is, in almost all sales, a condition of the buyer's offer. The business conditions must meet the buyer's expectations before the deal is finally closed. If there are any problems uncovered, this is the time they must be addressed.[17]

Due diligence is not fun; it's an invasive process, a peek behind the curtain. I'll say it: it sucks. But it's a necessary evil.

As much as any of us dread it, getting to—through—it with your hoped-for sale intact is the goal. To succeed, you need to do some advance planning and preparation, but the fact is most of us don't plan or prepare well enough.

Kenneth Marks, a longtime friend, fellow EO strategic partner for the Raleigh-Durham chapter, and managing partner of his firm, High Rock Partners (M&A and strategic advisors), says virtually everybody who successfully negotiates a sale does it with a substantial time commitment up front. "Depending on the level of preparedness, an entrepreneur starts preparing the company for sale up to two years out with some strategic activities, then building in monthly activities the year before." That's three years. Remember, earlier I said to allow for three to five years preexit, and another three to five years for the postexit transition. That added up to, generously, 5 + 5 = 10! A full ten years is entirely possible when you're starting from "contemplated sale" and ending at "new Core Purpose and new role."

What are these "strategic activities" and "monthly activities" that my friend Kenneth is talking about? The due diligence checklist I've

---

17   "Due Diligence Checklist—What to Verify Before Buying a Business," BizBuySell, accessed November 3, 2021, https://www.bizbuysell.com/learning-center/article/due-diligence-checklist-what-to-verify-before-buying-a-business/.

included will give you a much better feel for the puzzle pieces that will need to fit together well for the sale to ultimately happen.

Disclaimer: Due diligence is a complex process and should not be conducted without the assistance of your accountant and attorney. This list is just a sample to provide a feel for what due diligence entails.

1. Review and verify all financial information, including the following:

    □ Income statements, cash flow statements, balance sheets, general ledger, accounts payable and receivable

    □ Credit report

    □ Tax returns for at least the past three years

    □ All debts, their terms, and any contingent liabilities

    □ Analysis of gross profit margins

    □ Analysis of fixed and variable expenses

    □ Gross profits and rate of return by each product

    □ Inventory of all products, equipment, and real estate, including total value

2. Review and verify the business structure and operations, including the following:

    □ Articles of incorporation and amendments

    □ Bylaws and amendments

    □ Summary of current investors and shareholders

    □ All company names and trademark brand names

    □ All states where the company is authorized to do business

    □ All products and services, including production cost and margins

THE ME EXIT AND TRANSITION PHASE

- Business compliance requirements
- Marketing plan, customer analysis, competitors, industry trends
- Company's brand identity, including logo, website, and domain

3. Review and verify all material contracts, including the following:

   - All nondisclosure or noncompete agreements, any guarantees
   - Company purchase orders, quotes, invoices, or warranties
   - Security agreements, mortgages, collateral pledges
   - Letters of intent, contracts, closing transcripts from mergers or acquisitions
   - Distribution agreements, sales agreements, subscription agreements
   - All loan agreements, material leases, lines of credit, or promissory notes
   - Contracts between officers, directors, or principals of the company
   - Stock purchase agreements or other options

4. Review and verify all customer information, including the following:

   - All customer databases, subscriber lists, and sales records
   - Copies of standard communications and correspondence
   - All advertising programs, marketing programs, and events

- Purchasing policies and refund policies

- Any customer research data, whitepapers, or research

- All attorneys and law firms representing the company, areas of practice

- Pending litigation or threats of litigation

- Any unsatisfied judgments

- All insurance coverage and policies

- All professional licenses and permits

5. Review and verify all employee information, including the following:

   - Employee roster and organizational chart

   - Employee contracts and independent contractor agreements

   - Payroll information and employee tax forms

   - Human resources policies and procedures

   - Employee benefits, retirement plan, and insurance

6. Check for any legal issues, including the following:

   - Any outstanding legal issues or ongoing litigation that a prospective buyer needs to know about

   - Current representation

   - Proof of proper insurance

   - Review of licenses and permits necessary to operation

7. Review and verify all physical assets and real estate, including the following:

- Real estate, including office locations, warehouses, current leases and titles

- A schedule of all fixed assets, including product inventory, furniture, fixtures, and equipment

- Any automobiles or boats

8. Review and verify all intellectual property, including the following:

- All company's patents, trademarks, and copyrights

- Product inventions, formulas, recipes, or technical know-how

- All rights-owned data and digital information

- All work-for-hire or consulting agreements

As you can see, due diligence is a complicated, exhaustive process that gives the prospective buyers everything they need to determine what they're willing to pay for your company. That dollar value you had in your head when all this started? It will be stiffly challenged during due diligence. Having looked over the list, would you say your business is ready—at this moment—for a rigorous due diligence review? Or could there be some prework that needs doing prior to even considering putting the business up for sale, perhaps to get your administrative and revenue/profit house in order?

Here's what a former CEO (name withheld because they are actively involved with the business in confidential proceedings at this time) in the construction industry and a survivor of that big, gnarly process has to say about it: "We were growing 10 to 15 percent per year, but we needed professionals to help us build out our strategic plan. So when we got three unsolicited acquisition offers—for more than twice what I thought the company might bring—we signed that letter of intent. We thought we had the right bride. But we weren't nearly as joyful when we finally left, and we're still not today."

The CEO attributes a significant amount of the stress to his decision to maintain an ownership stake after the sale. Despite many words to the contrary, it turned out the buyer cared very much about maintaining a smooth revenue stream. "Every month mattered to the buyer in terms of the financials, and as entrepreneurs, we know that growing a business doesn't necessarily follow that model." He likens the feeling to "somebody else driving your boat," adding, "It may not be your way to hit the wake, but too bad. You start taking on water, but you can't do anything about it." In the end, the sale put an end to all the entrepreneurial creativity that the CEO and his team had used to build the business.

Looking back, the CEO wishes he'd never sold. Or that he'd "dated more first." He also wishes he'd had the support of someone who'd seen a lot of entrepreneurial exits and knew what to watch out for. That great team of acquisition experts that the CEO assembled handled the nuts and bolts, but he ended up wishing he'd found an executive coach to help him negotiate the personal and psychological difficulties of getting through the sale. He had seen a family member hire such a person during the sale of her business, and he thinks she did a better job than he did of handling "the gamesmanship and the psychological drudgery of due diligence," not to mention the "emotional balancing" necessary to get from letter of intent to exit.

As due diligence goes, his was relatively short—ninety days. But as you can see, even a short due diligence does not ensure a smooth one. Those stories you hear about the acquisition from hell? They aren't just stories: According to my friend Kenneth Marks and his surveys of the buyers he has represented, 50 percent of entrepreneurs will spend at least six to twelve months getting from letter of intent to bank deposit, and for another 15 percent of his clients, the sale process took one to four years. Suddenly my 5 + 5 = 10 equation for your transition phase doesn't sound so outlandish, does it? Yes, the first digit in my 5 + 5 = 10 equation is challenging, because it requires us to do the necessary prework that may or may not lead to an exit. It takes time and commitment. But the second "5" in the equation is more difficult, simply because it doesn't have the same nice, clean end point.

Rest assured that this CEO's story is ending great. His "bride" has actively pursued and reengaged with the CEO, working with him in the strategic planning process, realizing the significant value he and his leadership team can add to the future of the business, especially with their entrepreneurial instincts in a market space that's red hot. He's begun doing some executive coaching in the construction industry he loves, and to solidify his determination to give back, he's following through with a promise he made to himself: to complete his DBA, a doctorate of business administration! But getting from CEO to coach, with an acquisition in the middle, was difficult. He talks about the "emotional labor" of quietly negotiating a sale when four hundred employees knew nothing about it, of explaining his company's "lumpy" revenue to the buyer, of trying to time the sale to hit revenue peaks instead of valleys, and after the papers were inked, not having a clear understanding of what the buyer really wanted from the CEO and his team other than to "keep doing what you're doing." No, the only easy part of the sale was cashing the check. To him and his team, I say, "Well done," and to his buyer, I also say, "Well done," albeit a little delayed, to shift to and truly value the positive contributions entrepreneurs can bring postsale.

Whatever timeline the buyer gives you for due diligence, double it. If they put down the pen after signing a binding letter of intent and tell you all that's standing between you and the day of the wire is ninety days, assume 180. If they say one month, they're not even trying to be accurate—assume three. You will thank me for this advice when things drag on and start messing with your head. As stressful as due diligence, as the CEO says, the postsale period isn't all that fun either. Let's look at one view of that postsale period—the one where you work for somebody else, perhaps for the first time.

Intrapreneurship and the Increasingly Common Earnout

"Intrapreneurship is the act of behaving like an entrepreneur while working within a large organization."[18]

Suddenly the sale is finally complete, and the long-anticipated liquidity event has occurred. The day of the wire has come and gone, you've received your funds from the buyer, and the feeling of victory is something you'll never forget.

But except for all those zeroes in your bank account, it's almost anticlimactic, like crashing from the world's worst sugar high. My first day of the wire found Kristi and me on vacation. I remember padding my way into the hotel business center in my flip-flops to send the final fax that would seal the deal. After all the work, the stress, the second-guessing, the periodic temptation to just end the thing and put everyone out of their misery, this was it? It was all over with within a couple of minutes, leaving me and my flip-flops to head back out into the sunshine, blinking at the brightness.

You're not the boss anymore, although you may be requested to stay on in your own newly merged company for anywhere from

---

18 "Intrapreneurship," Wikipedia, accessed November 3, 2021, https://en.wikipedia.org/wiki/Intrapreneurship.

three to twelve months after the deal is completed, according to data collected by High Rock Partners.[19] For some sellers, however, the holdover period will be formalized in the sale documents and stretch out to two years, maybe more. It's called an employment agreement, and during that time you'll work not as the boss but as the buyer's employee. An earnout is often the solution when buyer and seller can't close the gap on a sales price. It's the buyer essentially saying, "Fine, if you think the company's worth that much, prove it by staying on board and using your time and experience to convince us." In other words, the earnout literally requires the seller to earn some of his or her own payout—sometimes a lot of that payout. In an article in *Inc.*, George Geis, an associate dean of the executive MBA program at UCLA's Anderson School of Management, cited surveys suggesting that owners of private companies have been taking between 40 and 45 percent of their total payout through an earnout agreement.[20] Other sources say, for high-tech or services companies, it's between 60 and 80 percent of payout.[21] Figures from 2016 indicate that 30 percent of private M&A transactions included an earnout, but the practice seems to be growing—and not just in traditional circumstances where "future cash flows are inherently uncertain,"[22] such as companies with

---

19   Kenneth Marks, "How Long Does It Take to Sell a Company?" High Rock Partners, July 11, 2019, https://www.highrockpartners.com/how-long-does-it-take-to-sell-a-company/.

20   Christine Lagorio-Chafkin, "How to Structure an Earn-Out," *Inc.*, March 11, 2010, https://www.inc.com/guides/earn-out-structuring.html.

21   "Should I Consider an Earn-Out When Selling My Business?" Morgan and Westfield, accessed November 3, 2021, https://www.morganandwestfield.com/ask-the-expert/should-i-consider-earn-out-when-selling-my-business.

22   Christine Lagorio-Chafkin, "How to Structure an Earn-Out," *Inc.*, March 11, 2010, https://www.inc.com/guides/earn-out-structuring.html.

high upfront R&D.[23] Legal observers report that the COVID-19 pandemic expanded the use of earnouts to include many different sorts of companies whose track record could be deemed unreliable as the result of lockdown-caused losses and layoffs. Interestingly, at the same time that buyers were increasingly demanding earnouts due to market uncertainties, sellers may have been less likely to agree to them. Why? Because many postclosing covenants that include an earnout prohibit the seller from making changes—downsizing, terminating management, selling assets, closing locations, etc.—that may be required to pilot the company through a recession or disruption that might occur during the earnout period.[24]

So now the docs are signed, and you've been paid, but the payout is partially dependent on proving out your presale projections—and the new boss is not the same as the old boss. The role shift required of you in an earnout can be jarring—and not just for you but also for the people who used to be your employees. You're no longer growing your company; you're growing somebody else's and doing it within the covenants the acquiring company imposed. Instead of leading a budget process in your own business, you will be participating in one that holds you accountable for hitting targets, perhaps for the first time in your career. If there's a board of directors, they're now in a position to fire you. You signed on the dotted line thinking this gig might be fun for a while. But now it feels like the walls are closing in—I felt that a year into the sale of my second business. To fulfill the terms of my earnout, I was working as an employee of the purchaser, and I shared a laundry

---

23   Javier Enrile, "Earnouts: Structures for Breaking Negotiation Deadlocks, Toptal: Finance Processes, accessed November 3, 2021, https://www.toptal.com/finance/mergers-and-acquisitions/structuring-earnouts.

24   Efren Acosta and Ron Scharnberg, "COVID-19 Crisis May Make M&A Earnouts More Attractive," Law360, September 23, 2020, https://www.law360.com/articles/1311289/covid-19-crisis-may-make-m-a-earnouts-more-attractive.

list of complaints with my Vistage and EO peer groups: I wasn't having much fun. I wasn't free to do what I could in the past. I didn't like all the silos of the parent company. There was too much bureaucracy and red tape. Nobody in management was listening to my ideas. All I wanted was to go back to being an entrepreneur right *now*.

My peers looked at me for a moment, then asked, "Are you done?"

"Yes," I said, and thanked them for listening. That ended the gripe session, or so I thought. But it soon became clear that everybody was irritated by what I'd said, and nobody felt sorry for me.

"Did you get paid for selling your company?" they asked. Yes, of course.

"Did you sign the employment agreement?" Again, yes, I did.

The concluding message from my peers that day equated to this: Shut up. Quit complaining and go to work. You don't always get what you want. Not every situation is going to bring you the best of everything. If you were smart, you would consider this as an opportunity to learn; why aren't you taking advantage of it?

That wasn't what I wanted to hear back then, but I now know it was what I *needed* to hear. I took their advice, knowing that my attitude was going to determine how the rest of my employment agreement would go and that what happened during that time could have an impact on the rest of my career. I formulated a way of thinking about this part of my postexit transition, which I now share with you:

When you sell your business, you are no longer an entrepreneur. You become an intrapreneur. If you elect to maintain a purely entrepreneurial mindset, you will lose a significant opportunity to learn as an intrapreneur during the time you spend in the organization that purchased your company. What you don't know that you don't know is that you very well might utilize your new insights and enhanced skill set in a future return to entrepreneurship.

> If you elect to maintain a purely entrepreneurial mindset, you will lose a significant opportunity to learn as an intrapreneur during the time you spend in the organization that purchased your company. What you don't know that you don't know is that you very well might utilize your new insights and enhanced skill set in a future return to entrepreneurship.

By choosing to listen and learn in my new role, I picked up new skills and new understandings of what to do and also on what not to do. Because I was working for a global company, I had the opportunity to travel and explore new cultures and business customs. I figured out how to be a productive intrapreneur—a good employee for my boss, yet also one who could operate with the drive and zeal of an entrepreneur.

Although an earnout can feel long, it really isn't. High Rock Partners found that very few entrepreneurs stay intrapreneurs with the company that purchased them for more than three years.[25] For me, the three-year employment agreement proved to be four for various reasons, and by the end, I was more than fine with it. Had I continued sulking and whining, I would have gotten out too early—one way or another—and I would have missed out on many valuable lessons and experiences. I stopped feeling I "had to" work off my employment agreement. Instead, I relished reporting directly to the CEO of a global company, as an intrapreneur able to share entrepreneurial wisdom. What wasn't there to like?

---

25   Kenneth Marks, "How Long Does It Take to Sell a Company?" High Rock Partners, July 11, 2019, https://www.highrockpartners.com/how-long-does-it-take-to-sell-a-company/.

Steve Shankin's company makes accessories for the utility terrain vehicles market, and he's another satisfied entrepreneur-turned-intrapreneur who attributes his positive experience to the way his new corporate role was framed and built out. "It wasn't just me selling my company. It was us building a new division." Shankin's buyer made the savvy choice to look at the acquisition as more than a set of tangible assets. "They really wanted and valued the leadership that I and my team could bring. They know there's a secret sauce that good companies or brands have, and they've worked hard not to ruin it." Now that he has been in his postsale role for over a year, he also noted that he would not have been as happy with the work if it was essentially just going to be doing the same stuff he did before, but just having more reporting and a boss—and a big bank account. In fact, he said, "I think I'd be counting my days until I'm out the door. A couple of the other entrepreneurs whose businesses we bought seem to be moving in that direction. The reason it's interesting and engaging to me is that I'm doing different things than I was able to do before, like acquiring companies and building the whole division. I go to work now because I like building things, and I want to see if I've got the chops to be successful in a different/bigger role. I like the challenge."

No doubt it helped that the corporate CEO had been an entrepreneur himself and could easily understand as Shankin processed the mix of emotions that come with a sale. The buyer has made over thirty acquisitions now, so this wasn't something brand new for them. Steve's boss, himself, sold them his company about seven years ago, so he knows firsthand what it's like for someone in Steve's position. It also helped that expectations on both sides of the deal were written down, referred to often, and managed as needed. "Like almost everything in life, I think it boils down to people and communication," Shankin concludes. "If someone's not excited with the future plans, it's likely not going to be a good fit. If it's the same stuff, more headaches, a boss, *and* you've got lots of money, it's super easy to see why people don't stick around after selling."

In other words, it's another example of how important it is to pick the right buyer—ideally, one that recognizes your skills, embraces your insights, and solicits your opinions. Find a true partnership, the kind that runs longer and extends broader than a typical earnout.

Mike Malone, who built MJM Investigations state by state and then internationally to become the outsourcing leader in his field, is another example of a sale gone right. His period of intrapreneurship, at *thirteen years* and counting, is with the UK-based corporation that kept him on to run businesses in ninety different countries and service 265 contracts worldwide. He has tripled revenues for his bosses, which wasn't hard to do, he says, because his new bosses instinctively followed some basic rules that would improve many a postsale intrapreneurship:

- Let the team of the acquired company keep its entrepreneurial spirit. (The leadership team, with whom Mike "shares the same heartbeat," is still almost entirely intact.)
- Clearly define corporate expectations up front.
- Help the acquired team maintain and build on its long-term strategic plan. Invest in them.
- Don't get in the details of the acquired team's day-to-day.

Mike hasn't loved every moment of his long intrapreneurship—certainly not the adjustment phase at the beginning, when there seemed to be so many small but irritating differences between the entrepreneurial world and the corporate—but he says the sale has helped him achieve what is most important to him: "It has allowed me to continue my journey."

Clearly, Mike did his part to make the postsale transition work, but for what he describes as his own reasons, "I integrated myself because I cared."

Yes, a successful intrapreneurship is about caring, the kind Mike Malone has always shown for his people, his company, and his business partners. It's also about choosing the right timing and the right fit, no doubt about it. Add in plenty of clear communication, flexibility, and mutual respect, and that's the recipe for a postsale intrapreneurship worth emulating.

What's Next?!

It's the effort to change stripes that has us tigers pacing our new cages just at a time when we're supposed to feel most free.

After an exit, it's inevitable that the world will feel different, maybe even foreign. If the exiting entrepreneur faces an empty calendar, this "freedom" will soon feel like a prison. That's because nothing is being created. For the first time since choosing to think of the self as an entrepreneur, the postexit entrepreneur doesn't have a clue what to create. No wonder depression is a significant risk in the postexit transition period.

But you are an entrepreneur down to your tiniest cell. Selling your company doesn't mean that's changed.

What follows the cash-out is similar to what precedes it—it's alien, confusing, and frustrating. So take your time. Enjoy having reached a summit. Relish having successfully built your company and navigating it through your exit. But when your thoughts turn toward the future, think with the end in mind, as Stephen R. Covey, the author of *Seven Habits of Highly Effective People*, explains when seeking to achieve a goal: "The mind must imagine what the eye cannot yet see."

In the previous chapter, I discussed the various roles. If you are unsure which role best suits you, chart your career path to date by the roles you've played. When I do this, I can certainly argue that I have been a leader, role-player, and creator, which means my future could involve any one of them. But when push comes to shove, I know I'm a creator at heart. I build businesses to scale and then turn them over to Leaders who are well suited to take the company far into its future.

Here's another way to look at your desired role: determine which role you'd never want to leave, or which role most energizes you—they may be one and the same. As I created my businesses, I had all the energy in the world, until the point where they just needed to be operated and grown profitably, which is a job best held by a Leader.

> Determine which role you'd never want to leave, or which role most energizes you—they may be one and the same.

Nowadays, I'm a role-player for my clients and readers—teaching and supporting, and feeling energized by it.

Once the top-line questions and issues have been considered, you can begin drilling down into the fine points of whatever role you seem to be gravitating to. Here are some possibilities, with discussion intended to help you do some further weeding.

PORTFOLIO ENTREPRENEUR

Expanding on the definition in the previous chapter, a portfolio entrepreneur is someone who holds active interest in more than one business at a time. Another defining characteristic is that portfolio entrepreneurs typically hire leaders to run the businesses, essentially reserving for themselves a role similar to chairman of each company (assuming majority control).

While some serial entrepreneurs proudly boast of being the brains behind a long string of companies, portfolio entrepreneurs tend to consider themselves guides for the organizations in which they take an interest. And if they're a *maximized* portfolio entrepreneur, their preferred boast might be that all of their companies (three, five, ten, whatever) are operating with vision and execution, aided by professional management whose goal is for the company to reach full potential.

That's a distinction from those serial entrepreneurs, with their nine-company track record, many of which I would diagnose as Bore-E-Gaged, a term I introduced in *The Second Decision*. They toggle quickly from bored to engaged and back again, and their companies often fail to meet their potential, mostly due to the lack of attention they receive from their founder.

But MEs who become portfolio entrepreneurs operate very differently, ensuring each business has the 100 percent focus it deserves to achieve its highest and best future. That takes a thorough commitment to our motto:

> Bore-E-Gaged, a term I introduced in *The Second Decision*. They toggle quickly from bored to engaged and back again, and their companies often fail to meet their potential, mostly due to the lack of attention they receive from their founder.

Know thyself. Accept thyself. Improve thyself. Accept others. Complement thyself.

A RESOURCE FOR OTHERS

As discussed earlier, becoming a resource in one form or another is a common lane for exiting entrepreneurs to choose.

Angel investors. These provide capital for a business start-up, usually in exchange for convertible debt or ownership equity. Angel investors often lend support early in the life of a company or when other sources of funding run dry. Typically, angels are wealthy individuals or groups investing their own money. With cash in hand and the need to do something with it, an entrepreneur postsale can be receptive to becoming an angel.

Venture capitalism. This is a form of private equity financing that is provided by venture capital firms or funds to start-ups, early-stage, and emerging companies that have been deemed to have high-growth potential or that have demonstrated high growth. This would be a less-common path for entrepreneurs in a postexit transition, as VCs are typically employees of firms or funds that exist to invest other people's money. But it's among an array of options.

Consultant/advisor/coach/mentor/teacher. I've mentioned these previously, but let me expand on them here.

Consultant—An expert or experienced professional in a specific field who offers that broad or deep knowledge to paying clients. Exiting entrepreneurs can consult on their industry or on specific management strategies or skills, or they can assist nonbusiness entities such as government. The thrust of the consulting can be quite general or very specific.

Advisor—This is similar to a consultant, except that his or her knowledge may be deeper, more cross-functional, or multidisciplinary. The role here is that of mentor or guide and is usually not task-specific. For exiting entrepreneurs, such a role could become a first step toward investing in a company, or adding it to a portfolio of companies.

Coach—Coaching supports an individual or a company in achieving a specific goal or set of goals, through training and guidance. There is demand for experienced entrepreneurs to play this role with younger or newer entrepreneurs and their companies, either ad hoc or by teaming up with a coaching company.

Mentor—Mentorship differs from some of the above advice-giving roles in that it tends not to be paid. It is a true helping role, in which someone older, more experienced, or having certain expertise offers to help a lesser person or organization navigate. Exiting entrepreneurs are prized mentors—if they can advise instead of boss!

Teacher—A teacher or educator differs from the other roles by having some form of curriculum that he or she seeks to deliver to a person or company that is happy to take on the role of student.

Use this chart to help you further define your postliquidity role. Circle the blocks and roles that speak to you.

	PASSIVE	ACTIVE
In Control—People	N/A	Majority Investor Portfolio Entrepreneur Entrepreneurial Leader-CEO Intrapreneurial Leader-CEO
Not in control—People	Investor	Minority Investor/Coach/Consultant/Mentor/Advisor
In Control—Financial Review	N/A	Majority Investor Portfolio Entrepreneur Entrepreneurial Leader-CEO Intrapreneurial Leader-CEO Consultant/Coach/Mentor/Advisor
Not in Control—Financial Review	Investor	Minority Investor/Coach/Consultant/Mentor/Advisor
In Control—Strategy Review/Setting	N/A	Majority Investor Portfolio Entrepreneur Entrepreneurial Leader-CEO Intrapreneurial Leader-CEO Coach/Consultant/Mentor/Advisor
Not in Control—Strategy Review/Setting	Investor	Minority Investor/Coach/Consultant/Mentor/Advisor

So what's next for you? Where do you currently reside on this chart?

TOOL: ME EXIT AND TRANSITION PHASE

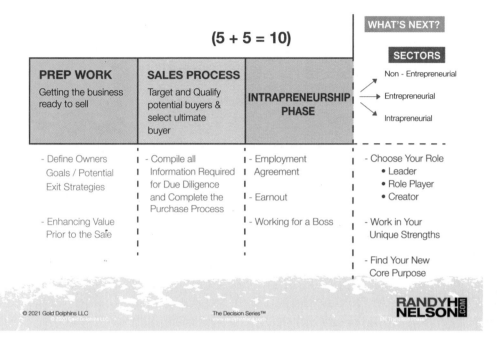

By first giving you an opportunity to think about what a postexit transition entails, and what role you may choose for yourself at the end of that period, I think you'll be able to see the usefulness of the next section of the book, the tools section, within a framework of how your career is likely to proceed.

MEQC—What's Next?!

Learn. Think. Decide. Implement.

Initials

1. Answer the five ME prep questions in the bullets below:

   • Do you want to be in (majority) control, or are you willing to give up control and remain a minority owner?

   _____

   • Do you want to build businesses for just yourself, and/or build to support or create for other entrepreneurial CEOs?

   _____

   • Day to day, do you want to play an active role, or are you okay with a passive role?

   _____

   • Do you want to increase the blend of your life and business at this point in your career, or are you okay with the blend you have now—which may be tilted toward business?

   _____

   • Is remaining visible and "relevant" important to you?

   _____

   _____

2. Grade your organization on the due diligence checklist, 1–10, with 1 not prepared at all, and 10 being fully prepared. What are your next steps, if any, after thinking about your current status?

   _____

3. Explain the different ME roles you can play in a postexit future and identify your preliminary role choice moving forward, taking into account your vision of what constitutes a perfect day.

    _____

4. What are your unique and exceptional strengths and abilities, and what are your areas of genius?

    _____

5. Describe your current thinking and planning around your own version of $5 + 5 = 10$. When do you think each part of the equation will occur in your career, taking into account the content of *The Fourth Decision* thus far?

    _____

6. What is your current Core Purpose? If this chapter has changed or revealed your new Core Purpose, explain the change. Given that, what might be your future Core Purpose at the end of your ME transition phase?

    _____

7. Describe in detail what you could learn as an intrapreneur, if you had the right "learning mindset" in place.

    _____

Signature: _____

Date: _____

A Wayfinder for the Maximizer: Where Have We Been? What's Next?!

This section focuses on the Decision Series Tools, additional resources for scaling leadership skills and roles within your organization(s) to help your business(es) reach full potential, with or without you at the helm. The tools in this section include the following:

The Self-Awareness Decision Tool (Revised), a practical development tool for all levels of leadership, revised here to help you get the right *qualified* people in the right seats doing the right things.

The Qual Card Development Tool to help you design new qual cards to build and scale qualified leaders who have your full trust and confidence, and who you've *verified* are capable of teaching and scaling without you, if needed or desired.

The Audit-Ready Decision Tool identifies, at each level of the Productive Growth Pyramid, your current state of play. The results lead to an action plan that you and your qualified leaders can use to establish a game plan for improving each block on the pyramid in a specific time frame.

The Three+ Business Models Tool takes us through the business models under which companies typically operate. As part of your qual card, you and your leaders identify which model you are currently using, which may be different from the one you *thought* you were using. The new awareness puts you in a place to establish action plans for your own maximization goals, as well as help your company reach full potential.

The Truth and Trends Tool gives you the guide that will combine your data and metrics with your gut feel and intuition to help you make better-calculated decisions faster and with more confidence. It will also be a critical component of the Revenue Lever Strategy Tool.

The Revenue Lever Strategy Tool helps you and your qualified leaders make better strategic decisions by doing a detailed analysis of where each of your revenue levers has been, is going, and ought to go to reach full potential.

The Three+ Decision-Making Models Tool takes us into the world of *must*, *should*, and *could*, in both our business and personal lives. It forces us to be more analytical regarding what ideas grab our attention and time.

The Nonnegotiable Decision Tool guides us to set our nonnegotiables for the next twelve months, by asking both life and career questions in different time frames. It drives us to think deeply about what truly needs to be nonnegotiable, both at work and in our personal life.

The N-MSC-T Alignment Tool puts all of your critical decisions, for both your business and your personal life, into one tool. It helps you outline the essential elements for aligning your work and personal lives, as well as aligning your efforts throughout the year.

The ME Bridge Tool guides you toward your *reset* as an ME. It defines the steps necessary to qualify you as an ME, helping you cross the bridge from entrepreneur to *maximized* entrepreneur.

Many of these tools work together, overlap, and build on one another. I've organized them in the order that makes most sense to me and seems to work best with clients, but if you need to jump around these tool chapters to make your own sense of them, have at it!

Now that you have the lay of the land for what lies ahead, let's begin our tool chapter of the Decision Series Tools with a discussion of Qual-E-Gaged.

CHAPTER 5

Qual-E-Gaged and the Qual Card Development Tool

The best leaders are those who can maximize
the potential of their people.
—CHIP CONLEY, AUTHOR OF *WISDOM @ WORK*

Let me start this tool chapter by reminding you that, in this book, the "ands" are everything. I hope you've already noticed this and retained it, but here are some examples to bring you back up to speed:

- Entrepreneurship *and* leadership

- Creativity *and* discipline

- Vision *and* execution

- Doing the right things *and* doing them right

Across the books I've thus far completed in the Decision Series for Entrepreneurs, I've introduced and made steady use of the "qual card" concept. Arising from my own experience with Navy qual cards, the concept is that we should self-qualify for the evolving work we do as entrepreneurs. In *The Second Decision*, you became a *qualified* entrepreneur, one who became fully self-aware of what you know and don't know, allowing you to choose the role you were best suited to play for the continued growth and well-being of your company, at its then-current age and size. In *The Third Decision*, you used a qual card–like set of nonnegotiables to become *intentional* about blending your personal life with your entrepreneurial life.

Now, in *The Fourth Decision*, I'm offering you the opportunity to introduce and implement the qual card concept in how you manage your own company. It's a step that takes you beyond merely being a successful entrepreneurial leader, to becoming a leader who is maximizing for the sake of his or her company's growth and longevity. It gives us a new kind of "and":

- Successful *and* maximized

Let me give you the backstory on this, because a funny thing happened along the path to this book. After a decade of working with clients worldwide in our Entrepreneurial Leadership Development practice, I suddenly recognized that a really good idea had been staring me in the face all along. In fact, how it happened reminds me of one of my favorite phrases:

The hardest thing to discover is the obvious.

Maximized entrepreneurs *and* qual cards. In a lightbulb moment, I realized I had been overlooking something that had been there all along. Look along with me at my thought process, most of which you'll recognize from previous chapters:

Know thyself. Check.
Approve thyself. Check
Improve thyself. Check.
Approve others. Check
Complement thyself. Check.

It seemed to me I had checked all of the blocks relating to self-awareness, along with some that encourage self-acceptance and involving others in the journey. I knew that any entrepreneur who could put all of this in place would be well positioned in a role that's right for his or her company's future. And that he or she has made room for others to assist in entrepreneurial leadership.

And that's where I saw the missing link, the key, and last step in becoming *maximized*. The work isn't done, I realized, until you've taken your leadership team and all of your employees through a similar self-awareness and role-qualifying process. In essence they, too, need to fill out their qual cards.

So the ME Equation, updated with a newly added word, "qualified," became:

Know Thyself *and Approve Thyself* +
Improve Thyself +
Approve and Qualify Others and Complement Thyself

Entrepreneur + CEO Mentality = Unconscious Competence = the ME Equation.

Here's another way to look at the same equation:

Getting the Right *Qualified* People in the Right Seats =
Unconscious Competence =
the ME Equation.

Getting the right things done right.

In other words, your self-awareness isn't enough, not for the good of your organization. Your people themselves need to combine the entrepreneur and CEO *qualified* mentalities. It's the only way to get the right things done right. How else can you maximize?

When I got to this point in my thinking, it all made sense. It just seemed a little easier said than done! But not anymore. The key, I realized, is to bring the qual card concept to the entire organization, not just the entrepreneur or CEO, or even the C-suite team. Whereas "The ME Exit and Transition Phase" discussed in detail the process that you, personally, go through ten or more years into your career, I'm introducing the qual card at this point to provide you the necessary— and until now, missing—link. It's the one that completes your journey from entrepreneur to entrepreneurial leader and, ultimately, to ME. That link is the qual card.

The qual card is where the military method meets the needs of entrepreneurial skill development. It's where the best of both worlds intersect. Indulge me for a few paragraphs as I explain why.

The Decision Series has always been about getting the entrepreneur qualified first, as a leader, role-player, or creator. Getting more leaders qualified leads to scaling leadership throughout your organization, which then leads to successfully scaling the growth of the business. "Qualified" raises the stakes in the above equation and pays big dividends when put to work in your organization.

Transform the individual, qualify the team, and scale leadership across your organization.

Let's review what "qualified" means to me so you can understand how I'm applying it to you and your company.

In 1983, I went through six months at the Navy Nuclear Power School in Orlando, Florida. (Think of this as getting an equivalent of a master's degree in nuclear engineering in half a year. Rapid-paced learning!) This was followed by six months at a Navy Prototype in Ballston Spa, New York, at first teaching and then actually working at a nuclear power plant so we could put our teaching to practical use. Then came three months at the Naval Submarine School, where we were taught all aspects of submarine operation. After a total of fifteen months of school, then and only then was I finally allowed to board a submarine for the first time. It was the ballistic missile submarine the USS *James Madison* (SSBN 627). There I joined the Blue crew for the next three years, working alternate patrols with a Gold crew.

It may surprise you to know that, even though I had been to school for fifteen months, I was still deemed ineligible to lead. I hadn't been qualified. And what I failed to mention above was that I couldn't begin submarine school until I was qualified at the Navy Prototype to lead the engineering plant.

Do you see the pattern? Teach. Qualify. Teach. Qualify.

In the Navy, there was never a time when I wasn't using my qual card to work on my next qualification. As soon as I was qualified in one area, then I was handed the next qual card. There was always a higher level to qualify for and achieve. And as always, I had to be qualified before I could lead.

Let me say that again: *I was not allowed to lead until I was qualified.* And I wasn't allowed to take the next step in my schooling, either, until I was qualified. As much as I or my fellow submariners felt ready to jump in and take more responsibility, it just wasn't allowed.

Other disciplines follow a similar protocol. Accountants have to pass the CPA exam. Lawyers must take and pass the bar exam. Medical professionals must be qualified (thank goodness!). Executive coaches can get certified, a level of qualification in itself. But the entrepreneurial sector? Qualified? That's a no!

Unlike the self-selecting process that makes us entrepreneurs, the Navy starts by choosing the right people for the job track, whatever it may be. Then the Navy ensures that everyone on that job track has proven their qualifications to do the right things and do them right. Not just on paper or, these days, on a screen—no, in the Navy you've got to prove your ability to do each necessary thing in a hands-on, demonstrated way. Another thing: in the Navy, credentialing isn't a matter of just putting in the time. Hours mean squat. You can't wait your way to the next qual card (or any skill that might be on it) just by putting in the time and expecting to be tapped for the next rung on the ladder. If you want to move beyond instruction and get qualified, you've got to take the initiative. You've got to step up and ask your higher-up to check you out and, hopefully, sign off on your card.

> If you want to move beyond instruction and get qualified, you've got to take the initiative. You've got to step up and ask your higher-up to check you out and, hopefully, sign off on your card.

Now, nobody in the Navy is going to just assume you've learned the material; you have to prove it—first during your supervised "under instruction" time, then in a final, hands-on quiz designed to look for holes in your knowledge-gathering. When you're seeking that signoff on your qual card, you have to demonstrate that you know what you're talking about. You have to show you've made the jump from theory to practice. The supervisor has to come away from the checkout confident that you're ready to quit having somebody looking over your shoulder, that you're in fact both ready to lead and to begin teaching others, when the time comes. Nobody but nobody in the Navy gets sent out on their own, with their bosses hoping for the best. Not even for a day. In *The Second Decision*, I created the Entrepreneurial Qual Card. It's different than the ones I knew in the military, because it's tailored to who we are as entrepreneurs. I did it because I knew we entrepreneurs are far, far from being the right butts the Navy wants in its seats. Consider:

When we start our first company as an entrepreneur, we have full autonomy to do whatever we want, whenever we want, with whomever we want, and day one we begin calling ourselves the CEO, the captain of our own ship. Qualifications? None needed beyond the guts required to actually start the company and a strong desire to be our own boss. Abilities? Just the stamina to work one hundred hours a week so that we never have to work a forty-hour week for anybody else ever again. Of course, a desire to be our own boss and the self-confidence to pursue that goal, whatever the cost, doesn't make us qualified to lead a growth company. Except in our own minds, of course.

In fact, I can easily picture an entrepreneurial CEO fishing off the deck of their own submarine in a lounge chair, relaxed and confidently saying, "I got this" ... truly believing that they will just figure it out ... no qualifications necessary ... how hard can it really be, right?

In *The Second Decision*, I challenged readers to choose their role for the next three years—leader, role-player, or creator—and to take the self-awareness journey necessary to get qualified for the role. Each chapter ended with a personal qual card to fill out, reflecting the basic knowledge requirements for running your entrepreneurial business.

The process I laid out was self-paced and self-policed. If you wanted to do it, you did; if you didn't want to, you didn't, because you're in charge and can do whatever you want!

Here, in *The Fourth Decision*, you're past all that, so I'm raising the stakes—from becoming qualified, yourself, to qualifying others in your organization(s) through qual cards.

Imagine for a moment that you have a meeting with a prospective "whale," and you have a new salesperson onboard. She's new to the company but relatively experienced and raring to go to prove herself. Do you send her to the meeting by herself, or do you send an experienced sales leader with her to both teach by example and make sure she doesn't do anything to screw things up? The latter, right? If so, you're well on your way to doing things the Navy way—choosing the right person for the job, making sure she's qualified for the task, and then watching over her until it's clear she's unlikely to blow the sale. But unless I miss my guess, there are plenty of other high-stakes situations in your business where employees aren't as vetted or supervised. Ask yourself this: Across the board, throughout your enterprise, *what are you doing to get your people qualified for the jobs they do?*

I'd venture to say not much.

When it comes to employing people, one of our biggest hurdles may be our own entrepreneurial attitudes and attributes. We believe in autonomy. We are comfortable with risk. We are self-confident enough to think we can do almost anything if we try. And we tend to assume that if we click well enough with our prospective hires, they can simply be wound up, set on a flat surface, and let go. The problem is that we, too, readily assume that our people are just like us—self-motivated, quick studies, fully autonomous in thought and action, and thus immediately ready to achieve or lead.

We like to think we tell our "right people" the "right things to do." But in my experience, most of us fall short in this area, and with good reason: in our early, fast-growth years, we hired as quickly as we could to keep up with the growth. Later, we gave our new hires the freedom to operate independently, rationalizing that we didn't want to micromanage them. We had bigger fish to fry, after all. New ideas to generate. Maybe even new companies to start. Opportunity was what we were after. It was the gift we gave our employees, and they loved it for the upward mobility it offered them.

But ten or more years into the business and possibly on the verge of deciding "What's next?!" for us, we need to ask ourselves this: Do we really know that our employees are qualified to do the right things right? And if we don't know, how do we find out?

I believe that without some accountability established within your organization(s), you simply cannot ensure that the training you have conducted has actually worked—that your trainees have been truly prepared—not only to lead but also to train other people to lead. *Without that accountability in place, you risk running an organization that does the wrong things right, or the right things wrong.* What you've got going may look good on the outside, but on the inside it's, well, a busy mess. Busy messes do not succeed long term, do not *maximize*, and certainly do not reach full potential. Qual cards give you the peace of mind knowing that the entrepreneurial leaders and

> Without that accountability in place, you risk running an organization that does the wrong things right, or the right things wrong.

employees with whom you have "complemented yourself," and given significant opportunities to, are indeed capable and qualified for doing the right things right. Period.

Now, you might think that what I'm really talking about is matching people to a job description and holding them to it. No. A job description is a formal account of an employee's responsibilities. Knowledge includes the facts, information, and skills acquired by a person through experience or education, the theoretical or practical understanding of a subject. Qual cards are knowledge requirements that link or lead to demonstrated competence.

I know that some organizations do a great job with their job descriptions, adding very specific metrics to ensure that the employee understands very clearly what he or she is accountable for at evaluation time. Most organizations also set annual or quarterly goals for their employees and hold them responsible for achieving them.

But something is still missing: that final step that ensures that necessary knowledge is actually acquired, put into use, and ultimately used to lead and train others in the organization on the same, both in theory and in practice.

MEs don't take an attitude of "set it and forget it." MEs ensure their organizations of continuing qualified leadership by developing qual cards up, down, and across the organization. This structure allows for the training and qualifying of future leaders and, when combined with systems and processes, assists organizations in their effort to scale toward full potential.

To illustrate how qual cards add accountability to knowledge requirements, consider one of my favorite diagrams:

TOOL: THE QUAL CARD

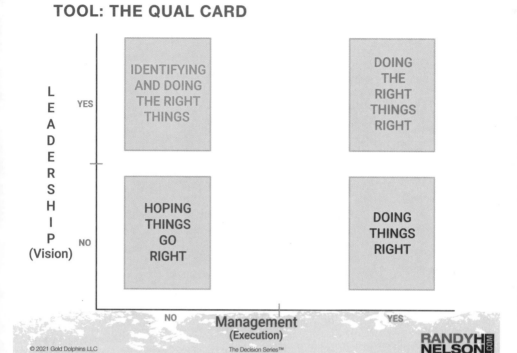

Those of you who are voracious readers of leadership and management books have most likely seen some variation of this diagram with different wording but with the same meaning. But I have come to think that this diagram is incomplete.

We all know that the more you scale your company, the more you need three key things to succeed and especially to *maximize*: processes, systems, and qualified leaders to help the organization reach its potential. We also know that setting goals and assigning responsibilities is the fuel that such efforts run on. But what if people complete training, only to begin *doing the wrong things right?*

TOOL: THE QUAL CARD

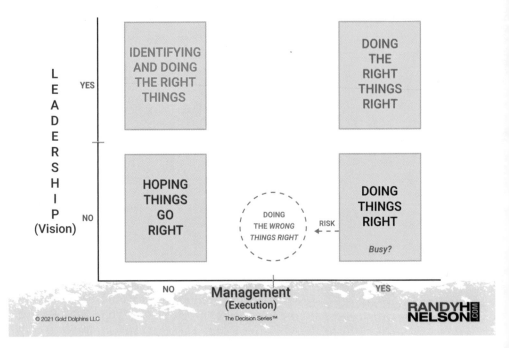

Successful organizations, ones that have been market or industry leaders for a long time, are *still* susceptible to doing the wrong things right. After years of doing the (wrong) things the same way, companies transform these things first into habits and then routines. Over time, the organization comes to view these well-worn procedures as "working." They become traditions in the same way that generations of a family might accept that the tips must always be cut off the Sunday roast with no one ever asking why. When at last someone does—a young bride in this story, but easily a new employee in a company—an honest answer reveals the wrongness of the tradition. Grandma's smaller roasting pan and oven could never hold an entire roast without cutting it down to size. Now it's viewed not only as a tradition but as "the right thing to do"—even though with today's larger ovens it's become "the wrong thing to do."

With this story in mind, ask yourself this: How many processes, structures, systems, and reports exist in your organization simply because they always have? What effect might this be having on your drive to *maximize*? If a few possibilities pop to mind, jot them down here:

_____

_____

_____

_____

_____

Then there's another situation to consider: What if your people are doing the *right things wrong?*

TOOL: THE QUAL CARD

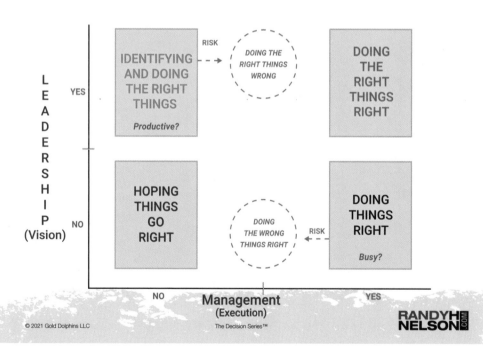

Whether it's "wrong things right" or "right things wrong," it's still wasted effort and no way to *maximize* a company's leadership corps. The organization as a whole is missing out on tons of upside potential and shareholder value. Indeed, when we give too much freedom to our employees without setting the right expectations, we set them up for failure.

That's right: *We* are at fault, not them. Let me give you an example from my own experience.

In the first decade of my entrepreneurial career, our business was growing at a pace of 50 percent year over year. We went from a handful of employees to over 250, from one office to nine, and from a standing start to $24 million in sales. We hired continually, and after giving the new employees their orientation briefing, we sent them on their way to do great things. We gave them freedom to do their jobs, lots of freedom, but we were too busy building the company to really oversee their performance. Then, in our leadership meetings, we gradually began complaining that our people weren't getting stuff done as "right" as we would have liked. Nobody doubted that our people were working hard, really hard. But they weren't meeting expectations, so after complaining about them for a while, we'd fire them, hire their replacements, and the cycle would start again.

That cycle was *my* fault. I had broken all three of the cardinal rules for MEs. I didn't know the rules back then, but I sure know them now:

1. Don't assume that your employees know what to do just because you hired them and gave them freedom to do their job.

2. Don't give your employees complete freedom to do their jobs without setting goals for them and making it clear what you expect them to do (job description, goals, metrics, etc.).

3. Don't assume your employees are qualified just because you trained them and gave them a job description with metrics. Hold them accountable for being qualified. Training without including some Navy-style qualification strategies just adds to the risk in the organization, and as we will discuss in future chapters, there is a lot to be said about *controlled risk* versus *pure risk*.

The mistake many leaders make, especially in growth companies, is assuming that the potential leaders they are considering promoting do indeed have the requisite knowledge for the position. The qual card process takes it a few steps further. It sets out your knowledge requirements in the form of qual cards, and

> That cycle was *my* fault. I had broken all three of the cardinal rules for MEs. I didn't know the rules back then, but I sure know them now.

then allows you to verify that the leader has the qualifications. The revised Self-Awareness Decision Tool will challenge you to come up with the specific qual cards and areas for qualification that are needed to scale leadership—your emerging leaders—as well as to move you toward full potential and away from doing the right things wrong, or wrong things right.

TOOL: SELF-AWARENESS DECISIONS

NAME/DATE	Baseline - "The Truth and the Trends"		
	1	**2**	**3**
You have been fired — Your successor has been wildly successful over the past 12 months. What did they do that (1) you didn't want to do, (2) you didn't know what to do, and (3) you didn't know how to do it?			

Assessments/Date Completed	"The growth of a company is limited by the growth of its leaders" "Double your personal capacity in the next 12 months" "The fatal flaw of a leader is their lack of self-awareness"			
Culture Index				
	Fact Finder	Follow Through	Quick Start	Implementor
Kolbe A				

CliftonStrengths 34	1	2	3	4	5
Top 5 Strengths					
	30	31	32	33	34
Bottom 5 Strengths					

Self-Awareness (Top 3 in Each)	1	2	3
Know Thyself — **What** are your greatest strengths/ your areas of Genius/Excellence? *Don't include strengths that you are just competent at (Genius/Excellence/Competence/Incompetence)*			
Accept Thyself — **What** are your greatest weaknesses - that if you don't improve upon or delegate to others - the company will underperform? *Which strengths are also weaknesses?*			
Improve Thyself — **What** specifically do you need to commit to improving in the next 12 months to double your personal capacity?			
Accept Others — **What** do you need to delegate in order to set the organization up to reach its full potential? *BY WHEN?*			
Qualify Others — **What** Qual Card (s) do you need to create in order to *delegate and verify*? *BY WHEN?*			
Complement Thyself — **Who** do you need to complement yourself with so that the organization is set up to reach its full potential? *BY WHEN?*			

© 2021 Gold Dolphins LLC   The Decision Series™   RANDY NELSON

Engagement Matters

In finding where your organization is doing "the right things wrong" or "the wrong things right," you must also consider levels of *engagement* among your various employees. Engagement matters as much for employees as it does for entrepreneurs.

In *The Second Decision*, I coined the term "Bor-E-Gaged" as a way of describing the entrepreneurial attention span—a short continuum that stretches from bored to engaged. Bor-E-Gaged is about being stuck smack in the middle or vacillating frequently from left to right. You're not engaged enough to truly focus on the business you're operating, and you're not mind-numbingly bored enough to cut the cord and move on. Stuck in between, your current company is suffering from your lack of engagement. There's nothing *maximized* about this.

Bor-E-Gaged entrepreneurs satisfy their entrepreneurial drive with quantity—the more the better.

Employees of entrepreneurial leaders can also suffer from Bor-E-Gagement.

Employee engagement is the by-product of the relationship between an organization and its employees—a very important one. An "engaged employee" is one who is fully absorbed by—and enthusiastic about—his or her work. This causes the employee to take positive action to further the organization's reputation and interests, with positive effects on the bottom line. But with continual access to the internet at anyone's fingertips, there are ample alternatives to work that are not only available but often right in the disengaged employee's

> **Bor-E-Gaged entrepreneurs satisfy their entrepreneurial drive with quantity—the more the better.**

153

face. Push notifications exist to exploit exactly this sort of distraction. And this, too, impacts the bottom line—and *not* in a positive way.

Consider Gallup's international study on the *State of the Global Workplace*, which found that only 20 percent of employees worldwide are fully engaged at work. In other words, only about one-fifth of workers are psychologically committed to their jobs and likely to be making positive contributions to their organizations.[26]

Conclusion? While entrepreneurs can shift from bored to engaged by becoming more entrepreneurial, their employees go almost entirely the opposite direction, becoming less interested and letting their productivity dwindle.

What this information shows us is how important it is to boost your people's ability to become self-aware of their state of mind—just as you have as boss. Entrepreneurs need to recognize the difference between boredom and active engagement so that they can manage themselves appropriately for the good of their company and its future. We also need to recognize that we can be the cause—and often are—when our employees display a lack of engagement. Here is where opportunity meets the qual card. Instead of Bor-E-Gaged, choose **Qual-E-Gaged**.

> While entrepreneurs can shift from bored to engaged by becoming more entrepreneurial, their employees go almost entirely the opposite direction, becoming less interested and letting their productivity dwindle.

One of the critical differences between a successful entrepreneur and a *maximized* entrepreneur is the focus on quality versus quantity. *Said*

---

26   "A Global Pandemic. And Its Impact on Global Engagement, Stress and the Workforce," Gallup, accessed November 3, 2021, https://www.gallup.com/workplace/349484/state-of-the-global-workplace.aspx.

another way, it's not just the number of businesses you start; it is—or ought to be—the number of great businesses you build that also achieve their full potential and assist employees in meeting theirs.

A Qual-E-Gaged ME embraces the need to have qualified leaders in his or her organization, ones who can position the organization to reach its potential. By ensuring that the leaders are qualified, the ME provides opportunity both for themselves as well as for the potential leaders in their own organizations who are ready to move up and take on more responsibility.

TOOL: THE QUAL CARD

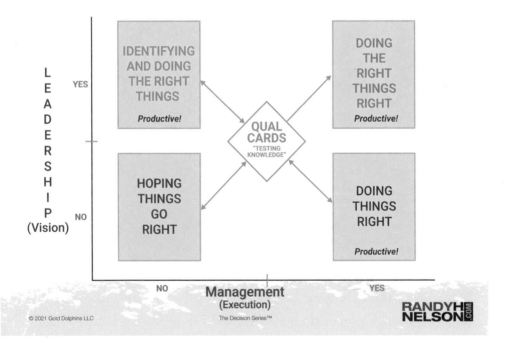

The Qual Cards

There are four qual cards every Qual-E-Gaged ME should introduce into his or her organization(s). Along with these, since no two organizations are alike, the company should devote the time and focus necessary to develop qual cards specific to their own individualized needs. Identifying and developing specialized qual cards for your company isn't easy, but customizing them for best fit in your business is the truly *maximized* way to implement the Qual-E-Gaged concept. (For additional help in identifying qual card opportunities and developing the ones that will serve you best, visit my website, www.randyhnelson.com, and find out how to get involved with this part of our Decision Center practice.) Here are the four basics to give you a starting point:

1. **The CEO Qual Card**—Prior to replacing themselves or placing a CEO in charge of one of the companies they own, an ME ensures that any replacement will have proven themselves qualified to take over the day-to-day leadership of their organization, rather than simply assuming they can. As part of filling out the CEO Qual Card, the potential CEO successor should also fill out the EQC, which was developed for *The Second Decision*, their nonnegotiables from *The Third Decision*, and the MEQC that was developed for *The Fourth Decision*.

2. **The Leadership Development Qual Card**—This qual card can be used for the top leadership, second-tier leaders, etc. in your organization. To scale properly, you need to build a cadre of leaders who can take on more responsibility when needed. This card can be customized to work for your organization.

3. **The Emerging Leader Qual Card**—Any organization has high-potential employees, and the Emerging Leader Qual Card gives them the opportunity to proactively prove, through their own initiative, that they not only want to take on a larger portion of responsibility, but that they are willing to get qualified to do so.

4. **The Senior Leader Qual Card (Outside Hire)**—Outside hires fail, unfortunately. A lot. This qual card is necessary for the senior leaders you may hire from outside your organization. Many have all the experience and expertise you seek, but they are still newcomers to your culture and the entrepreneurial way you build and run your businesses. Ensure they become qualified in your culture, and in the specific ways your organization works that are different from where they came from, and you will increase the long-term potential for great impact and success from these hires.

Remember, an entrepreneur faces a few pitfalls when starting on organizational qual cards. First, there's the entrepreneur's own tendency toward being unwilling to build structure, cultivate expertise, or delegate. Second, there's the entrepreneur's potential for getting bored (Bor-E-Gaged). Third, there's the likelihood that the entrepreneur has fallen short of true self-examination (lack of self-awareness). Now I'm setting a higher bar: it isn't enough to learn how to delegate. We need to *delegate, verify,* and *qualify.* These qual cards, used diligently, ensure that *when qualified leaders in your organization teach others, they teach the right things and see that the lessons are properly implemented.*

Now that you're beginning to think about the qual cards you could devise to serve your organization, it may help to see a couple of pages from my Navy qual card. Let it spark your thinking: What general knowledge would you want to sign off on prior to appointing a replacement CEO?

> We need to *delegate, verify,* and *qualify.* These qual cards, used diligently, ensure that *when qualified leaders in your organization teach others, they teach the right things and see that the lessons are properly implemented.*

COMSUBLANTINST 1552.6D
COMSUBPACINST 1552.1J
1 0 FEB 1983

LINE OFFICER SUBMARINE
QUALIFICATION CARD

Name __RANDALL H. NELSON__   Reporting Date __26 NOV 1984__

A. PREREQUISITES

*Signature   Date

1. Qualified as Diving Officer of the Watch.

2. Qualified as Officer of the Deck (surfaced and submerged).

3. Qualified as Duty Officer.

4. Qualified as Engineering Officer of the Watch (nuclear trained officers).

5. Qualified as Engineering Duty Officer (nuclear trained officers).

6. Qualified as Weapons Duty Officer (SSBN officers who have completed the Weapons Officer course at NAVGMSCOL, Dam Neck/TRITRAFAC, Bangor).

7. Meets the minimum time requirements as established in the basic instruction.

B. KNOWLEDGE REQUIREMENTS

1. Discuss the following submarine force mission concepts and operations:

   a. Approach

   b. Attack

   c. Opposing ASW ships and screens

   d. Coordinated Tactics/Direct Support

*Signatures must be from an officer qualified in submarines. If the designated officer is not qualified, that officer's department head will sign.

Enclosure (8)

As you can see, the Navy's qual cards are 100 percent thorough and complete. But yours don't have to be in the beginning—or ever! All you need is a means of measuring knowledge and establishing accountability. In the Navy, I had to be qualified in multiple positions before getting my final qualification. So think: What general knowledge would you want a CEO to have prior to starting—finance, marketing, sales, IT, HR? Each of these should be added to the CEO Qual Card, just as the Diving Officer, Duty Officer, and Engineering Duty Officer blocks were included on my Navy qual card.

COMSUBLANTINST 1552.6D
COMSUBPACINST 1552.1J
1 0 FEB 1983

*Signature   Date

    e. Mining

    f. Photo-reconnaissance

    g. Swimmer operations

    h. Strategic deterrence

    i. Transitors

    j. Anti-submarine operations

    k. Reconnaissance/intelligence/surveillance

    l. Landing and recovery of personnel

    m. Under ice operations

    n. Search and rescue

    o. Blockade and Quarantine

    p. Navigational and hydrographic data collection

    q. MEDEVAC and HUMEVAC

   2. **Characteristics of Soviet Surface Warships and Aircraft including Initial Detection and Contact Evasions**

    Ref: 4, 21, 22, 55, 66, 91, 92, 127

    a. Explain the visual, ESM and Sonar recognition and classification techniques for Soviet surface warships and aircraft.

    b. Discuss the expected initial acoustic detection range for Soviet surface warships based upon their radiated noise and active sonars.

   3. **Strategic Weapons Systems Capabilities (if applicable)**

    Ref: 6, 30, 31, 80, 81, 112, 113

Enclosure (8)   2

Bear in mind, though, that a CEO doesn't need to be an expert in all areas—not any more than I needed to be an expert on every system on the submarine. I did have to understand, overall, how the submarine operated in every area, and that's the level of knowledge a CEO (or a replacement CEO) should be able to demonstrate. What the qual card process helps you ascertain is *whether your newly qualified leader has the knowledge necessary to teach the right things.* With experience, the rest then falls into place.

Start your qual card process by developing a systematic checkout procedure aimed at revealing whether the employee actually has the knowledge necessary to be deemed qualified. Don't get hung up on testing each fact or detail. But I do recommend that no qual card be signed off unless there's a sit-down Q&A with whomever you establish as the proper signing authority. *Pro forma* sessions aren't what we're after here; we want to make this an opportunity to probe the depth and breadth of our potential leaders. Testing on knowledge is the bulk of what needs to happen, but each checkout should aim to measure wisdom and insight as well.

Recognizing the difference between knowledge and experience is absolutely critical to qual card success. Before you offer someone the opportunity to gain experience, you have to verify that he or she has the knowledge necessary to get qualified and take that next step. Experience is what it takes to move from teaching the right things poorly to teaching them well—we all start out lousy at our jobs, don't we? I certainly did. I was still awful as a leader even after the Navy qualified me to lead and let me start standing watch on my submarine. I needed experience, and the same is true for the leaders in your organization.

> Experience is what it takes to move from teaching the right things poorly to teaching them well—we all start out lousy at our jobs, don't we? I certainly did.

If reading this far has you thinking that developing a qual card process is too much work to take on, remember Desmond Tutu's old saw about how to eat an elephant—"one bite at a time." Your first few bites don't have to be big or particularly precise. The point is merely to take matters a step or two beyond what you're doing now, which is likely just the dangerous assumption that your people know what they are doing because they were taught.

Time now to look at an actual Leadership Development Qual Card. The example below comes from one of my clients in Dublin, Ireland. This global leader in healthcare, technology, and services developed its qual card to get the process started for its global managers. Each of the topics displayed has knowledge requirements embedded in it, but the specifics are omitted here. This was a first-iteration Leadership Development Qual Card developed for a face-to-face work session with the leadership team:

- Know your revenue and EBITDA off the top of your head.

- Be willing to admit your vulnerabilities and mistakes to your peers.

- Be on a path to personal growth.

- Know your culture index and what it means about your blind spots.

- Know your transformational vision off the top of your head.

- Be trustworthy (don't hide the bad news or your problems).

- Be scrappy, down-to-earth, and focused on results, not title and position.

- Hire great leaders who can execute your transformational vision.

- Know your top three metrics off the top of your head.

For the opportunity to see a Leadership Qual Card with more detail included, I would like to thank one of my long-term clients, Entrust Global Group, a portfolio of global brands ranging from collectibles to healthcare. As you can imagine, it's important for me to be careful not to include information that could compromise a strategic advantage or highlight negatives instead of positives in my examples. Entrust gave me permission to share its customized Individual Business Unit Qual Card. The company is using it to qualify leaders who are preparing to take a unit-level helm position.

Entrust's qual card sets out knowledge requirements that are quite specific, with a signature block and date for each—similar to what I saw in the Navy. Once the prospective leader feels that he or she is knowledgeable enough about the topic, it's time to seek out an expert within Entrust and ask for a "checkout." If they demonstrate knowledge to the signer's satisfaction, the signoff occurs. If they don't, they are sent back to deepen or broaden their knowledge. Again, the key aspect for any qual card is that it identifies the basic knowledge requirements needed for the position the person is seeking to qualify for. With those established, it's then up to the prospective leader to take the initiative to do their learning and get their qual card signed off. It's going to feel new in your organization because it *is* new. Instead of just promoting someone who's been there long enough and "feels ready," you now know that they are qualified and ready to begin racking up experience. This worked great in the military, and it's working great with clients whom I've introduced it to.

Entrust—Individual Business Unit Leadership Qual Card

Name _____

Company _____

Title _____

Knowledge Requirements

1. Be qualified in the Entrust "Rocks" Qual Card.

   Signature: _____

   Date: _____

2. Explain in detail the financial reporting system within Entrust, to include the daily, weekly, monthly, quarterly, and annual reporting requirements.

   Signature: _____

   Date: _____

3. Submit the annual budget to the Entrust Senior Leadership and get approved.

   Signature: _____

   Date: _____

4. Explain the priority of the metrics that you are accountable for as the Individual Business Unit Leader. Explain in detail the following financial terms:

   □ Contribution margin

   □ Gross margin per product

   □ Concept of the acronyms YTD, TTM, LTM, H1, and H2

- ▫ COGS

- ▫ EBITDA

- ▫ Cash flow

- ▫ Leading and lagging indicators

- ▫ Revenue levers

Signature: _____

Date: _____

5. Discuss the Entrust shared services philosophy and process in detail, to include the following:

   - ▫ Shared service's full understanding of the business unit strategy and goals.

   - ▫ Description of shared services capabilities across disciplines.

   - ▫ Have a meeting with shared services to get their input on what's next in your business, including bringing their market expertise to your business.

   - ▫ Full understanding of when to use and when it is okay not to use shared services.

Signature: _____

Date: _____

6. Explain in detail your answer to the following question: If the Board of Directors fired you today, and your replacement was very successful in making changes over the next twelve months, what are the three major changes they would make?

   - ▫ You did not know what to do.

    □ You did not know how to do it.

    □ You chose not to do it.

Signature: _____

Date: _____

7. Explain in detail the use of the Strengths Finder Assessment, the Kolbe A, and the Culture Index at Entrust, including how you use the results of the assessment to set your leadership team up for more success, utilizing the *know thyself, improve thyself, complement thyself* self-awareness model. Take all three assessments.

Signature: _____

Date: _____

8. Describe in detail the difference between lagging and leading indicators. List the top five lagging and top five leading indicators for your role on the qual card and explain in detail.

Leading Indicators	Lagging Indicators
1.	1.
2.	2.
3.	3.
4.	4.
5.	5.

Signature: _____

Date: _____

9. COGS—five years' numbers/percentage/data-sorted percentage—lead the development of the COGS reports for your business, along with an analysis of the COGS reports and implementation of *What's Next?!* mentality for the business.

    Signature: _____

    Date: _____

10. Explain in detail the metrics process of collecting three to five years of data, setting current fiscal year targets (budget) and then setting Three-Year Strategic Rocks (X to Z growth)— *The Decision Series Tools—The Truth and Trends.* As part of this process, include both leading and lagging indicators. Produce the report as part of this process.

    Signature: _____

    Date: _____

11. Explain in detail the revenue levers process and illustrate your knowledge by preparing your organization's five revenue levers (X to Z), ultimately connecting them to Three-Year Strategic Rocks for the organization.

    Signature: _____

    Date: _____

12. Rate your organization in terms of being "audit ready" on the Productive Growth Pyramid in each block on a scale of 1 to 10, with 10 being the most prepared and audit ready, and explain your plan for improving each of the areas.

    Signature: _____

    Date: _____

13. Explain the Gold/Diamond/Fool's Gold/Cubic Zirconia slides in relation to the Three+ Business Models.

    Signature: _____

    Date: _____

14. Implement the start/stop/keep survey into your organization. Bring the results and explain the changes you have made after the survey was conducted.

    Signature: _____

    Date: _____

15. Explain the defendable differentiators in your organization and illustrate how they are being built as part of your overall strategy.

    Signature: _____

    Date: _____

16. Discuss the three nonnegotiables for yourself and your top leaders.

    Signature: _____

    Date: _____

17. Final qualification

    □ All blocks signed

    □ Final oral interview completed by qualified senior leadership

    Signature: _____

    Date: _____

Finally, let's talk about a very particular type of qual card, the Senior Leadership Qual Card (outside hire).

As I've already indicated, hiring an experienced leader from outside your organization is a tough mission, one that's difficult to get right. The success rate just isn't strong when we try to onboard people who come from a very different kind of business environment. A new hire coming into an entrepreneurial environment from something more traditionally corporate is going to be a fish out of water, at least at the start.

Yet despite the temptation to say, "That's too big a cultural shift; I'll skip outside hires," it's seldom possible to avoid them. The more we grow our companies, the more likely it is that the experience we seek will come from leaders born and bred somewhere else. It's then natural to want to honor that experience by turning the new hire loose to do what he or she does best. Why else would we make the hire? Why hobble a thoroughbred?

But when we yield to this urge to over-respect outside experience, we violate cardinal rule number one, which is assuming that a person experienced in leading elsewhere is qualified to lead in *our* organization. Smaller is different than bigger. Entrepreneurial is most definitely different than corporate. It's all too easy to find your new hire has sparked a culture clash—with you, with other leaders within your company, and with the people they were brought in to lead. That's why it's so important that outside hires at a senior level understand that, even though their knowledge and skill is what's attractive about them, it doesn't mean it's automatically and thoroughly transferrable to their new job. The ground rules of the hire should include an expectation that the senior newbie will put in the time and effort to learn the ropes as they exist in your organization. Those who don't or won't want to do that shouldn't be hired.

Let's take a look at another of my favorite diagrams.

TOOL: CORE VALUES / PERFORMANCE

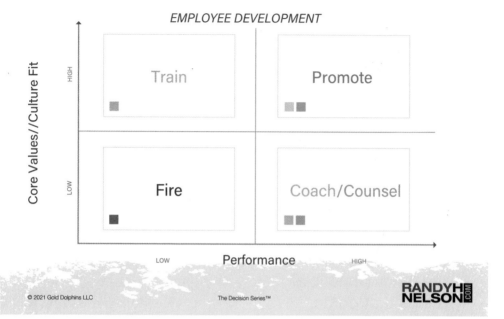

If a senior outside hire consistently performs poorly and doesn't culturally fit in your organization, then that person should find a better fit somewhere else, and sooner rather than later—that's the "fire" block. It's also obvious that a high performer who proves to be a great fit should be promoted (through the use of qual cards).

Now, to the other blocks: the employee who is a great cultural fit but an inconsistent performer needs training. That's not difficult. But the trickiest situation is the fourth block, the high performer whose values make him or her a bad fit for your organization, culturally speaking. If you've ever dealt with somebody like this, and eventually had to let them go, you probably remember the reaction from within the organization: "Why did it take you so long? That person was poison."

What could you do instead? Well, never let things get that far. Create a qual card specifically for the outside senior hire, one that ensures they are trained and qualified in the values and culture of your company. Don't just hope for the best or assume that your culture will train the candidate. Often, it works the other way around.

At this point, I suspect this all sounds like more work than you want to "get bogged down" with. Entrepreneurs love to go fast and in many directions; for us, speed and activity always feel good. But I'm a firm believer in the many beneficial things that come from "slowing down to speed up." Qual cards help you do it, and do it well. If you truly want to *maximize*—to not only complement yourself by bringing in needed skills but also truly build the kind of leadership that will allow you to someday replace yourself—you need to take a more deliberative, careful approach. That's how you can ensure that you've got the right people doing the right things right.

> I'm a firm believer in the many beneficial things that come from "slowing down to speed up."

Below is an example of some of the knowledge requirements you might fashion for a senior outside hire's qual card:

Senior Leader (Outside Hire) Qual Card

Name _____

Company _____

Title _____

Knowledge Requirements

1. Describe in detail the company's Core Values and Core Purpose and give examples of how you have exemplified and/or struggled with each of them throughout your career.

   Signature: _____

   Date: _____

2. Explain how you as a leader will ultimately provide lasting impact within your organization through the qualification system—teach the teacher.

   Signature: _____

   Date: _____

3. Explain the Culture Performance 2 x 2 slide in detail, describing all four blocks and the need for qual cards for experienced hires to help with their transition to an entrepreneurial leadership culture.

   Signature: _____

   Date: _____

4. Discuss your assessment results and how they will complement and/or clash with other leadership.

   Signature: _____

   Date: _____

5. Explain the Leadership and Management slide, to include the need for qual cards to minimize the chances of doing the right things wrong, and/or the wrong things right.

   Signature: _____

   Date: _____

6. Complete three "Under Instruction" visits with clients with a qualified leader.

   1. _____ Date: _____

   2. _____ Date: _____

   3. _____ Date: _____

   Signature: _____

   Date: _____

7. Discuss the main differences between operating in your previous organization compared to the current entrepreneurial organization, and the adjustments you will proactively need to make to succeed.

   Signature: _____

   Date: _____

Final Qualification—All Blocks Signed and Oral Interviews Completed

Obviously, what I just shared is an abbreviated qual card. It will need to be customized and fleshed out through plenty of deliberation at the leadership level. But as I've said before, it can be done more simply, at least to begin with.

To conclude the chapter, I've included another tool that should help your organization design qual cards that the Revised Self-Awareness Decision Tool identifies for you in the "qualify thyself" blocks:

TOOL: "QUAL CARD" DEVELOPMENT

Company Name: _____

Division: _____

Job Title: _____

Step One – Identify
What qual cards do you need to create? Utilize the Self-Awareness Decision Tool (Qualify Others blocks) to help you decide!

1. _____

2. _____

3. _____

Step Two – Develop
List the general knowledge requirements for each qual card. Each knowledge requirement will be followed by a signature block and date. Develop an overall list of knowledge requirements. Be careful not to make the qual card so long and onerous that few will want to complete it. The next step allows you to ask more in-depth questions around the general knowledge requirements to ensure that the person has a strong grasp on each of them.

Step Three – Verify
This is another critical success factor for the qual card. The person who desires to get qualified must take the initiative to seek out the "expert" in each knowledge requirement and ask them for a "check-out". At this point the expert will ask questions to ensure that the person truly has the general knowledge required to get their qual card "signed off" for that specific line item on the qual card.

Step Four – Qualify
Once all the blocks of the qual card are completed, there will be a final oral interview by the leader/overall expert as a final check-out prior to signing off on the person being qualified. By being able to identify the knowledge requirements first, then verify that the person has a firm grasp of them, and then finally qualifying them, the qual card process will build speed and trust in the critically important delegation process necessary to grow organizations to reach their full potential.

The Decision Series™

RANDYH NELSON

In the next chapter, I will introduce you to another tool that can be installed in your organization's tool inventory—the Audit-Ready Decision Tool. But before you turn the page and begin that journey, test your knowledge of this chapter by working through the MEQC. Don't rush—there's a lot of detail here that requires your attention and consideration.

MEQC—What's Next?!

Learn. Think. Decide. Implement.

Initials

1. Discuss the three cardinal rules for MEs:

    - Don't assume that your employees know what to do just because you hired them and gave them freedom to do their job.
    - Don't give your employees complete freedom to do their jobs without setting goals for them and making it clear what you expect them to do (job description, goals, metrics, etc.).
    - Don't assume your employees are qualified just because you trained them and gave them a job description with metrics. Hold them accountable for being qualified. Training without including some Navy-style qualification strategies just adds to the risk in the organization and, as we will discuss in future chapters, there is a lot to be said about *controlled risk* versus *pure risk*. _____

2. Complete the Revised Self-Awareness Decision Tool and explain all of your answers in detail. _____

3. Explain in detail the difference between an entrepreneur who is Bor-E-Gaged and a *maximized* entrepreneur who is Qual-E-Gaged. How are they the same? How are they different? _____

4. Develop the CEO Qual Card for your organization(s). _____

5. Develop a general Leadership Development Qual Card for your organization. _____

6. Develop a specific Leadership Development Qual Card for a hire you intend to make. _____

7. Develop the Senior Leader (outside hire) Qual Card for your organization. _____

Signature: _____

Date: _____

CHAPTER 6

The Audit-Ready Question and Decision Tool: The Growth and Busy Pyramids

When you clearly understand that success is a process, not an event, you are encouraged to follow the right process to create the success you are capable of having.
—ZIG ZIGLAR

In the world of the ME, the difference between merely being success-ful and becoming *maximized* starts with an audit-ready mindset. The IRS audits personal tax returns to ensure they are correct, and there are heavy fines to pay when someone is found to be out of compli-ance. What if the same held true for entrepreneurs? What if you, as a *maximized* entrepreneur, set up your organization(s) to the highest level of performance and were willing to be audited to see if you were truly attaining your highest goals for your company's potential? This is the essence of being audit ready. Some of you are already doing this with your financial statements. Some aren't.

In the financial world, there are three levels of compliance:

1. **The compilation**—A compilation refers to a company's financial statements that have been prepared or compiled by an outside accountant. With compilations, or compiled financial statements, the outside accountant converts the client's data into financial statements *without providing any assurances or auditing services.*

2. **The review**—A financial statement review is a service under which *the accountant obtains limited assuranc*e that there are no material modifications that need to be made to an entity's financial statements for them to be in conformity with the applicable financial reporting framework, such as GAAP (generally accepted accounting principles) or IFRS.

3. **The audit**—An audited financial statement refers to a provider's financial statement that has been taken to the highest level of detail and rigor. It has been prepared in accordance with GAAP and *has been audited* by an independent certified public accountant in accordance with generally accepted auditing standards.

What if you, as a *maximized* entrepreneur, set up your organization(s) to the highest level of performance and were willing to be audited to see if you were truly attaining your highest goals for your company's potential?

In my workshops and as part of my coaching and consulting practices, I offer what I call the Audit-Ready Question, which takes the familiar financial concepts and seeks to spread them throughout your organization. It also sets you up to work with the Audit-Ready Decision Tool.

The concepts behind this tool are timeless. It can be used alongside whatever else you are currently using to build your business and can be tailored to your needs, then returned to your bookshelf as a reference for the future. In short, it's a building block.

For an overview of how this works, let's take a look at the Productive Growth Pyramid (see figure). I was inspired to develop the pyramid shape after seeing a version of it in a workshop for Verne Harnish's *The Rockefeller Habits*. The boxes are consistent with most operating systems today; the words are a bit different since everyone has their own customization of the business model.

TOOL: AUDIT-READY DECISIONS—THE PRODUCTIVE GROWTH PYRAMID

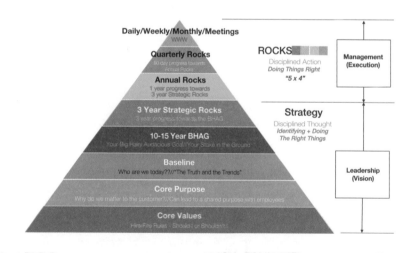

The larger we grow our organizations, the more at risk they are of succumbing to the typical reasons for business failure. Of the top ten reasons companies crash and burn, two come to mind that fit well here:

- Dysfunctional management—lacking vision, focus, planning, standards, and other requirements of good management

- Operational mediocrity—not having the right people in the right seats

Now let me ask you a simple, yet complicated question:

If I were to spend a month inside your organization, auditing each of the blocks above, what would I find?

Start at the bottom of the pyramid, with Core Values. This is, of course, the well-known concept developed by author Jim Collins, one of the world's most highly respected business thought leaders. My tool also uses his terms Core Purpose and BHAG (big hairy audacious goal), but if you prefer to use a different set of terms, please do—just keep the intent consistent.

Need a definition to get started? Here's the one for Core Values provided by Collins, the term's originator:

> *Core Values are the handful of guiding principles by which a company navigates. They require no external justification. For example, Disney's core values of imagination and wholesomeness stem from the founder's belief that these should be nurtured for their own sake, not merely to capitalize on a business opportunity. Instead of changing its core values, a great company will change its markets—seek out different customers—in order to remain true to the core values on which it was founded.*[27]

I propose that Core Values be established and taught at home (with accountability built in for violations), because without them, rules don't have any meaning or foundation. It's like letting your teens hang out with just anybody, act any way they want, and come

---

27 Jim Collins and Jerry I. Porras, *Built to Last: Successful Habits of Visionary Companies* (New York: HarperCollins, 2002).

home anytime they choose—because you trust them to make good choices. When I present this information in my talks, the audience's response, of course, is always nervous laughter. We all know that's not enough guidance. You have to build a foundation of values and purpose before you can trust kids to make good choices. Same goes for adults, right?

If I were inside your organization, would I find it audit ready in the category of Core Values? If your answer is yes, then your Core Values have been designed and implemented at an audit-ready level, and the CEO or entrepreneur is confident that these Core Values are guiding behavior and decision-making throughout the organization. If no is your answer, it indicates an honest recognition that there's more work to do in this area, especially if the company aims to move from being merely successful to *maximized*. On average, based on research over the past decade, I find that half the people in any given speech or workshop claim to be audit ready in the category of Core Values. What's your honest answer, yes or no, to the Audit-Ready Question on Core Values?

Core Values—5/10 = 50 percent
Your organization: Yes _____ No _____

I'll have a bit more to say on the subject of Core Values later on, but for now, let's move up the pyramid to Core Purpose. Jim Collins defined it well in his *Harvard Business Review* article titled "Building Your Company's Vision," which he cowrote with Jerry Porras:[28]

Core Purpose is an organization's most fundamental reason for being. It should not be confused with the company's current

---

28   Jim Collins and Jerry I. Porras, "Building Your Company's Vision," *Harvard Business Review*, September–October 1996. Retrieved from https://hbr.org/1996/09/building-your-companys-vision.

product lines or customer segments. Rather, it reflects people's idealistic motivations for doing the company's work. Disney's Core Purpose is to make people happy—not to build theme parks and make cartoons.

Collins and Porras use an exercise to help an organization discover its Core Purpose. It involves getting all leaders and key personnel into a room and asking them, "Why do you matter to the customer?" Collins advises the group to continue asking itself the same question until it can settle on a single answer—which should reveal the company's Core Purpose.

When I do this exercise with my own clients, I find that initial answers tend to center on the company's products (quality, ingenuity, etc.) and services (customized, reliable, etc.). It takes some prodding and reframing to get people to begin identifying why the company's existence matters to the customer outside of its products or services. In trying to drill down to a true Core Purpose, it often helps to ask what customers would likely miss most if the company disappeared. Think of it this way—if your company went out of business, what kind of gap would you leave in the market that you currently serve?

To flesh out this question a bit, let me share some of my own experience. My first company, which I cofounded in 1991, was among many businesses hit hard in the aftermath of the 9/11 attacks. We were forced to downsize the company by over 70 percent. At many points, we felt perilously close to losing the company altogether. I'm proud to say that Orion Talent is alive and well today, having helped over fifty thousand veterans transition from military to civilian employment over the past thirty years. For this company, the question "What would the world miss if the business failed?" has an easy answer. Support for veterans would have suffered significantly in this country, and untold numbers of our dedicated service members would have failed to enjoy the good jobs and prosperous postmilitary life they so richly deserve.

The Core Purpose for Orion Talent? Originally, helping ex-military personnel build successful civilian lives. It is interesting to note that over time Orion has evolved to also include recruitment process outsourcing (RPO) services, widening its purpose beyond military talent to supply more of what its customers need as a one-stop solution. The company's Core Purpose has most likely evolved to include these outsourcing services as well.

From the numerous audiences I have asked to honestly assess their company's audit-ready stance in this area, I've obtained the following data. I ask you to also take your own reading of the situation in your company:

Core Purpose—3/10 = 30 percent**[29]
Your organization: Yes _____ No _____

That's right—only 30 percent of the leaders I've worked with believe that their company's Core Purpose has been discovered and discussed through their organization. Most have had to acknowledge it's likely unclear to their people why what they do matters to customers. This is a significant problem. The ME fully understands that without an identified and shared Core Purpose between leaders and employees, the organization is at risk of losing great people along the way, ones who don't feel connected to the company's basic cultural understanding. When Core Values and Core Purpose are established, a strong corporate identity can't help but follow. This makes it much easier for the organization to know what opportunities to say yes to

---

29   **I've found that certain companies have nailed their Core Purpose but continue to miss badly with their Core Values. The 30 percent average includes many such companies, ones I'd later learn scored poorly on Core Values but were very clear on the Core Purpose of their organization.

and which require a firm no—which, of course, makes everything about running the company easier.

In chapter 9, I will share much more information on how to improve your business and personal decision-making. Personally, I have plenty of experience in trying to figure out who I am, what I'm doing, and why I'm doing it. As I transitioned from being an entrepreneur and building businesses for thirty years to a new career trying to help entrepreneurs build their businesses, my peer groups worked hard to pin me down: Why was I doing all this writing, coaching, teaching, mentoring, and advising? Having been successful at building and selling multiple companies and, together with my wife, raising six kids who were now grown adults raising their own families, why did I feel it necessary to keep working instead of stopping and smelling the proverbial

> When Core Values and Core Purpose are established, a strong corporate identity can't help but follow.

roses? I gave them many answers, most of which were initially vague. But continued questioning and challenging brought me to the point that I could satisfy them—and myself—with a true Core Purpose:

> *"To unlock and maximize the inner entrepreneurial leader ... by getting the entrepreneur right ... first ... at every stage of your entrepreneurial career."*

Okay, that's two blocks done, Core Value and Core Purpose. As we prepare to move up the blocks of the pyramid illustration that guides our discussion of the audit-ready decision, I invite you to pause and consider: If just 50 percent of typical organizations can report discovering and living their Core Values, and only 30 percent can answer yes to the Core Purpose question, what kind of audit-ready numbers might we find moving further up through the blocks? Will they be better? Or do the numbers keep going down as we move up the pyramid? Place your bets.

Coming soon is the BHAG—the big hairy audacious goal, as Collins named it. But first I want to pause and talk a bit about data. I spoke lots about numbers and data in the "Cash," "COGS," "Metrics," and "Reset" chapters in *The Second Decision*.

Next up is *baselining*. It's a concept you'll need to understand and get comfortable using throughout the remainder of *The Fourth Decision*.

To become a *maximized* entrepreneur, the prerequisite of which is ten years of experience in starting and running companies, you can't say you don't have data—you have at least a decade of it. But how can you use it to make the jump from merely being successful to becoming truly *maximized*? Data is a yellow brick road—it'll lead you where you need to go. I often tell my audiences that if I knew nothing about their business, but I had all of their data, then I would be in the position to ask all of the right questions necessary to help them to make better decisions for their company's future. Yes, true—I could make Gold Level decisions, even without knowing what the company really does for its customers! And if I truly understood the business and had the necessary intuition to combine with the metrics, then I would be able to mine not only for Gold but also for Diamonds. That's the basics of baselining. You, as ME, embrace data and

> That's the basics of baselining. You, as ME, embrace data and combine your metrics with the intuition you've developed by piloting your company to success—and thereby teach yourself to make Diamond Level decisions. Not once or twice, but consistently.

combine your metrics with the intuition you've developed by piloting your company to success—and thereby teach yourself to make Diamond Level decisions. Not once or twice, but consistently.

Let me show you below what I mean in a 2 x 2 matrix:

TOOL: THE GOLD-DIAMOND MINE

MAKE BETTER, CALCULATED DECISIONS FASTER, AND WITH MORE CONFIDENCE

Most entrepreneurs find it easy to operate at the Cubic Zirconia Level. They have some data and track some metrics, but mostly they trust their gut.

There are *some* successful entrepreneurs who operate at the Diamond Level, but not nearly enough. They trust their gut (use their intuition) and track numbers, but not enough to make consistently good decisions. Ask them why, and the answer is almost always the same: it's hard to find the right numbers.

That's where baselining comes in, the goal of which is to mine data at all levels of the organization for the purpose of not just making better decisions—Diamond Level decisions—but to *make better-calculated decisions faster and with more confidence.*

The *maximized* entrepreneur embraces data, period. They are as insatiable in collecting it as they are in pursuing excellence in general. On the other hand, entrepreneurs who are merely successful can and often do remain satisfied at the Cubic Zirconia Level, *especially if their results are in line with their expectations.*

In the pyramid, you might wonder this: Why does the baselining block come after Core Values and Core Purpose but before the BHAG? Because to do otherwise would be putting the cart before the horse. The behaviors (Core Values) you build your business on form the foundation of the company. While the Core Values never change, the Core Purpose can change as markets evolve. Yet both of these are statements rather than data. They are building blocks that, while specific, are not quantifiable. They illustrate how you act and why you matter. The data—important as it is—comes later, followed by the metrics. And only then is the organization in a position to seriously entertain goal-setting with a BHAG. That, my friends, is why baselining comes after Core Values and Core Purpose but before BHAG.

> The *maximized* entrepreneur embraces data, period.

Again, all it takes to make at least Gold Level decisions is to know the right questions to ask—which requires data. In fact, I don't work with a new client until we baseline their data, because it puts the truth right out there in front of us. Remember, entrepreneurs are optimists. They see opportunity in everything, including difficulty. I'm good with that. I accept that personality trait. But we need to start by looking at the truth, in the form of data. That's what we'll use as a baseline for any further discussion.

But not data alone. Tracking numbers by themselves limits the decision-making power you have available to you. Including *trends* with your data allows you to set the right targets for the current budget year for each of the metrics that you track. By comparing where you are today with your projections for a year from now, you can build in the audit-ready mindset and blend it with continuous improvement.

> In fact, I don't work with a new client until we baseline their data, because it puts the truth right out there in front of us.

Let me give you an example. A client of mine (to remain anonymous) had some issues with the company's leadership team. This outfit was in real trouble, suffering massive discontent among upper management. I was called in to facilitate a meeting to get to the bottom of it. Utilizing the baselining methodology, I decided that to make progress with them, we had to establish where they stood with their Core Values, from an audit-ready perspective. I asked each of the leaders to state, yes or no, whether each of the company's five Core Values were in place and effective in the organization.

	TODAY
Core Value 1	0/15
Core Value 2	1/15
Core Value 3	0/15
Core Value 4	4/15
Core Value 5	3/15

Each of the fifteen leaders in the room spoke their mind, and when we baselined each of the Core Values, the reality of the situation became abundantly clear. For the first Core Value, not a single leader gave it a yes, and in fact, they were laughing at how bad they were on this one. From there, things improved but not by much. And these were the people responsible for leading the organization!

Baselining is critically important for a few reasons:

- It tells *the truth*, whether we want to see it or not.

- It shows us *the trends*.

- It raises our confidence in making decisions for the future by allowing us to ask great questions.

In the case of this leadership team, the truth was all out in the open now, and the dialogue they had that day set the tone for the future. But one question was nagging at me as I looked around the room at a group of leaders who were obviously at odds with each other. I asked, "Why are you still here?" It was a nod at the obvious fractures in the culture of this particular company. The frowns I had been facing turned to smiles.

"We love the company and what we do for our customers. We matter greatly!"

Aha! For this group, the Core Values were a mess, but the Core Purpose was clear. (Remember the ** notation earlier?) To repeat, what I've found is that certain companies (around 30 percent) have nailed their Core Purpose but continue to miss badly with their Core Values.

In six months, I met again with my unnamed client company, and the results were as follows:

	TODAY	SIX MONTHS LATER
Core Value 1	0/15	4/15
Core Value 2	1/15	6/15
Core Value 3	0/15	5/15
Core Value 4	4/15	9/15
Core Value 5	3/15	10/15

If we had never baselined, we would have left the room with irritated people pointing fingers at one another, and in six months, the results would have been much like the first meeting. But that's not what happened. Improvement happened, and the leaders were excited. If we had been satisfied at the compilation or review level, we wouldn't have come close to reaching the audit level. We wouldn't have discovered the Diamond Level data with which to make better decisions. This leadership group left the second meeting knowing there was still a long way to go, but they had made a start by finding their *baseline!*

As we know, building businesses for the long term is all about continuous improvement. You really can't do it without baselining, because that's what allows us to take measurements that help us decide to grow from X to Y, whatever Y may be. Baselining can be done at all organizational levels and with all sorts of metrics. The Truth and Trends diagram can help with the basics of how to baseline.

TOOL: THE TRUTH AND THE TRENDS™

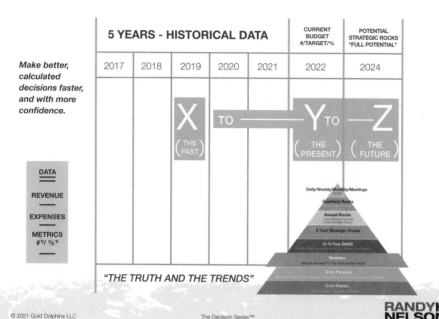

1. Put together five years of historical data for the metrics/data that you track. You may have a practice of using a specific term for your metrics, such as key performance indicators (KPIs). If so, go with the intent of my training, which is to compile all of the metrics/data you can, regardless of what you call them.

2. If the enterprise or business segment isn't yet five years old, and/or you don't have that kind of history available for what you're looking at, then start to collect data on a weekly, biweekly, monthly, and quarterly basis. This will give you additional data points quickly. From a standing start, no data, you can have thirteen data points to analyze at the end of a single quarter. So get started tracking weekly.

3. The five years of data give you the truth. Now analyze the trends, adding in your intuition to understand in better detail why the metrics are improving, getting worse, or holding steady.

4. Set the target for the current fiscal year budget cycle and then be consistent about reviewing it.

5. The three-year target for the metric for 2024 potentially becomes your strategy for that metric. To grow from the current metric, we will have to explain how we will make the improvement from X to Y to Z quantifiable and specific. We will also have to identify specific accountabilities for improvement—whose job is it?

6. Baselining consists of two separate components. First, it's baselining your metrics over a five-year period, then setting the current-year targets and potential Strategic Rocks for the future. Second, baselining includes all the blocks of the Audit-Ready Decision Tool to ensure that the organization is making broad, consistent improvement.

Historical data	Historical data	Historical data	Historical data	Historical data	Current-year target	Three-years-out target
2017	2018	2019	2020	2021	2022	2024

The data you compile by baselining includes both your leading and your lagging indicators. The practice requires us to chart this data for a visual representation of the truth—what's really happening (or not) in your organization. It then affords us an opportunity to compare and contrast as we wish, revealing trends we might not otherwise have noticed. The ME, who has also baselined each of the building blocks (Core Values, Core Purpose, etc.), combines everything with an initial audit-ready number, then conducts a new baselining exercise in three months, six months, or a year, as desired.

In this chapter, you are watching the audit-ready results come in one at a time for the building blocks, which are the same for every organization in the world. Successful entrepreneurs learn. *Maximized* entrepreneurial leaders learn and implement, both at high levels. They baseline *everything*. I don't have data on who's baselining, as I didn't expect my clients and audiences to be doing something I hadn't yet taught

> The ME, who has also baselined each of the building blocks (Core Values, Core Purpose, etc.), combines everything with an initial audit-ready number, then conducts a new baselining exercise in three months, six months, or a year, as desired.

them. But I can definitely ask you! My educated guess is 20 percent.

Your Organization—Baseline: Yes _____ No _____

On to the BHAG. To introduce or refresh you on the concept, Collins and Porras define this as

"Ambitious plans that rev up the entire organization. They typically require ten to thirty years' work to complete … Vivid descriptions paint a picture of what it will be like to achieve the BHAGs. They make the goals vibrant, engaging—and tangible … It has a clear finish line, so the organization can know when it has achieved the goal."

Note: I prefer to look at a ten- to fifteen-year time frame because I can see, feel, and touch ten to fifteen years more easily than I can two or three decades.

One of the interesting things about my experience with entrepreneurs and CEOs is the very real differences I see in learning the terminology versus implementing it. If I ask the question "Does everybody have a strategy in their organization?" the answers are universally yes, because all entrepreneurs and CEOs believe they have a strategy. The same would be true with Core Values and Core Purpose, as well as one-year plans and daily activities. Everybody says, "Yup, got those." That's why I don't ask about "having"; I ask about implementing, which is a higher-level audit-ready question.

Successful entrepreneurs have made the commitment to vision and execution in their organizations. But *maximized* entrepreneurs ensure that things are not only getting done but being done at an audit-ready level.

The BHAG must also be "clear and compelling." In our Decision Center coaching and growth advising practice, I've found that once a client slows down long enough to have the BHAG brainstorming session, the likelihood of it being discovered and put into place rises significantly. This is especially true when the organization's Core Values and Core Purpose (along with Defendable Differentiators, which we'll discuss later) are also clear and concise. Without the BHAG, the Three-Year Strategic Rocks (the next block in the pyramid) lead the "begin with the end in mind" discussion for strategic planning. But a clear and compelling BHAG becomes the starting point for subsequent strategic discussions. Whereas I have chosen to utilize Jim Collins' terms for the first few blocks of the pyramid, I now choose "Rocks," popularized by Stephen Covey in his book *The Seven Habits of Highly Effective People.* Rocks and goals are synonymous and interchangeable.

My data suggests that very few companies have a stated BHAG. What about you?

BHAG—<1/10 = 10 percent max

Your organization: Yes _____ No _____

Perhaps the most compelling of all my observations over thirty years of building businesses, helping others build them, or hearing from peers with business-building experience is this:

Three-year strategy—2.5/10 = 25 percent

One-year business plan—9/10 = 90 percent

Think about these results for a minute. Of the data points that I gathered over a six-year period, and observed as a member of peer groups for forty-plus years, asking entrepreneurs and CEOs to make the audit-ready decision for both the strategy and the business plan question, nearly everyone had an annual plan. Very few had a strategy—and among those who said they did, even fewer could say the strategy is understood throughout the organization. Digging deeper into the details, I consistently found the number of entrepreneurs and CEOs who could claim a *quantifiable and specific* three-year strategy was vanishingly small.

The *maximized* entrepreneur has clarity for the future, in the form of Three-Year Strategic Rocks. The merely successful entrepreneur does not, at least not most of the time. And I will tell you why: it's the sheer difficulty of it. Entrepreneurs who are not otherwise committed to becoming maximized and achieving true entrepreneurial leadership find it much easier to punt on this, and you'll see this tendency exemplified in an upcoming anecdote.

Where organizations do self-identify as holders of three- to five-year strategies (I chose Three-Year Strategic Rocks), closer questioning reveals they are more likely to be goals—really just revenue and profit targets set for the time span. These are not strategies; they are outcomes. Strategies are very different. In the "Vision" chapter of *The Second Decision*, I outlined some of the questions that should be asked to come up with a true strategy and also outlined the Vision and Execution Checklist to evaluate your leadership at an audit-ready level.

TOOL: VISION AND EXECUTION CHECKLIST

Audit ready status (Check the one that applies)	CEO Plan	CEO Value (And Why?)	Performance Rating	Where Are You?	Next Grading Period - Board of Directors (BOD)	Employee Response
☐	Three-year/ One-year and Quarterly plan	Disciplined Thought and Action	A	2 steps ahead	Promote	Excited/ passionate
☐	Specific One-year/ Quarterly plan	Disciplined Action	B	1 step ahead	Train and promote	"I'm in, but I want to see more."
☐	General One-Year/ Quarterly plan	CEO is sitting in his/her comfort zone	C	On the same step	Train	On the bubble
☐	A quarterly plan is all we can manage."	"I'm too busy!"	D	1 step behind	Counsel— train	"Why am I listening to you?"
☐	Today's plan may or may not be in place	Banking on hope and hope alone.	F	2 step behind	Progressive discipline	Active on the Job Boards this afternoon

The Decision Series™

RANDYH
NELSON

As I've taken the same questions to my audiences and clients, a good portion of them reported "strategy" that sounded like a *Dilbert* comic strip, where the boss mentions that the visionary leadership plan for boosting sales is "to invent some sort of doohickey that everyone wants to buy."[30]

---

30   Scott Adams, "Dilbert," April 17, 2004, https://dilbert.com/strip/2004-04-17.

And these were very successful companies, with savvy, heads-up leaders! Yet nearly every company's so-called strategy was an annual plan with a budget showing growth from the current year to the next. Why? Because it's easier to do that.

In chapter 7, I will delve into the three most prevalent models of the one-year budget and the three- to five-year strategy that exist in industry today. For now, it suffices to take a not-very-satirical look at the classic entrepreneur's "strategy." Imagine the company has gathered everyone together for the unveiling of a strategy for the next several years. It goes like this:

"I am so excited to be here today! We are a $10 million company, and I have racked my brain over the past three months trying to come up with the right strategy for where we are today and, man, am I excited to share it with you! Everybody ready? Here it is. From $10 million in revenue today, we will become, in just three years, a $34 million company!"

Exciting, yes, but every sensible employee in the audience is wondering exactly how that growth will be accomplished. There are no details. And therefore there is no strategy. Throwing a dart would be as predictive.

Those who are committed to becoming a *maximized* entrepreneur, one who is truly audit ready, can't just throw a dart and call it good. To truly reach ME status when it comes to strategy, you're going to have to pass Jim Whitehurst's test. Jim was the chief operations officer of Delta Air Lines and then became the CEO of Red Hat, an open-source software company that has been purchased by IBM. Most recently, he was the president of IBM, so he is indeed a mover and a shaker in the leadership world. Since he's been based in the Raleigh, North Carolina, area for some years, I've had the pleasure of hearing him speak on numerous occasions, as well as hosting him at various meetings. When I heard what he did for his organization as it pertains to strategy, it stuck.

As we all know, plenty of companies survey their customers and track their scores, following up with strategies intended to achieve measurable improvement over time. Jim goes about it differently. He surveys his *employees* to determine how well they understand the very specific strategy of the company overall. The lower the resulting score, the more he sees need for improvement. Jim knows that his employees are where the rubber really meets the road. He's dedicated to developing the right strategy *and implementing it* by ensuring that it's been communicated and reinforced throughout the organization. Surveying customers? That's a lagging indicator. Working instead on the leading indicator—employee comprehension—well, that's what I call an audit-ready strategy.

In my experiential data-gathering, I've found that a merely successful entrepreneurial company can get away with annual budgets and a less-than-clear three-year strategy. The *maximized* entrepreneur, however, will not accept this. He or she wants all the blocks to become audit ready and thus prepared to be held accountable for the results—as has been the practice of Jim Whitehurst at Delta, Red Hat, and IBM.

The ME understands that without a clear strategy to guide the organization, it runs the risk of becoming a company less focused on producing and more than likely just staying busy. This, too, is something that I've seen proven over and over again:

The majority of entrepreneurial organizations are busy, not productive.

Let's look at the audit-ready results of the remaining blocks in our model:

Quarterly—6/10 = 60 percent

Your organization: Yes _____ No _____

Weekly/Monthly—8/10 = 80 percent

Your organization: Yes _____ No _____

Daily—8/10 = 80 percent

Your Organization: Yes _____ No _____

Whereas 90 percent of the organizations I've polled had an annual plan in place and a budget to go with it, only 60 percent of organizations broke down the annual plan into quarterly plans that support the overall annual plan. A slightly higher percentage of these organizations had some sort of weekly or monthly meeting schedule in place, and the same 80 percent knew what they had to do today. Of

> The majority of entrepreneurial organizations are busy, not productive.

course, with "to-do" lists chockablock with action items, it's invariably far more than any human can achieve in a day!

This brings us to the "Busy" and "Productive" arrows on our illustration.

TOOL: AUDIT-READY DECISIONS—THE PRODUCTIVE GROWTH PYRAMID

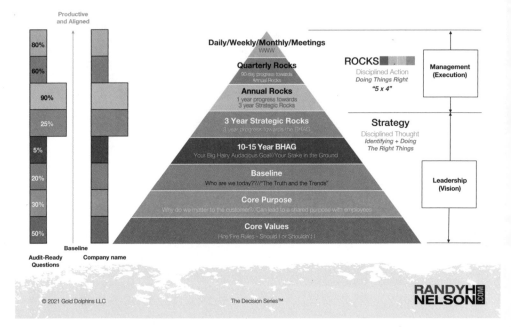

If your organization has become audit ready, with Core Values and Core Purpose defined and working well, baseline data mined for better decision-making, a BHAG and/or company three-year (audit-ready) strategy in place—all followed by an annual plan that supports the strategy and quarterly/monthly/weekly/daily meetings, which support the annual plan—then it's highly likely to be aligned up, down, and across the org chart. That's a *productive* organization, set up to meet its full potential, with everybody marching forward to the same music. Productive organizations are ones that have their top priorities in sharp focus. As we'll see later, these are the organizations best positioned to level up, not just by meeting strategic goals but by having the laser-like focus and discipline to know which opportunities they should let pass by.

Let's consider the less desirable alternative before we move on:

TOOL: THE "BUSY" GROWTH PYRAMID

If the three-year strategy is not in place, then the organization tends to move forward with the "beginning in mind budget" guiding daily activities, as opposed to the "end in mind strategy" calling the shots. Whereas the Productive Growth Pyramid is on firm ground with Core Values at the base of the model, the Busy Growth Pyramid is highly unstable and lacking firm ground upon which to stand. Normally, the organizations that operate this way tend to be very *busy*, allowing what feels urgent to take priority over what's truly important. Such organizations are under the mistaken impression that this is how progress is made—by choosing frenzy over true strategy. Organizations that are habitually busy tend to leave tons of potential on the table, choosing revenue growth over profit, and indiscriminately saying yes to opportunity when they ought to say no. Inside such companies, it can feel a lot like being on a treadmill you can't get off, but there are ways of pulling the plug and switching from "busy" to "productive," and we'll take a closer look at them in a later chapter.

Daily plans and meetings	B	80 percent
Weekly plans and meetings	A	80 percent
Monthly plans and meetings	S	80 percent
Quarterly plans and meetings	E	60 percent
One-year operating plan (budget)	L	90 percent
Three-year strategy	I	25 percent
BHAG	N	10 percent
Baseline		*20 percent*
Core purpose	E	30 percent
Core values	D	50 percent

Such organizations are under the mistaken impression that this is how progress is made—by choosing frenzy over true strategy.

In the Navy, I couldn't have become *qualified*—have my qual card signed off—without understanding all the systems and processes on the submarine, both big picture and in detail. When you conduct an audit-ready exercise, you're putting yourself in a similar position—looking top-down into your organization to see how it's functioning at all levels. You start with the baseline of today. Just as my goal as a sailor was to enhance my knowledge a bit every day, ours as leaders must be to improve from that baseline, then find the new baseline and improve again.

We are successful entrepreneurs who know how to build companies. That's good, but it shouldn't be where we top out as leaders. Taking the next step, becoming MEs, requires us to understand where our actions and inactions are causing our companies to fall short of their full potential, and which strategies are critical to moving forward in that direction. To test you right away, I have included two very different audit-ready examples for you to analyze. Take a look and decide what the next step for each company should be.

COMPANY A:

Daily plans and meetings	B	100 percent
Weekly plans and meetings	A	100 percent
Monthly plans and meetings	S	100 percent
Quarterly plans and meetings	E	100 percent
One-year operating plan (budget)	L	100 percent
Three-year strategy	I	0 percent
BHAG	N	100 percent
Baseline		100 percent
Core purpose	E	100 percent
Core values	D	100 percent

What is the issue facing this company?

So what is your conclusion regarding this company?

If you guessed that this organization is at risk of being disrupted, you're right. Every block of the business model is functioning at a high level except for longer-term strategy. The team is meeting the budget targets every year, which indicates that it excels at execution. But the risk is competitive. Because the company is only looking out as far as the next year, it faces the possibility of missing a disruptive event of some kind, which would leave it strategically unprotected and unable to react.

LET'S LOOK AT COMPANY B.

Daily plans and meetings	B	100 percent
Weekly plans and meetings	A	50 percent
Monthly plans and meetings	S	0 percent
Quarterly plans and meetings	E	0 percent
One-year operating plan (budget)	L	0 percent
Three-year strategy	I	0 percent
BHAG	N	0 percent
Baseline		0 percent
Core purpose	E	0 percent
Core values	D	0 percent

So how does this company look to you, being that it only passes the audit-ready test at the daily level? What would you do next?

This company is in the manufacturing business and leads its industry in what it produces. Customers are willing to wait for these products, and wait they do because the company is always running behind, operating reactively year after year, just hoping that the pace will soon slow down and overtime hours will decline. But what I know, and you don't, is that such a day hadn't come, and wouldn't have ever arrived until it confronted the truth (baselined its data), identified the trends, and committed to becoming an audit-ready company reaching to achieve its full potential.

The importance of "and." The more I've asked the Audit-Ready Question, and the more combinations I've seen of audit results, the more it's become obvious to me that truly *maximized* entrepreneurs know how to do it all at once. They've figured out how to fully embrace not the either-or decision but the "ands" of becoming an entrepreneurial leader. To be audit ready, they know that they must *improve themselves and complement themselves* with people smarter and better than themselves. They have to shoulder a more leader-like approach to their business(es), especially if there are two or more, and this stance requires *creativity and discipline.* Knowing how to start and run a business, even to do it over and over again, is not enough. Becoming truly *maximized* is a matter of understanding both *entrepreneurship* and *leadership* and toggling well between the two.

What the colors mean. The ME recognizes that the areas highlighted in blue in the previous charts are where disciplined *thought* is necessary, and these areas make up the visionary component of the CEO task. The areas highlighted in yellow, meanwhile, make up the disciplined *action* component of leading the

> Becoming truly *maximized* is a matter of understanding both *entrepreneurship* and *leadership* and toggling well between the two.

business, and it's where execution takes place. You can't have one without the other:

- Vision without execution is hallucination.

- Execution without vision is meeting budget, and doing only what is necessary to do so.

"What's next?!" That's the key question now and always. To move forward, the ME must have a plan to get to the upper right block of the Leadership/Management illustration, which is labeled "doing the right things right." MEs do this by employing the Audit-Ready Decision Tool to check the data on where they are operating and to decide what to do next. When the ME gets the disciplined thought right (vision), they are doing the right thing(s). When they get the disciplined action (execution) right, they are doing things right. Once again we see it's an "and" proposition. You need to get both things right. When you add qualified leaders to the equation, you're setting up the organization to scale leadership and growth!

If MEs have a slogan, it is this one I've been using throughout the book: "What's next?!" As I've said, the question helps us identify the next step to take, but with its exclamation point, it also signals an urgency to take that step before it's too late. In the context of this chapter, *"What's next?!"* establishes an audit-ready orientation that ensures our organizations move well beyond mere success, to achieving full potential.

> If MEs have a slogan, it is this one I've been using throughout the book: "What's next?!"

TOOL: THE QUAL CARD

		NO	Management (Execution)	YES
L E A D E R S H I P (Vision)	YES	IDENTIFYING AND DOING THE RIGHT THINGS		DOING THE RIGHT THINGS RIGHT
	NO	HOPING THINGS GO RIGHT		DOING THINGS RIGHT

© 2021 Gold Dolphins LLC   The Decision Series™   RANDYH NELSON

In the companies I work with, only 30 percent of these failed companies identified with having an audit-ready Core Purpose and 25 percent had a strategy in place. What if 70 percent of this group had Core Values and strategy not just in place but implemented? Would the 70 percent failure rate be reduced? Yes, I think it's clear that failure rate would come down, simply because these companies would have embraced strategy and adopted a continuous improvement mindset.

In *The E-Myth*, author Michael Gerber concluded that every company was founded by somebody who is a combination of three different personality types: the entrepreneur, the manager, and the technician.[31, 32] In a subsequent book, *The E-Myth Revisited*, Gerber found that the internal makeup of a typical founder or CEO is 10 percent entrepreneur, 20 percent manager, and 70 percent technician. That's a problem, because the technician is a doer, somebody who believes that thinking gets in the way of work. Gerber says that this pie chart of a founder's personality goes a long way toward explaining why so many companies fail. I agree. Once again, my advice is to *know and accept thyself, improve thyself, accept and qualify others,* and *complement thyself*—my favorite definition of self-awareness. Companies—and their leaders—who become audit ready can't help but know where they fall short enough to require improving themselves and complementing themselves.

Before we leave this chapter, let me insert an important caveat: this stuff works best when the leader in question has ample experience with self-examination. A lack of self-awareness is the fatal flaw of many an entrepreneurial leader.

The growth of a company—its likelihood of reaching full potential—is limited by the growth of its leaders (or the lack of it). Successful entrepreneurs who seek to become MEs should be analyzing themselves even as they're analyzing their companies. The aim should be to become so self-aware that you could label yourself as audit ready as your company. Indeed, knowing yourself is as important as baselining your data because you identify necessary improvements and commit to making proactive decisions to address them. Of course, this includes any and all changes—up to and including your own

31   Randy Mayeux, "The E-Myth Revisited by Michael E. Gerber—Here Are My Six Lessons and Takeaways," 15 Minute Business Books, February 17, 2020, http://www.15minutebusinessbooks.com/blog/2020/02/17/the-e-myth-revisited-by-michael-e-gerber-here-are-my-six-lessons-and-takeaways/.

32   Tyler DeVries, "The E-Myth Revisited: Why Most Small Businesses Don't Work and What to Do About It," Tyler Devries Book Summaries, accessed November 3, 2021, https://tylerdevries.com/book-summaries/the-emyth-revisited/.

future. To emphasize the importance of gaining true self-awareness, both internal (understanding yourself from the inside out) and external (from the outside in … how people see us), let's take a look at the research from Dr. Tasha Eurich, named one of the top 30 emerging management thinkers in the world by Thinkers50. She came to one of the biggest conclusions in self-awareness research—95 percent of people believe they are self-aware, but only 10-15 percent of people actually are self-aware! Indeed, a lack of true self-awareness can be the fatal flaw of a leader. Given the gaps you see between baseline and full potential, do you have the skills to get the company there? Or do you need to "complement thyself" with people who bring the talents and disciplines your company needs?

> **95 percent of people believe they are self-aware, but only 10-15 percent of people actually are self-aware! Indeed, a lack of true self-awareness can be the fatal flaw of a leader.**

It's not a question you ask yourself just once. MEs keep that one an open question day in and day out, all the way up to when you reach the point of asking yourself, "What's next?!"

MEQC—What's Next?!

Learn. Think. Decide. Implement.

Initials

1. The ME commits to a baselining approach—
   the Truth and Trends—to all aspects of his
   or her business, ensuring that all company
   metrics/data/KPIs for the past five years are
   measured as a baseline and compared with
   both a current budget target and a strategic
   target three years out. _____

2. The ME commits to becoming a fully productive organization utilizing the Audit-Ready
   Decision Tool independently or alongside
   other operating and leadership systems
   currently in use. _____

3. The ME completes the Audit-Ready Decision
   Tool on a quarterly basis, filling in the audit-
   ready numbers for each of the blocks of
   the Productive Growth Pyramid. Using the
   baseline data gathered, the ME uses the
   Audit-Ready Decision Tool to set specific
   targets and establish action steps needed for
   improvement in all blocks shown in the model. _____

4. The ME completes the Vision and Execution
   Checklist in parallel with the Audit-Ready
   Decision Tool, setting specific targets for
   improvement for the next quarter. _____

5. The ME develops a customized qual card
   for the organization, building the Productive
   and Busy Growth Pyramids into the current
   operating system to verify alignment with leadership on the overall company business model. _____

6. The ME commits to the philosophy of the "ands," and to consistently improving his or her self-awareness through the philosophy of *know thyself, improve thyself, and comple-ment thyself*, as discussed earlier in this book. _____

Signature: _____

Date: _____

CHAPTER 7

Three+ Business Growth Models

Don't measure yourself by what you have accomplished, but by what you should have accomplished with your ability.
—JOHN WOODEN

Risk-taker = the entrepreneur
Controlled risk-taker = the *maximized* entrepreneur

When we play it too safe, risking very little, the returns are minimal—whether that's in life or in business. When we risk everything, the returns can be much worse or far greater, depending on circumstances, skill, and luck. We know this well because we're risk-takers.

But are we really risk-takers? I mean, at this stage of our career, and when compared to our entrepreneurial peer group? I'd say the answers to both questions are yes—and no.

How many of you have taken that investment quiz given by your broker, the one that helps gauge how much risk you're willing to take for the returns that you might realize? If you did, how did you answer? Minimal risk? Maximum risk? Somewhere in between?

To the outside world of nonentrepreneurs, we *are* risk-takers. Every time I ask regular folks to describe an entrepreneur, *risk-taker* always comes up first. But actual entrepreneurs are slower to grab that term, because we don't necessarily think of ourselves that way. How can it be a risk to do things we have supreme confidence in our ability to win at doing? We have so much confidence, in fact, that we've chosen the path of autonomy—the ability to be *in complete control of our own decisions* as we grow our companies.

Aha!

If we are risk-takers in control of the decisions we make every day, does this make us controlled risk-takers?

Well, that depends on the decisions we make.

Neil Blumenthal, the cofounder of Warby Parker, said that he used a different strategy to grow his billion-dollar eyewear brand: *minimizing risk.* And to him, "the key to minimizing risk is threefold: be flexible, take small steps, and make informed decisions."[33]

Let's look at how MEs can become better informed, with an eye toward minimizing or better controlling your risk as you grow.

We'll start with the very key decision we make in our organizations—what sort of strategy to pursue. In the last chapter, I shared that only about 30 percent of entrepreneurial leaders actually *have* a strategy in place. Yet over 90 percent have an annual budget in place. The question is obvious. Why a budget, but no strategy?

The truth is this: *Prior to being asked to make the audit-ready decision, at least 75 percent of the leaders told me that they* did *have a strategy in place in their organization. But in the final analysis, they actually did not.*

---

33   Mariyam Khaja, "Neil Blumenthal: How to Grow a Billion-Dollar Company Without Taking Huge Risks," *Inc.*, July, 22, 2020, https://www.inc.com/mariyam-khaja/warby-parker-neil-blumenthal-risk-decision-making-strategy.html.

In this chapter, we'll delve into where and how these disconnects on strategy occur. We'll discuss risk and business models, looking into the three common model types with which entrepreneurs build their businesses. And then, we'll build in the qual card process to help solidify the learning and, ultimately, implementation of the strategic model I recommend for MEs: the Full Potential Growth Model.

There's a big difference between achieving but underperforming, and *reaching your full potential.* That's why I chose to open this chapter with the John Wooden quote. Each of us has his or her own potential. The same goes for the companies we build. "Full potential" is a bit hard to measure—it's sort of like telling kids to do their best, leaving them to wonder, *What's that?* Well, it's different for everybody, but like grabbing for the brass ring, making the reach is worth it because it increases the likelihood of securing it.

The chart depicts the difference between those who overachieve (getting the very most out of the limited talent they have) and those who underachieve (wasting a portion of their talent through lack of work ethic or a disinterest in working continually to double their personal capacity). Decide for yourself what names to put in the blocks, and while you are at it, put your name in one of them. Need inspiration? Search for Rudy Ruettiger and Notre Dame football on the internet, and read one of the greatest overachieving stories ever.

The reality in the entrepreneurial space (or any space, probably) is that hard work beats talent when talent doesn't work hard.

TOOL: TALENT / WORK ETHIC

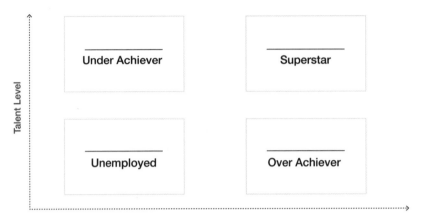

The Decision Series™   RANDYH NELSON.COM

The *maximized* entrepreneur focuses on maximizing talent *and* work ethic at the same time. All you have to do is look at the greatest basketball players ever to play in the NBA, such as Michael Jordan and LeBron James. They always had the talent to be the best, but their fierce desire to win—and to work harder than anybody else—is what made them superstars in the league. In fact, Michael Jordan, arguably the best of the best, never took a day off. He knew that fans came from around the world to watch him, and he never wanted to show them less than his full, winning potential each night. What if we—or our organizations—lived by that same commitment?

*Ask yourself this: Where does your **work ethic** and **desire to improve** align with your **talent** for the sake of the organization(s) you lead and its/their future?*

Now let's turn toward the strategic business model you've chosen for your company or companies. Does what you're doing match up with what you intended to do? As the "Audit-Ready" chapter revealed, there's a big difference between setting an intention and seeing what's really happening in your company.

Bring your audit-ready mindset to the different models in this chapter. Consider this a second audit of your strategy, with a closer look at your chosen model and how well you're operating under it. As you read on, keep in mind the following quote:

The most dangerous phrase is "We've always done it that way."
—REAR ADMIRAL DR. GRACE MURRAY HOPPER

Ideally, our entrepreneurial leadership skills grow and mature as we do. We become better leaders, better listeners, and hopefully learn to ask better questions. Of course, leadership also entails decision-making—and consequences.

The *maximized* entrepreneur understands and embraces all of this. *The ME is fully aware of the choices that need to be made to maximize (or not) their organization(s). MEs don't continue doing things the same way if they don't work; they are constantly moving forward with a continuous improvement mindset—for themselves, their team, and their organization.*

Oops, what's that breathing down the CEO's neck? It's one of those elephant-in-the-room moments we've seen in each of the books in the Decision Series.

"I suppose I'll be the one
to mention the elephant in the room."

The Second Decision elephant was that you might not be the right person in the right seat in your own company. It introduced the roles of leader, role-player, and creator and invited you to both self-identify your right role and commit to becoming a *qualified* entrepreneur.

The Third Decision elephant is one we all work hard not to see—that even though you love the autonomy of running your own business, you might not love the entrepreneurial life you are building. By establishing a set of nonnegotiables with which to find a better blend, you become an *intentional* entrepreneur.

The Fourth Decision elephant? It's not okay to run a very successful entrepreneurial business that just happens to leave a significant amount of potential on the table. Key to seeing the fallacy and dealing with it is to understand the Bore-E-Gaged mindset, an ambivalent middle ground between boredom and engagement. That's what's required to quit fooling yourself that you're committed to reaching full potential for yourself and your organization. *Maximized* organizations understand fully that successful organizations can fall further behind the market leaders if they don't embrace full potential and the *maximized* mindset. That's true even when they are growing—especially when their competitors are growing faster or better than them!

The reality is entrepreneurs have only a few days in their career (at most) when they're truly judged on how well they and their companies have lived up to potential: when a buyer accepts the price you set for your company, and the day of the wire, when your liquidity event occurs and the funds hit your bank account. Did that buyer pay for full potential? Or did they value the company at something less than that? You didn't build your company to fall short of its true potential, did you? *Or did* you?

> *Maximized* organizations understand fully that successful organizations can fall further behind the market leaders if they don't embrace full potential and the *maximized* mindset. That's true even when they are growing—especially when their competitors are growing faster or better than them!

When I first noticed that few businesses operate in audit-ready condition, mostly due to not having a real strategy in place, I was determined to figure out why. How could leaders think they had a strategy in place when, in truth, they did not? The answer? Risk aversion, with an added dollop of inertia. It just feels inherently risky to select a strategy, implement it, and reinforce it. It's much more comfortable to stay inside that comfort zone we all prefer, which has us creating one-year growth-and-profit plans (i.e., budgets) year after year.

Strategy is hard, no doubt. But to *maximize*, we must choose, set, and execute strategy.

The Models

Through my research I started to see distinct patterns emerging. Ultimately, it was clear to me that there are three different models being used throughout organizations:

1. The Decision Series Numbers Growth Model—*lower risk*

2. The Decision Series Entrepreneurial Growth Model—*higher risk*

3. The Decision Series Full Potential Growth Model—*controlled risk*

And now for the big reveal, the answer to my how-could-they-say-they-do-when-they-don't question. It's a fourth model I identified after the other three:

4. The Subjective Strategy Growth Model—*busy risk*

Each of the models is intended to accomplish the same things—to build a three-year strategy for the organization and establish a structure of one-year budget/operating plans. But each model behaves differently in practice, as we'll see.

> Strategy is hard, no doubt. But to *maximize*, we must choose, set, and execute strategy.

Admittedly, reaching full potential is rare—both in reality and as a stated goal. Why? Because theory is often missed in practice. Vision and execution are misaligned.

Many entrepreneurs are doing

the right things right. *But too many are either doing the wrong things right, or the right things wrong.* Committed as they are to growth, and successful as they are quarter after quarter in that metric, too many are leaving tons of potential on the table.

While chewing on the hows and whys of this, I developed this very complicated-looking tool, which I'll simplify as we move through the remainder of this chapter.

TOOL: THE DECISION SERIES "FULL POTENTIAL" GROWTH MODEL

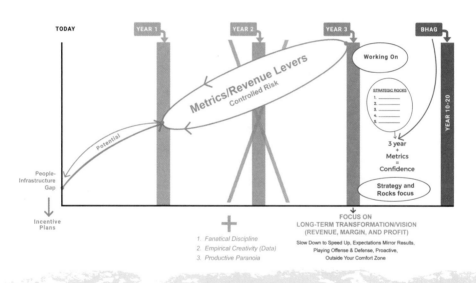

This version of the chart is hung on walls at Farragut, one of the leading workers' compensation and property tax solution providers in the United States. Its CEO, Shail Jain, is determined to see his company reach its full potential, just as his corporate logo clearly states!

Now, let the simplification of that chart begin.

THE DECISION SERIES NUMBERS GROWTH MODEL

The first model that I observed is the classic one-year budget model. Organizations that operate in this manner are successful at growing revenue and Annual Rocks (which could include both revenue and EBITDA) on a year-over-year basis. But they tend to spend less time focused on strategy and differentiating the business from the competition. These organizations are operationally focused, as opposed to strategically focused. From the previous chapter, recall the audit-ready organization that had perfect scores in all blocks except for strategy. This would be the poster child for model one, the Numbers Growth Model. Such companies can be knocking it out of the park with profitable growth, but they are at risk of being disrupted due to their complete lack of focus on future strategy.

This model starts with where we are today and projects out a year at a time. This hyperfocus on the year ahead steers toward its companion, an operating budget/plan for the current fiscal year. So who operates this way? Three common examples include the following:

1. Companies that operate on a go-forward budget cycle (year one, two, three, etc.)

2. Bottom-up budget organizations

3. Public companies that have promised certain targets to the investment community

Let's take a closer look.

The companies that operate on a go-forward budget cycle can be successful organizations that consistently grow year over year. For them, a growth rate target involving either revenue or EBITDA is typical, with the aim of showing year-over-year growth. Here's a common example: an edict comes down from the top establishing a particular percentage growth target (say 7 percent) in the next year. When the budget cycle begins, the target is right there, and management builds the organization to meet the target. When leadership is asked to also forecast year two and year three for the senior executives, the numbers exercise continues until an agreed-upon growth rate is in place, whether that's the same 7 percent year over year or a different rate of growth for years two and three. It's the numbers that dictate the actions. Sure, there may very well be strategy backing the numbers that support the growth projection, but the goals of the company are driven by revenue and profit numbers first and foremost, with strategy coming in third (or worse). If the employees were to listen to their CEO talk about the vision for the future, it would all center on the continued growth of the company; specifics on anything else are likely limited.

Does this work? Certainly it does. Are there risks associated with it? You bet.

Here's the caution. Remember that disruption and innovation are opposite sides of the same coin. The organization can always meet its growth targets by cutting costs, even when revenue is not increasing. But costs can only be cut so much, and that makes it a short-term strategy at best. The longer-term strategy is increasing revenue.

The organization that operates on the Numbers Growth Model can operate efficiently and profitably every year, year after year, and still *be at risk—mainly by being disrupted.*

The second type of organization that operates on a Numbers Growth Model relies on a "bottom-up" budget process. Organizations that have been doing it this way for years are particularly good at the process but run the risk, as do the organizations of the first type, of growing below full potential. Is 7 percent the maximum growth rate, or could it be 17 percent, or even 37 percent? The top decision that needs to be made each year for the bottom-up budgeting model crowd is "What number will we promise?" Should they reach high, running the risk of overpromising but underdelivering? Or will they underpromise and overdeliver? Most companies, of course, greatly prefer to have their results exceed expectations—to provide a good surprise instead of a bad one.

The third type of organization in this group, the public companies, are driven to meet the financial forecast they put out to "the street." It's their primary, if not only, target. Their publicly traded stock price, after all, depends on maintaining investor confidence that they can and will deliver consistently on their promises.

Let's now dig deeper into the particulars of the Numbers Growth Model, particularly with regard to what happens in year one. The decisions made during the budget process, and ultimately the promises that go along with the budget, are driven by today's conditions in employment, infrastructure, people, etc. Or to say it another way, because there's concern of not having the right people, systems, and infrastructure in place to promise full-potential growth, the safe route is taken. The numbers promised are ones within their comfort zone to reach, driven by leadership's strong desire to overdeliver by the end of the year. Typically, we set revenue and profit targets, and, over the year, the model is driven by comparing budget to actual. Because the plan is year to year, there can't be a focus on strategy. Even if the executives ask for a forecast for years two and three, the model will be built by adding a percentage of growth to each year to satisfy the C-suite, or whomever above them or outside the company they're making promises to. In this model, the focus is on

- execution—reacting to whatever is in the way of making budget and fighting through the difficulties to reach revenue and profit targets,

- short-term results that will normally exceed expectations—the underpromise and overdeliver mentality, and

- operating within their comfort zone versus stretching themselves beyond it.

In a sports analogy, the strategy is to play defense rather than offense and to not let anything get in the way of achieving the promised budget. It's the lack of strategy present in this model that makes it defensive. It exemplifies a "working in the business" mindset (instead of "on the business"), with a focus on the tactical actions necessary to achieve the goals and objectives set forth for the upcoming year.

Ultimately, this model is built to an extent on a paranoid mindset. A worried or pessimistic management team is promising a level of growth it is confident it can pull off, thus allowing managers to keep their jobs. This is what makes the Numbers Growth Model a lower-risk model. Growth happens, yes. But it's less than the company's full-potential growth because the projection made each year is within the organization's comfort zone.

Yes, it absolutely works. It lowers risk and guarantees consistent growth—along with unachieved potential.

But that's not to say there's no risk in the Numbers Growth Model. Once this model's budget habit of underpromising and over-delivering is in place, there's always the threat of the "annual potential gap." You see what I'm talking about in my illustration. Pay particular attention to the growing gap year over year, compounding the potential for underperformance.

TOOL: THE DECISION SERIES "NUMBERS" GROWTH MODEL

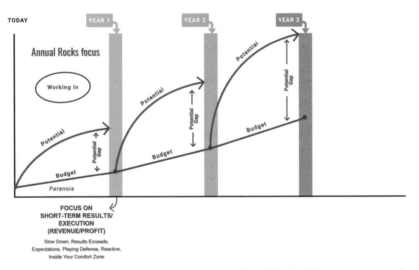

The green line represents the full potential for the organization over the next year, and the red line represents the annual promises that end up in the budget. The obvious problem with this type of budgeting is that when the next year comes, the same process will yield similar results. Year after year the organization will always operate with an expanding potential gap and fail to reach its full potential.

In the end, this is often a very successful model for strong, operationally excellent companies that can promise a certain percentage of growth each year, and who excel at consistently delivering the required Annual Rocks. Organizations can be successful year in and year out, making their revenue and profit targets. Every year is repeated, like Groundhog Day. The desire for longer-term strategy plays second fiddle to the need to meet the budget submitted and, ultimately, any hope of implementing a strategy dwindles.

Looking back at the 2 x 2 financial matrix that I introduced in the previous chapter, we see that the Numbers Growth Model would fit into the upper-left quadrant. Questions and decisions are led by numbers, ensuring that the goals are met. The Numbers Growth Model is naturally more driven by data and metrics than strategy and intuition, which take a back seat to the omnipresent need to hit the targets. The company that operates under this model tends to react to whatever gets in the way of achieving its projected growth percentage just to stay on track. This keeps the company operating at a slower pace than it would under one of the other models.

TOOL: GROWTH MODELS

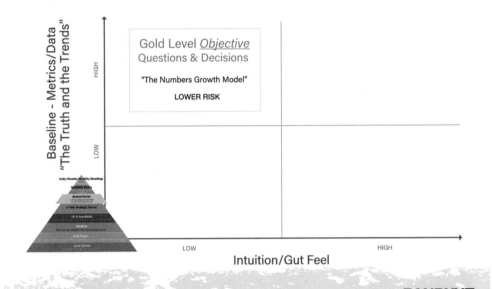

The Decision Series™ RANDYH NELSON

While the Numbers Growth Model virtually promises consistency, predictability, and performance, it exposes the company to an important competitive risk. Operating well, the company may fail to notice changing needs and demands in its industry—and, by failing to maintain a competitive differentiation in its market, the company may fall further behind its peers each target-achieving year. To counter the natural effects of the model within an organization, the following actions can be implemented:

1. Ensure that investments in strategy continue to occur by setting aside an investment account. List it below the profit and loss line or make an "off the income statement" adjustment. This allows the leader to become an "and" leader—focusing on meeting the annual targets, as well as investing in the competitive future of the business.

2. Conduct a thorough audit of the market and the competition to determine whether you are in the position to be disrupted or to become a potential disrupter.

3. Allow a greater infusion of intuition from company leaders, thus nudging the organization closer to making Diamond Level decisions.

In conclusion, the Numbers Growth Model is a "working in the business" model, focused primarily on meeting and exceeding short-term results and expectations.

Is this your organization?

TOOL: THE DECISION SERIES "NUMBERS" GROWTH MODEL

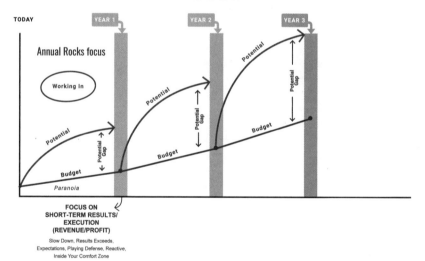

RANDYH
NELSON.COM

THE DECISION SERIES UNDISCIPLINED ENTREPRENEURIAL GROWTH MODEL

Grow. Fast. Now.

In the Entrepreneurial Growth Model, the major motivator of the Numbers Growth Model gets turned on its head. Instead of focusing on underpromising and overdelivering, the fast-paced, growth-minded entrepreneur who prefers this model would rather overpromise and underdeliver. In one way of paraphrasing it, "Let's shoot for the stars and see where we end up!"

Imagine being an employee of this visionary entrepreneur, listening as the boss reveals the marching orders for the upcoming year: "I've done a lot of thinking over the past month," she begins. "We ended last year at $10 million in revenue, and I've been going back and forth on what's the right strategy for us to put in place, so we move the organization forward. Well, I figured it out, and I'm so excited to tell you! In three years, we are going to be a *30-million-dollar company*. Who's in? Who's excited like I am?"

Raucous applause follows. But in case you don't know what your people are thinking when they hear something like this, it's roughly this: "Great idea. Where are the details on how this is supposed to happen?"

So far, this sounds exactly like the scenario I described for the Numbers Growth Model, but there's a key difference. This time, instead of pulling numbers out of the air based on somebody's sense of what could be an appropriate growth percentage for the year ahead, the impetus is coming straight from the entrepreneurial CEO's gut. And what do we find there? Plenty of aggressive optimism, always extremely light on specifics. That J-curve or hockey stick growth is gonna happen *just 'cause we want it to so bad!*

Is this approach risky? Absolutely. It's every bit as risky as the Numbers Growth Model can seem (at least outwardly) safe. It's built on all the hunches and optimism that would be total anathema to Numbers Growth Model folks. And because followers of the Undisciplined Entrepreneurial Growth Model ignore data and metrics that would be beneficial in making better decisions, adherents go gung ho at their company's peril.

TOOL: THE DECISION SERIES "UNDISCIPLINED ENTREPRENEURIAL" GROWTH MODEL

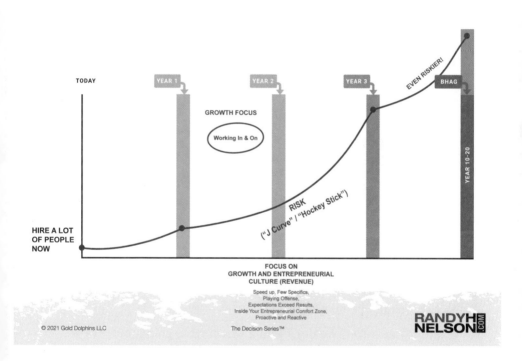

In addition, the operational efficiency we see in the Numbers Growth Model is lacking in this one. The research shows that a high percentage of entrepreneurs operate in the Cubic Zirconia quadrant, and while it may look good to them, from the outside we can see that everything is not as real as it appears to be. Could the entrepreneur make better, more calculated decisions faster and with more confidence if they included more data and metrics? If they paid more attention to the Truth and Trends of their business? Most definitely.

TOOL: GROWTH MODELS

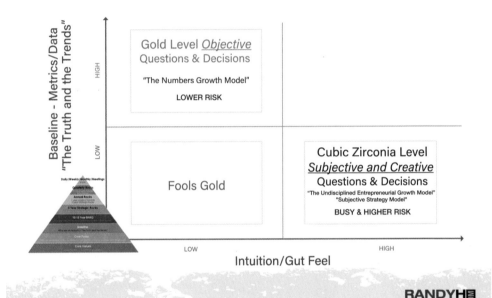

The Decision Series™   RANDYH NELSON

Examples of those operating by the Entrepreneurial Growth Model include the following:

1. Start-ups. "We don't know where we're going, but let's *go!*"

2. Companies that haven't yet put an operational system in place.

3. Companies that are led by entrepreneurial leaders who are full of ideas, driven toward change, and yet lacking in the right operational leaders (and potentially the discipline as

well) to hold the organization accountable for executing its plans.

In this model, not only is full-potential growth desired, but the goal or target is actually something greater than that. Imagine evaluating a company that operates this way. You'd see a group of vibrant people in motion, like constantly busy. The lack of specifics that is characteristic of the *Undisciplined* Entrepreneurial Growth Model (we will simply call it the Entrepreneurial Growth Model from this point on) results in frenzied employees doing everything they can to blow out any goal that may have been set. While Numbers Growth Model companies play defense, the Entrepreneurial Growth Model outfit plays only offense—and a hurry-up offense at that. But those who build a business under the Entrepreneurial Growth Model are just as much operating within a comfort zone as are those who prefer numbers. It's just that it's the *entrepreneur's* comfort zone, where shooting for the stars is par for the course (note that I included the Subjective Strategy Model in the diagram … more on this busy and higher risk model soon!).

One of the good things about the Entrepreneurial Growth Model is that it encourages experimentation. Employees are rewarded for all the things they try in pursuit of success at a level nobody could have predicted. This proactive approach is the most attractive aspect of the model. Unfortunately, there are as many things about it that are reactive as proactive.

TOOL: THE DECISION SERIES "UNDISCIPLINED ENTREPRENEURIAL" GROWTH MODEL

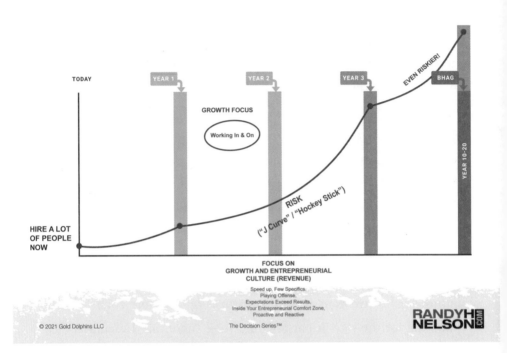

The seduction of this model is that it reminds us of the excitement, the creativity, and the confidence of early entrepreneurship. It's what created our addiction; it's what lures us to new enterprises again and again. And it works! That is, until the company hits its first speed bump. A great entrepreneur and investor described the results best: "Only when the tide goes out do you discover who is swimming naked" (Warren Buffett).

That missing bathing suit? It's called discipline, and it's sorely lacking in Entrepreneurial Growth Model companies. Life on a hockey stick curve of growth is great until reality sets in, in the form of slowed growth. That is when the need for strategic specificity is revealed. It's where this particular model breaks down. Without the discipline of strategy, the company will never reach its full long-term potential.

To emphasize what ought to be obvious here, the strategy of the Numbers Growth Model comes from a growth rate that is predictable and achievable. The strategy of the Entrepreneurial Growth Model comes from a growth rate that is higher, just higher. But both models fall on their lack of strategy and specifics.

Ultimately, both the Numbers and Entrepreneurial Growth Models produce companies that end up among the 70 percent that are so lacking in effective strategy that they can't pass the Jim Whitehurst test—that employees can clearly understand and articulate the organization's quantifiable, specific strategy. But the company working under the Entrepreneurial Growth Model also risks being among the 10 percent that either don't have an operating budget in place, or the one they have isn't effective.

Here are the correctives for those who may be stuck in start-up mode with an Entrepreneurial Growth Model:

1. The first step, of course, is to become fully aware that the company is operating under the Entrepreneurial Growth Model, with its notable lack of specifics. Along with this, the entrepreneurial leader needs to commit to complementing his or her approach with discipline—both in the mindsets of the people he or she hires and the systems that are implemented.

2. Then, rather than just hiring lots of people and setting bigger BHAGs, the entrepreneurial leader must commit to making greater use of data and metrics to make better and more proactive planning decisions. Richard Branson may say he's made most of his decisions on instinct—and wow, he's made

some good ones—but we mere mortals need data backing us up.[34]

3. Finally, the entrepreneurial leader must face the fact that a new attitude toward change is in order. Too much of it isn't fun and exciting. It's harmful to the goal of creating a full-potential organization.

THE DECISION SERIES FULL POTENTIAL GROWTH MODEL

Now comes a third model, one that involves strategy and EBITDA, along with vision and execution and creativity and discipline. (I've left those "ands" in there to emphasize them.) It involves having a three-year strategy in place, and then setting an operational plan to move year by year toward your three-year goal. Most operating systems advise entrepreneurial leaders to operate this way. But the model we've been taught, the one most of us are using, will *not* get us to our full potential. It makes us successful, but *not audit ready*, *not maximized*. Achieving success simply does not equate to reaching full potential. You've got another gear or two—or five—that your business hasn't reached yet.

Achieving success simply does not equate to reaching full potential.

Unlike the Numbers Growth Model, where executives set the goals based on a declared percentage of revenue and profit growth that is unrelated to any specific strategic plan, the Full Potential Growth Model starts with setting the Three-Year Strategic

34 Marla Tabaka, "Iconic Entrepreneurs Use Their Intuition to Succeed. What You Need to Know About Following Your Gut," *Inc.*, September 30, 2019, https://www.inc.com/marla-tabaka/iconic-entrepreneurs-use-their-intuition-to-succeed-what-you-need-to-know-about-following-your-gut.html.

Rocks. It's a model that's built backward rather than forward. Rather than moving one year forward from today (the Numbers Growth Model) or creating a "hockey stick" with no specificity on what the strategy is to accomplish the growth, the Full Potential Growth Model emphasizes starting with Strategic Rocks that are hammered into the organization to a level that passes the Jim Whitehurst test. It also uses Stephen Covey's "begin with the end in mind" mentality to answer a key question:

"What—specifically—will success look like three years from today?"

TOOL: THE DECISION SERIES "FULL POTENTIAL" GROWTH MODEL

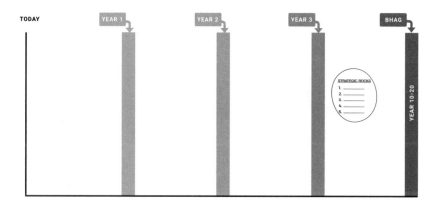

The above chart shows us why this third model works so much more effectively than the first two. The Full Potential Growth Model makes perfect sense, at least in the abstract. But in practice, it's another example of success having little congruity with reaching full potential or becoming *maximized*. After we look at the details of how the model works, we can talk about how to make it work better.

As I've said, the Full Potential Growth Model begins with setting your Strategic Rocks, by pounding some stakes into the ground firmly enough that there isn't anybody in the organization who doesn't know the plan. (Stick a pin in that.)

The next step in this model is to completely forget about year two—it doesn't matter at this point. To review the outline in *The Second Decision* of why a "no year two" methodology works, instead of setting Annual Rocks to move the company year by year toward its Strategic Rocks, this model has us focusing only on the Strategic Rocks in year three and Annual Rocks in year one. That's the foundation for adding a set of Quarterly Rocks that move the company toward its Annual Rocks every ninety days.

TOOL: THE DECISION SERIES "FULL POTENTIAL" GROWTH MODEL

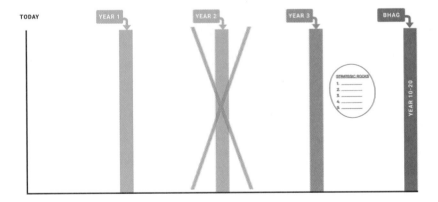

The next step in the model is critical because, if done well, it's what will set the organization up to reach its full potential with high confidence. However, if done poorly, it's also the step that ensures even the best companies among us will succeed only in posting a(*nother*) good year. I'm referring to Revenue Levers, which are so critical that they get their own chapter in this book (see chapter 8). Here's a preview: Revenue Levers are what allow risk-takers and non-risk-takers alike to become *controlled* risk-takers, by doing their Truth and Trends work, as I call it, to set better Strategic Rocks. For now, though, let's move forward, assuming you've set those Strategic Rocks in a way that identifies what progress toward achieving full potential means to your organization.

TOOL: THE DECISION SERIES "FULL POTENTIAL" GROWTH MODEL

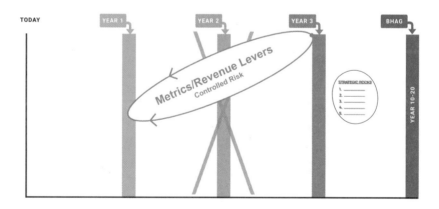

The single most important mistake entrepreneurial leaders make in setting strategy is to set very general Strategic Rocks; they rely on subjective strategy that lacks quantifiable outcomes and specificity. With the Full Potential Growth Model, rather than connecting to the potential gap budget (as does the Numbers Growth Model), the Full Potential Growth Model connects at year one to the full potential of the organization. Then the Annual Rocks move the organization year by year toward its Strategic Rocks.

TOOL: THE DECISION SERIES "FULL POTENTIAL" GROWTH MODEL

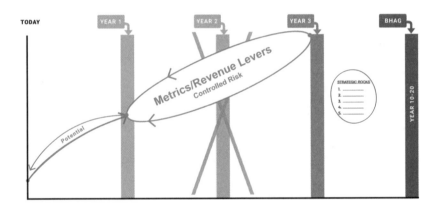

Here's another distinction of this model: rather than creating a potential gap each year like the Numbers Growth Model, the Full Potential Growth Model identifies the people-and-infrastructure gap that exists *today*, to better understand the reasons the organization could fail to reach its one-year Annual Rocks at full potential. While the Numbers Growth Model restricts growth due to a lack of people and infrastructure, and the Entrepreneurial Growth Model adds (mostly) people (frantically) to keep up with growth projections, this model sidesteps these problems. This third model is strategically aimed at achieving what we want: full potential. It has the right Rocks in place, and it identifies up front the people and infrastructure necessary to fully achieve the Rocks. Once the gaps have been identified, and the right people, systems, and infrastructure are in place, the next critical step is to establish the incentive plans needed to align the efforts of the organization with its strategy.

TOOL: THE DECISION SERIES "FULL POTENTIAL" GROWTH MODEL

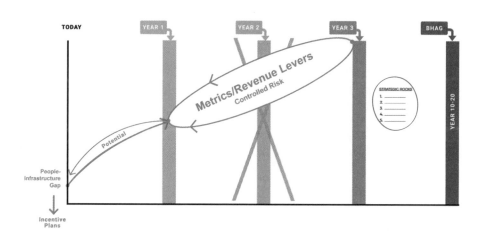

Some of the other differences of the Full Potential Growth Model include the following:

- Proactively working on and working in the business

- Focusing on both the short- and long-term strategy and EBITDA focus

- Controlled risk and metrics focus

- Playing offense and defense

- Expectations that mirror results

- Consistently operating a bit (or more) outside the comfort zone (which is perfectly okay!)

- Slowing down to speed up

- Setting both a BHAG and a three-year strategy

Notice all the "ands" here—that small word is so critical for the ME.

TOOL: THE DECISION SERIES "FULL POTENTIAL" GROWTH MODEL

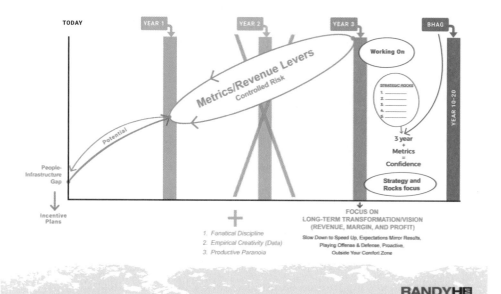

Borrowing from the genius of Jim Collins's *Great by Choice*, I've also added these three attributes to the Full Potential Growth Model:

- Productive paranoia

- Empirical creativity

- Fanatical discipline

The Numbers Growth Model was built on a mindset of paranoia. The Entrepreneurial Growth Model is characterized by overconfidence. The Full Potential Growth Model, meanwhile, features an attitude of "productive paranoia." Here, we're taking risks—but risks that are more controlled because better data and metrics are involved. More to come on this.

The role of the leader in the Full Potential Growth Model is to commit to the "ands": vision and execution, creativity and discipline, strategy and Annual Rocks, etc.—all while employing fanatical discipline to ensure everything works together well. Empirical creativity figures in too. Collins defines it as firing small bullets (testing new products, technologies, services, and processes) to see what works and what doesn't, before firing a cannonball. Your Quarterly Rocks are a great place to try firing some bullets!

Expanding on the concept of empirical creativity, it's to ensure that the leader under a Full Potential Growth Model analyzes the Truth and Trends before making any controlled risk decisions with their strategy. What I'm doing here is connecting data and strategy to better enable us to inject more controlled risk into our leadership. But there's still a role, big or small, for intuition—always. When the leader combines Truth and Trends with what his or her gut's saying—while also getting to the Diamond Level for both questions asked and decisions made—then the organization is set up to at least make the reach for that full-potential strategy. Basically, you're first identifying what full potential looks like, and then putting in place the right systems and processes (and incentive plans) to go after the goal.

TOOL: GROWTH MODELS

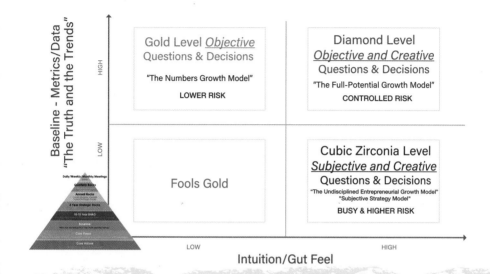

This way of approaching the issue of moving beyond success to reaching full potential makes sense, but why do things sometimes go wrong with the models we choose, even when they seem to make perfect sense on paper?

To drill into that a bit, it's time to look at a *fourth* model, the Subjective Strategy Growth Model, which comes into play when one or more of the following rears its ugly head in the organization:

1. Setting only revenue and profit growth as your strategy versus putting some stakes in the ground for Strategic Rocks that are both quantifiable and specific.

2. Developing Rocks that are activity-based (i.e., explore this, develop that, improve this, etc.) versus outcome-based X to Y growth.

3. The Strategic Rocks set are not goals for the company as a whole but rather lower-level goals, such as for a department or division.

4. The lack of firm and consistent leadership from a CEO/COO (or other leader), which can lead to Rocks not being set up across the organization—or anywhere at all!

TOOL: THE DECISION SERIES "SUBJECTIVE STRATEGY" GROWTH MODEL

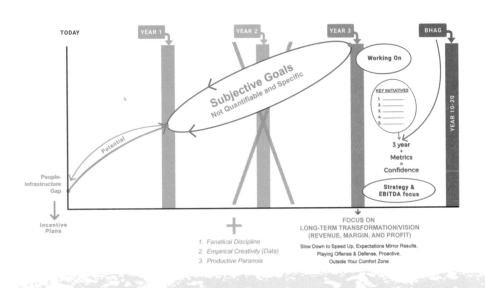

A whopping 70 percent of companies lack an implemented strategy, and here's why:

1. Use of the Numbers Growth Model, in which strategy always takes a back seat to hitting your numbers.

2. Use of the Entrepreneurial Growth Model, where there can be almost too much strategy, yet not enough focus to execute what can be an ever-changing strategy. Example? Saying yes to everything, which results in doing too much with too little process and accountability.

3. Use of the Subjective Strategy Growth Model, where the reason for a lack of strategy is a habit of setting subjective goals. When one critical piece of the model turns red, it throws everything else off, and things start falling like dominos. Another way to think of this is by imagining your favorite band, one you love to listen to. What happens if one member isn't doing their job? When one thing goes wrong, other things turn red—go bad—too.

TOOL: THE DECISION SERIES "SUBJECTIVE STRATEGY" GROWTH MODEL

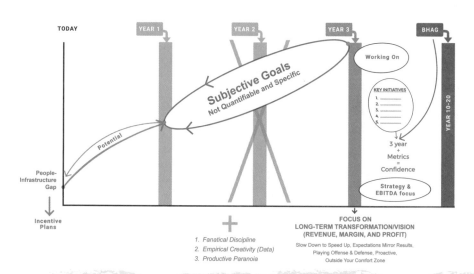

The Decision Series™

RANDYH
NELSON.COM

Here are some additional takeaways from this chapter's discussion of the Three+ Business Growth Models:

- Starting out, an entrepreneur can live with putting any model in place—it's a time when you're appropriately busy driving sales and proving the company's staying power. In audit-ready thinking, this is *compilation,* the lowest level of financial review.

- The *qualified* and *intentional* entrepreneur commits to putting a model in place, and with it, adding the discipline and instituting the processes that will make the company successful over the long term. Think *review*, the middle level of financial review.

- The *maximized* entrepreneur is willing to be audited to determine whether he or she has fully committed to a model that is not just in place but truly guides operations going forward. MEs understand that commitment, implementation, and follow-through are critical to reaching the company's full potential. Being very coachable by nature, true MEs are willing to blend their talent and work ethic to remove any impediments that would prevent their companies from becoming everything they can be. Think *audit* (or audit ready), the top level of financial review.

MEQC — What's Next?!

Learn. Think. Decide. Implement.

Heads up! Read the "Revenue Lever Strategy Tool" chapter (the next one) prior to moving on to the remaining qual card knowledge requirements for this chapter. That's right, I want you to **stop right here** and come back to the remaining questions on this MEQC after reading the next chapter!

Initials

1. Describe in detail the three main business growth models introduced in this chapter, along with the fourth, which helps identify where even installing the right model can fall short.

   _____

2. Identify which model most resembles your company's current approach to strategy. Identify "What's Next?!"

   _____

3. With an audit-ready mindset and methodology, identify the ways in which your current model sets your organization up for falling short of reaching full potential. Identify "What's Next?!"

   _____

4. Commit to the Full Potential Growth Model and work the action steps necessary to transition to this model. Develop the ongoing execution plan that is consistent with the Audit-Ready Decision Tool (and your quarterly rhythm) to update progress.

   _____

   Signature: _____

   Date: _____

CHAPTER 8

The Revenue Lever Strategy Tool

*Risk is like fire: If controlled it will help you. If
uncontrolled, it will rise up and destroy you.*
—THEODORE ROOSEVELT

By this point in your reading, you've learned that setting business strategy is hard and that, no surprise, not many companies do it well. In this chapter, we'll take the next step toward self-improvement and organizational improvement by looking at what Revenue Levers are, how to identify your company's levers, and why they're so useful for controlling your risk-taking as you seek that Holy Grail—reaching full potential. Via the Revenue Lever Strategy Tool, which helps you and your qualified leaders make better strategic decisions, I'm sure of your success. How sure? This sure:

I guarantee you will make better-calculated decisions faster and with more confidence by implementing the Revenue Lever Strategy Tool. This is one of the brand promises of the Decision Series for Entrepreneurs.

A brand promise is a value or experience that a company's customers can expect to receive every single time they interact with that company. The more a company can deliver on that promise, the stronger the brand value in the minds of customers and employees. And there's simply nothing more critical than creating value.

My brand promise is structured to be a leading indicator for you in your entrepreneurial leadership journey. (Recall that a lagging indicator tells you how you have performed in the past; a leading indicator predicts how you will perform in the future.) My aim is to prepare you to make better decisions on a daily basis, which will lead to improved performance—for you as an entrepreneur, for your organization, and even for the quality of your personal life. But simply wanting to do better won't get you there, and making decisions faster won't get you there either. What *will* get you there? Deciding what to do and what not to do, calculating the pros and cons faster and with more confidence—that's what will get you there, with greater speed and accuracy than in the past. In short, **making better-calculated decisions faster and with more confidence.**

To set better strategy going forward, each of us has to get serious about making some resolutions:

- It's time to be decisive, a trait shared by great leaders. The core of good leadership, after all, is good decision-making.

- It's time to make decisions with speed and conviction. This is one of the four traits shared by successful CEOs as reported in *Harvard Business Review*'s 2017 article "What Sets Successful CEOs Apart?"[35]

- It's time to exercise the power of your intuition. This is one of the four rare qualities of highly successful executives as detailed by Marcel Schwantes in "4 Rare Qualities of Highly

---

35 Elena Lytkina Botelho, Kim Rosenkoetter Powell, Stephen Kincaid, and Dina Wang, "What Sets Successful CEOs Apart: The Four Essential Behaviors That Help Them Win the Top Job and Thrive Once They Get It," May–June 2017, https://hbr. org/2017/05/what-sets-successful-ceos-apart.

Successful Executives, According to the Execs Themselves" in *Inc.*'s June 2018 issue.[36]

- It's time to take calculated risks. This is one of the five leadership team traits that all top CEOs share, according to Mark Moses, CEO of Coaching International.

Now, you may wonder why the guy who's always advocated slowing down to speed up is now telling you the opposite—to just plain speed up! Isn't that what I mean when I talk about making decisions faster and with more conviction? Or when I talk about making better-calculated decisions with confidence, doesn't that imply I'm fine with you taking the study and deliberation out of it?

Not exactly.

Decision-making success starts with preparation, just as it does in sports. If you're the head coach of an NFL football team, you wouldn't just field your team and tell them to execute. You and your assistant coaches would sit down and watch the opposing team's film. That way you can study how they've performed in the past (find their baseline), because you know that's the best way to predict how they'll play against you. Then you'd make a game plan that includes some contingencies, just in case the other team surprises you. Nothing about this is mysterious. You do these things to be ready. You want to be able to *make better-calculated decisions faster and with more confidence* during the game. Without preparation, it's just not possible.

That's all I'm asking you to do—to prepare so you can execute under pressure. And it *does* require you to slow down to speed up. How can you find your baseline if you don't slow down enough to

---

36   Peter Cancro, "4 Rare Qualities of Highly Successful Executives, according to the Execs Themselves," *Inc.*, June 21, 2018, https://www.inc.com/marcel-schwantes/4-signs-that-prove-youre-an-effective-leader-according-to-4-wildly-successful-ceos.html.

take a good look at it? How can you speed up if you haven't taken the time to gather your data, tap into your intuition, and be ready to make the right decisions in a timely fashion?

What I'm really advocating is that you—and this time, also your leaders—become Qual-E-Gaged (see chapter 5). To use your data to enhance your intuition's ability to guide you to better decisions. But in this chapter, I'm also asking you to use your data to become more certain of who you are today—instead of who you *think* you are—by analyzing with the Truth and Trends Tool. I've mentioned Truth and Trends before in this book, but now's the time for us to look at how to go about determining what's reality right now and where things are headed.

I hope you're starting to see that I'm not trying to erase the intuition aspect of making decisions—far from it. Rather, I'm trying to boost its importance by giving it a firmer foundation on data. That's how you build confidence in your decisions—by building your gut feelings on the solid ground of sound reasoning. Now, for the brand promise that I mentioned earlier to work, you need to hold up your end of it. So for this chapter, your job is to create an improved strategy by the study of your revenue levers.

Uncertainty Is the Enemy of Good Decision-Making

I think we can all agree that there's really only one thing that holds us back when we seek to make decisions with speed and confidence: uncertainty. And I'm confident that the Revenue Lever Strategy Tool will set you up for much more certainty, leading to more controlled risk in your strategic decision-making.

Of course, we will never have perfect information—or all of the information we could use. But if you make the effort to gather the data to prevalidate your hunches, you'll have much better luck finding "the 70 percent solution" that makes a bottom-line difference. The Revenue Lever Strategy Tool gets you to that point of "Yeah, this seems to be our best bet."

TOOL: GROWTH MODELS

In looking at the 2 x 2 matrix again, what if we could shift to the upper right? Wouldn't having metrics and data on our side help risk-adverse decision-makers ask better Gold and Diamond Level questions as they attempt to build out a strategy and, ultimately, make "controlled risk" strategic decisions at the Diamond Level?

When we set *crappy* strategy, it's because we don't want to make mistakes, or we are not willing to take the risk. But mistakes are inevitable if you want to *maximize* your potential, and great entrepreneurial leaders and CEOs take risks and make mistakes. Mark Zuckerberg, the often-controversial founder and CEO of Facebook, states, "I just take more chances, and that means I get more wrong. So, in retrospect, yeah, we have certainly made a bunch of mistakes in strategy, in execution. If you're not making mistakes, you're probably not living up to your potential, right? That's how you grow."[37]

Jeff Bezos, Amazon's founder and current chairman, says that a common pitfall for larger organizations is "thinking about decision-making as one-size-fits-all."[38] He divides decisions into two categories, which must be communicated to the team:

- Type 1 decisions are irreversible—they have to be made slowly and thoughtfully after consulting data and key players, since there's no going back once the decision is made.

- Type 2 decisions are reversible—they can be made quickly, with only a partial understanding of the consequences, since the decision can later be revoked or changed if necessary.

When it comes to irreversible decisions, your Strategic Rocks, there are ways to ensure that you're making better-calculated choices— by slowing down to speed up and using your data, thereby improving your success rate. Of course, you might argue that everything is reversible, but if so, at what cost to the company or to its reputation?

---

37   Mark Moses, "Great CEOs Make Mistakes—You Should Too," CEO Coaching International, accessed November 3, 2021, https://ceocoachinginternational.com/framework-better-decisions.

38   Ibid.

For those of you who have succeeded throughout your career by relying on your gut alone to make business-building decisions—congratulations! But please recognize that you're the exception, not the norm. Give the gut a rest. Take the ME challenge and begin adding five-year data to your future decision-making. I guarantee it will make a difference.

So where do you fall? Are you a risk-taker, or are you more careful? Are you okay with making mistakes, or do you try to avoid them at all costs? When it comes to taking risks, again, most entrepreneurs are more comfortable moving the ball forward at a careful pace than putting themselves out on some strategic ledge. That would put you in what I call the "controlled risk" group. In fact, when I ask my audiences about "controlled risk-taking," the majority of the audience, and sometimes as much as two-thirds, raises hands.

Once again, it's all about the word "and." In this case, the preference I'm homing in on is strategy *and* controlled risk.

Now, using the below 2 x 2 matrix, let's look at what my definition of controlled risk includes.

TOOL: GROWTH MODELS

The Decision Series™

RANDYH
NELSON

Note the reference to Objective and Creative ("Creative Objectivity") in the upper-right corner, the Diamond Level. "Objectivity," by necessity, includes data, but "subjectivity"—as shown in the lower-right quadrant, the Cubic Zirconia Level—does not. While data may be used to some extent by practitioners in the Cubic Zirconia Level, the true focus of its entrepreneurial leaders is on their own gut and intuition.

What allows these leaders to shift from subjectivity to objectivity and from Cubic Zirconia to Diamond Level decision-making? It's just a matter of applying the Revenue Lever Strategy Tool to combine intuition with metrics. This is all it takes to transform non-risk-takers into leaders who are much more capable of taking controlled risk and making calculated decisions with more confidence.

There's an additional benefit to those MEs who use the Revenue Lever Strategy Tool to adjust their approach to risk: it spreads out the responsibility from a sole leader to an entire team. It effectively scales decision-making, which in turn scales the company. Let's reduce this to an equation of sorts:

Revenue Lever Strategy Tool (plus intuition and metrics) = controlled risk—and scaled decision-making.

Disclaimer: I'm not down on risk! We must and we will take risks, and sometimes 100 percent on gut instincts alone. And I am all for making mistakes. Every successful entrepreneur must make some, or you are simply not trying hard enough! But we're not all Richard Branson, who as I mentioned earlier maintains he makes most of his decisions on guts alone.[39] What I'm offering is a tool for the rest of us. Sure, you can set great strategy without using the Revenue Lever Strategy Tool, but as you will see, this is a scalable and repeatable process that all leaders, regardless of their risk tolerance, can embrace and put to use.

Jeff McDonald and Neil Herding, leaders in the two major consulting practices of Farragut, my client in the workers' compensation and property tax solution space, are two very satisfied users. By deploying the Revenue Lever Strategy Tool, Farragut made the transition from lower risk to controlled risk and cemented its longstanding commitment to achieving full potential.

Director Neil Herding says he found it "powerful" to examine five years of data and use it "to identify Truth and Trends that enable me to look three years out from today and ask, 'Where should we be to reach our full potential?'" Using the data as a foundation, he then "used my intuition to be comfortable in taking controlled risks

39   Marla Tabaka, "Iconic Entrepreneurs Use Their Intuition to Succeed. What You Need to Know About Following Your Gut," *Inc.*, September 30, 2019, https://www.inc.com/marla-tabaka/iconic-entrepreneurs-use-their-intuition-to-succeed-what-you-need-to-know-about-following-your-gut.html.

for growing the business. I was able to create a three-year strategy for growth in my division. This three-year strategy allowed me to focus on what I needed to do in the current quarter to get me closer to my one-year goals, which then gets me closer to my three-year goals."

While Neil highlights the "power" of the Revenue Lever Strategy Tool, Farragut vice president Jeff McDonald chooses the word "magic." "The magic for us was, first, the lever examples Randy provided were themselves the right growth strategies to consider—comprehensive, tangible, and actionable." There was also magic, he says, in the analysis of past data to project future performance and set goals three years out, as Neil described above. "Ultimately," McDonald concludes, "our new and more actionable growth strategy incorporated our past, present, and future perspectives."

So there you have it: controlled risk-takers making better decisions faster. Neil and Jeff point out that these are truly calculated decisions made by harnessing both intuition and data. The Revenue Lever Strategy Tool is helpful both for those who consider themselves pure risk-takers and for those who consider themselves risk averse.

But the tool won't get you there without your full participation. And for it to work well, you'll need to bring with you all that's been discussed in the previous chapters. So for a quick backgrounder, recall these points before moving on:

- You need to embrace baselining and understand how it fits

> There was also magic, he says, in the analysis of past data to project future performance and set goals three years out, as Neil described above. "Ultimately," McDonald concludes, "our new and more actionable growth strategy incorporated our past, present and future perspectives."

into the Productive Growth Pyramid. Go back to chapter 6 if you need a refresher, because this chapter is built on that concept.

- A lack of strategy is woefully common among companies, even in very high-performing companies (as discussed in the previous chapter and depicted in the Full Potential Growth Model figure).

- Entrepreneurial organizations are at high risk for running "busy organizations."

- Entrepreneurial organizations, even when operating success-fully, tend to have "okay" strategies, subjective strategies, or no strategies in place.

- There are Gold Level and Diamond Level questions and decisions, and less desirable counterparts: Fool's Gold and Cubic Zirconia Level questions and decisions.

- There are Three+ Business Models: Numbers, Entrepreneurial, Full Potential, and Subjective Strategy Growth; these have respective counterparts—lower, higher, controlled, and busy risk.

TOOL: THE DECISION SERIES "FULL POTENTIAL" GROWTH MODEL

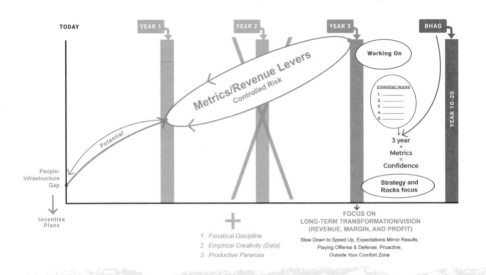

Your Truth and Trends

In the previous chapter, I provided a brief description of the concept of Truth and Trends. Now let's look at the actual nuts and bolts of identifying your Truth and Trends. Take a few minutes to absorb the Truths and Trends Five Years' Historical Data chart, because it sets the stage for a Revenue Lever strategic exercise that's coming up.

TOOL: "THE TRUTH AND THE TRENDS™"

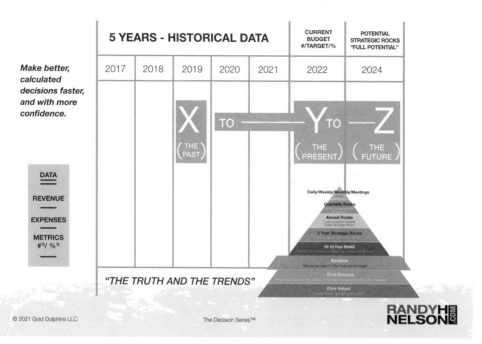

A familiar element of the chart is the Productive Growth Pyramid in the lower-right corner, but with the baseline block extended out on both sides. The *maximized* organization commits to baselining its data as a consistent operational practice. This puts the reams of key data that you have by now in place to be readily used in helping company leaders *make better-calculated decisions faster and with more confidence.*

The Truth and Trends analysis starts with inputting your data/metrics into an Excel spreadsheet covering the previous five years—this is your Truth. Once the data is in the spreadsheet, then the entrepreneurial leader is in a great position to analyze the Trends. You start the process by choosing the metrics that are most important to you, but in general I would say "the more the merrier" when it comes to the data you'll use to baseline your Truth and Trends. Here are some common examples of useful data:

- Revenue and expenses

- Productivity measures (revenue/employee, revenue/salesperson)

- Customer metrics/data

- Production metrics/data

- Sales metrics/data

- Geographical metrics/data

- Product metrics/data

The Truth and Trends analysis answers two questions: **Who are we today? And why?**

Obviously, these are questions that require us to "slow down to speed up." By slowing down long enough to baseline the business on all its important metrics, the ME can analyze the Truth and Trends first (X), then attach a target to the current fiscal year's budget for growth in that metric (Y). This is all you need to undertake the Revenue Lever exercise that's coming up.

But first, consider: If you had this Truth and Trends data available to your organization right now, would you use it? Why wouldn't you, right? These data points are your truth. They show your trends, your baseline. They clearly reveal who your company is today, and anything outside of this data set is just speculation or hope. What's more, the data gives you the opportunity to learn from your past to help predict and determine the future. Baselining via Truth and Trends is so important that it's one of the first three steps I take with any new client. We start with reviewing the company's Core Values and Core Purpose, then move toward creating the baseline. You can see how these three tasks are represented in the bottom three blocks of the Productive Growth Pyramid.

Then we "begin with the end in mind." We use the Revenue Lever Strategy Tool to take full advantage of the results of the Truth and Trends analysis. This is how our Decision Center clients and I drive toward establishing Three-Year Strategic Rocks—and X to Z growth.

Column Y is the current year's target for whatever metric you have analyzed, and three years out is where we'll see the X to Z growth, some of which will end up as your Strategic Rocks. You will see the phrase "full potential" listed on the chart, and that is the end result of using the Revenue Lever Strategy Tool. When you complete the exercise, you'll be able to see what full potential growth looks like for *every potential lever in your organization.* That's what any ME should get most excited about—achieving full potential.

THE TRUTH AND TRENDS	CURRENT YEAR BUDGET	REVENUE LEVER EXERCISE	STRATEGIC ROCKS
"Who are we today and why?"	*"What does X to Y growth look like this year?"*	*"Where should we be in three years—full potential growth?"*	*"Where will we be in three years, our stakes in the ground?"*
X ➡	Y	➡	Z
Baseline *all* levers	Growth in the current fiscal year	Evaluate full potential growth of each lever	Choose the top levers to become Strategic Rocks showing X to Z growth in three years

Make better-calculated decisions faster and with more confidence with your data-driven intuition!

To keep us moving, let's turn to a *Harvard Business Review* article titled "Three Rules for Making a Company Truly Great," which concluded as follows:[40]

1. Better before cheaper—in other words, compete on differentiators other than price.

2. Revenue before costs—that is, prioritize increasing revenue over decreasing costs.

3. There are no other rules.

Your Truth and Trends results will help with both number one and number two above, your revenue and expenses, and the Revenue Lever exercise will clearly focus on achieving number two.

Let's start with expenses. In the "Numbers—Good or Bad?" chart, "Percentages—Apples to Apples Better?" chart, and "Data Sorted— Truth and Trends" chart, you see the same company's expenses through three different lenses—the numbers (income statement), percentages (of revenue per expense item), and data sorted (highest expense to lowest) to reveal Truth and Trends.

If you were analyzing this company, what Gold Level questions could you ask in each of the different views to ultimately help this company make Diamond Level decisions? Do you find that you can ask better, more confident questions with the "Data Sorted—Truth and Trends " view?

---

40   Michael E. Raynor and Mumtaz Ahmed, "Three Rules for Making a Company Truly Great," April 2013, https://hbr.org/2013/04/three-rules-for-making-a-company-truly-great.

NUMBERS—GOOD OR BAD?							
	2017	2018	2019	2020	2021	2022	2024
REVENUE	1,000,000	2,500,000	3,250,000	4,750,000	6,000,000	8,000,000	12,000,000
EXPENSES							
Rent	100,000	225,000	260,000	310,000	450,000	500,000	575,000
IT	45,000	90,000	150,000	190,000	210,000	240,000	300,000
Payroll	400,000	1,150,000	1,500,000	2,400,000	3,100,000	3,800,000	5,200,000
Legal	7,000	20,000	25,000	50,000	55,000	65,000	80,000
Accounting	7,000	10,000	13,000	16,000	19,000	25,000	27,500
Travel	90,000	280,000	295,000	510,000	770,000	825,000	1,100,000
Office Supplies	50,000	15,000	25,000	30,000	40,000	50,000	60,000
Marketing	180,000	375,000	425,000	626,000	810,000	1,300,000	840,000
TOTAL EXPENSES	879,000	2,165,000	2,693,000	4,132,000	5,454,000	6,805,000	8,182,500
PROFIT	121,000	335,000	557,000	618,000	546,000	1,195,000	3,817,500

PERCENTAGES—APPLES TO APPLES BETTER?							
	2017	2018	2019	2020	2021	2022	2024
REVENUE	1,000,000	2,500,000	3,250,000	4,750,000	6,000,000	8,000,000	12,000,000
EXPENSES							
Rent	10.0%	9.0%	8.0%	6.5%	7.5%	6.3%	4.8%
IT	4.5%	3.6%	4.6%	4.0%	3.5%	3.0%	2.5%
Payroll	40.0%	46.0%	46.2%	50.5%	51.7%	47.5%	43.3%
Legal	0.7%	0.8%	0.8%	1.1%	0.9%	0.8%	0.7%
Accounting	0.7%	0.4%	0.4%	0.3%	0.3%	0.3%	0.2%
Travel	9.0%	11.2%	9.1%	10.7%	12.8%	10.3%	9.2%
Office Supplies	5.0%	0.6%	0.8%	0.6%	0.7%	0.6%	0.5%
Marketing	18.0%	15.0%	13.1%	13.2%	13.5%	16.3%	7.0%
TOTAL EXPENSES	87.9%	86.6%	82.9%	87.0%	90.9%	851%	68.2%
PROFIT	12.1%	13.4%	17.1%	13.0%	9.1%	14.9%	31.8%

DATA SORTED—THE TRUTH AND THE TRENDS™							
	2017	2018	2019	2020	2021	2022	2024
						Target	Target
REVENUE	1,000,000	2,500,000	3,250,000	4,750,000	6,000,000	8,000,000	12,000,000
EXPENSES							
Payroll	40.0%	46.0%	46.2%	50.5%	51.7%	47.5%	43.3%
Marketing	18.0%	15.0%	13.1%	13.2%	13.5%	16.3%	7.0%
Travel	9.0%	11.2%	9.1%	10.7%	12.8%	10.3%	9.2%
Rent	10.0%	9.0%	8.0%	6.5%	7.5%	6.3%	4.8%
IT	4.5%	3.6%	4.6%	4.0%	3.5%	3.0%	2.5%
Legal	0.7%	0.8%	0.8%	1.1%	0.9%	0.8%	0.7%
Office Supplies	5.0%	0.6%	0.8%	0.6%	0.7%	0.6%	0.5%
Accounting	0.7%	0.4%	0.4%	0.3%	0.3%	0.3%	0.2%
TOTAL EXPENSES	87.9%	86.6%	82.9%	87.0%	90.9%	851%	68.2%
PROFIT	12.1%	13.4%	17.1%	13.0%	9.1%	14.9%	31.8%

Before we leave these charts, let me emphasize the importance of having multiple years of data powering your Truth and Trends. What if I just gave you the current year's numbers, a single set of data points, versus a set that includes five years' worth of your history? How would you make better-calculated decisions faster and with more confidence? I'll answer that for you: *you can't* and *you won't*, period.

One of the workshops I remember most was the exercise I did with Beckett, one of my long-term clients, during a leadership team retreat in Dallas. Beckett has been the most trusted resource for collectors for over thirty years. I asked groups of leaders to decide what numbers they would put in the current year (it was 2020) after analyzing their Truth and Trends data. Here's what happened:

- All six teams of leaders came up with similar targets, numbers, and percentages after analyzing expenses charted in each of these three categories.

- All six teams of leaders came up with Gold Level questions for me about the data, even though they knew nothing about the hypothetical company in the exercise.

- When I started the exercise with only one year's worth of data and asked them to commit to numbers for the coming year, only two teams came up with actual numbers, and they varied greatly. The other four teams said they needed more information to make a good decision, and I agreed completely.

Of course, after the exercise, we moved quickly to their own data so that they could make decisions on their own company. Doing a Truth and Trends analysis can help anyone—even leaders who lack strength in the financial realm—make better-calculated decisions as they pertain to their expenses (and other metrics). By looking at both numbers and percentages—the latter allowing the leader to compare different revenue levels over the years, in an apples-to-apples comparison—you're putting yourself in a position to ask better Gold and Diamond Level questions about the data. A number can look great when you're just comparing it to the numbers of previous years. But the percentage approach is what keeps your data "like" and allows you to really compare and analyze the trend.

The Revenue Lever Strategy Tool

After a long drumroll intended to explain why you should be interested in making use of the Revenue Lever Strategy Tool, here's the rim shot: The Revenue Lever Strategy Tool is, by definition, *anything in your business that can be wiggled like a joystick to produce results.* This can mean growing revenues to reach full potential, and we already know we can achieve that growth by utilizing both intuition and metrics. But we need to add one more growth component: *our understanding of the customers that we support and the industries they serve.*

The essence of the Revenue Lever Strategy Tool is identifying all the levers that make up your current business, then deciding which levers to set as part of your Strategic Rocks for moving the company forward (along with M&A and new ideas/Rocks for the future). Using the Revenue Lever Strategy Tool requires us to clearly identify at least five levers and then, using related data and metrics combined with intuition, come up with X to Z growth projections or goals.

To kick off an exercise using the Revenue Lever Strategy Tool, I'll pull from another *Harvard Business Review* article, "The 6 Ways to Grow a Company," by Gino Chirio, which details six strategies that businesses could choose to focus on to promote growth:[41]

1. *New processes*: Sell the same stuff at higher margins. Cut production and delivery costs, automate for efficiencies, cut fat in the supply chain or manufacturing, or use robots.

2. *New experiences*: Sell more of the same stuff to the same people. Increase retention and share by powerfully connecting with customers.

3. *New features*: Sell enhanced stuff to the same people. Add improvements that drive incremental purchases.

4. *New customers*: Sell more of the same stuff to new people. Introduce the product to new markets with needs similar to your core, or to markets where it might address different needs.

---

41   Gino Chirio, "The 6 Ways to Grow a Company," *Harvard Business Review,* June 14, 2018, https://hbr.org/2018/06/the-6-ways-to-grow-a-company.

5. ***New offerings***: Make new stuff to sell—not just enhancements. Find new needs to solve within existing markets or invest in a new category.

6. ***New models***: Sell stuff in a new way. Reimagine how to go to market by creating new revenue streams, channels, and ways of creating value.

Chirio points out that the term "innovation" is often the catch-all term for what we do when we seek to grow. What's more, it's often associated with geniuses turning start-ups, such as Google, Apple, and Amazon, into goldmines. (I might add, into Gold or Diamond mines.) According to a series of surveys conducted by Maddock Douglas, some 80 percent of executives recognize that the success of their company depends on the introduction of new products and services.[42] Yet more than half of those execs also noted that their company did not have enough resources dedicated to innovation.[43]

I've seen this myself: even the companies that have allocated resources to innovation devote insufficient time and focus to bringing the innovation to fruition. And as you've already seen from my own data, just 25 percent of companies have anything resembling a great strategy to begin with. The reason? As we've already concluded, setting strategy is just plain hard to do!

When we seek to "innovate," it's not just a matter of declaring it to git 'er done. The first step on the path to year-over-year growth by innovating is understanding where growth can come from. But just as "innovation" is too broad a term, identifying growth opportunities can also slice things too narrowly.

42   G. Michael Maddock, Luisa C. Uriarte, and Paul B. Brown. *Brand New: Solving the Innovation Paradox* (Hoboken, New Jersey: John Wiley & Sons, 2011).

43   Gino Chirio, "The 6 Ways to Grow a Company," *Harvard Business Review*, June 14, 2018, https://hbr.org/2018/06/the-6-ways-to-grow-a-company.

Here's how Chirio groups each of the six categories into opportunities for growth and begins evaluating budget needs.

A SAMPLE INNOVATION BUDGET ALLOCATION MODEL
Innovation budgets are finite, so distribute scarce resources to reduce risk and focus on best bets.

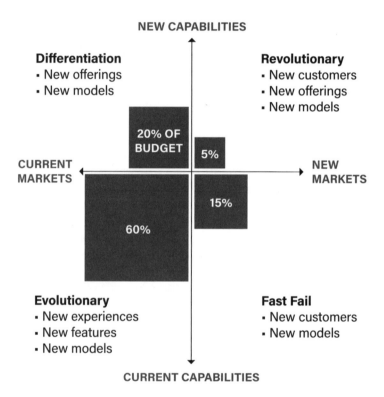

For the purposes of this chapter, we won't spend time on creating new capabilities for new markets, the upper-right quadrant of the chart. We are focusing on the areas that we have the Truth and Trends data available to us currently. But overall, the Strategic Rocks that you set in your organization could also do the following:

- Lead to new Strategic Rocks, through the Truth and Trends Tool, that combine data with intuition.

- Focus on completely new ideas that come through the intuition-laden strategic discussions of the leadership team. For new ideas that have not been tested, consider making them Quarterly Rocks instead of Strategic Rocks until you have enough data to start committing more resources and focus to the idea.

- Aid with M&A Strategic Rocks, which will come through the strategic discussions of the leadership team and, of course, with a heavy dollop of intuition. During due diligence (and to some extent, before it), you can most definitely analyze the Truth and Trends of the company you are considering acquiring, and I would highly encourage that process as a means of validating metrics instead of relying on the sellers' representations.

Revenue Lever Strategy Tool Exercise

Let's start with a hypothetical example—a $10 million, twelve-year-old business that we'll call the Maximized Company, or MaxCo. I'm not going to tell you what products or services the company provides, depriving you of any gut feel or intuition about its prospects. Instead, we'll just start baselining the company in various ways. Remember, each company needs at least five revenue levers for the purposes of this exercise.

THE TRUTH AND TRENDS	CURRENT YEAR BUDGET	REVENUE LEVER EXERCISE	STRATEGIC ROCKS
"Who are we today and why?"	*"What does X to Y growth look like this year?"*	*"Where should we be in three years—full potential growth?"*	*"Where will we be in three years, our stakes in the ground?"*
X ➡	Y	➡	Z
Baseline *all* levers	Growth in the current fiscal year	Evaluate full potential growth of each lever	Choose the top levers to become Strategic Rocks showing X to Z growth in three years

Let's go through this in stepwise fashion:

Revenue Lever Strategy Tool—*The ME's Full Potential Strategy Exercise*

1. Identify every lever that affects how the company brings in revenue.

2. Utilize data/metrics to develop each Revenue Lever.

The goal is to go back five years (three years minimum, or you won't be able to analyze trends) and create a history for each lever. The purpose of this step is for you to see the data, trust the data, and then fully understand the *Truth* and *Trends* of your levers. So for this company, the revenues are below:

	2017	2018	2019	2020	2021
Revenues	$4.5 million	$6.5 million	$8 million	$9 million	$10 million

Now comes the challenging part, number 1—identifying *all of the levers* in your business that ultimately show how you make your revenues. Here are some examples of revenue levers:

    a. Number of customers and revenue/customer

    b. Number of products sold and price/product

    c. Number of services sold and price/service

    d. Markets/industry segments served

    e. Customer retention and turnover

    f. Geographic locations—number of offices/revenue per office

    g. Countries/revenue per country

    h. Salespeople/revenue per salesperson

    i. Method of sales delivery (direct, internet, etc.)

    j. Market share

For each lever in the list, conduct the same exercise as you did for revenue—go back five years (minimum of three) to create the history of each of the levers. Each lever will have a quantity component (number of customers) and a productivity component (revenue/customer) that, when multiplied together, will yield the overall company revenue, as you see below. The purpose of this step is, once again, for you to see the data, trust the data, and fully understand the Truth and Trends of your levers. Let's start with the number of customers our friends at MaxCo have.

	2017	2018	2019	2020	2021
Number of Customers	250	400	500	700	800

The next step is to connect the lever to the company revenue. To do this, you will simply divide the company revenue by the revenue lever you are baselining, in this case the number of customers. This will yield the revenue per customer below. You will start to see some trends as you baseline.

	2017	2018	2019	2020	2021
Revenue/ Customer	$18,000	$16,250	$16,000	$12,875	$12,500

You have now identified a lever for the company that connects to the overall company revenue:

- 250 customers x $18,000 revenue per customer = $4.5 million in revenue in 2017

- 400 customers x $16,250 revenue per customer = $6.5 million in revenue in 2018

For most businesses, it will be necessary to get more granular as the revenue lever process moves forward. But bear in mind, *one of the critical success factors with the Revenue Lever Strategy Tool is to embrace the following: as long as you have consistently/inconsistently kept up with data, then every year will be comparable when it comes to data.* I say this because almost every client wants to "clean up their data" prior to starting the exercise. But your data will work even if the accuracy is just 60 or 70 percent because you will still see Truths and Trends when the data is compiled. Trust me on this, please. If you have great data, fantastic, but comparing crappy data to crappy data is okay! Now, back to the exercise.

Where customers are concerned, not all are created equal. Our hypothetical MaxCo has three different levels of customers: large, medium, and small. When the information was baselined, the following Truths and Trends for the different levels of customers emerged:

	2017	2018	2019	2020	2021
Number of Large Customers	10	12	14	15	20
Number of Medium Customers	50	75	80	80	90
Number of Small Customers	190	313	406	605	690

	2017	2018	2019	2020	2021
Large Customer Revenue	$1 million	$1.4 million	$2 million	$2.4 million	$2.8 million
Medium Customer Revenue	$1.5 million	$2 million	$2.5 million	$2.9 million	$3.2 million
Small Customer Revenue	$2 million	$3.1 million	$3.5 million	$3.7 million	$4 million

	2017	2018	2019	2020	2021
Revenue per Customer, Large	$100,000	$116,667	$142,857	$160,000	$140,000
Revenue per Customer, Medium	$30,000	$26,667	$31,250	$36,250	$35,556
Revenue per Customer, Small	$10,526	$9,904	$8,621	$6,116	$5,797

Remember, I still haven't told you anything about what MaxCo does. I've only given you its baseline data for customers of varying size over the past five years. If you were on the leadership team and in charge of strategy, what Gold Level questions would you ask at this point? How would you set the targets for growth for customers at each level over the next three years, growing them from X (Truth and Trends) to Y (Budget) to Z (Strategic Rocks)? Tough question, isn't it, because you don't have any knowledge pertaining to industry, customer, or company. Because you lack that data, you also lack the intuition/gut feel as to what to do next.

See how data and gut work together?

If we look only at Truth and Trends, the company is growing sales nicely every year, but the number of small customers is outpacing the growth of the medium and large ones. We also notice that revenue per customer is decreasing year over year in the small-customer category, indicating more effort and possibly investment, with less return. This is fairly typical in companies of all kinds. But it's the kind of thing you can only really see and measure if you baseline. That's what prepares you to ask great Gold Level questions, which, in turn, lead to *making better-calculated decisions faster and with more confidence.* Which, as you recall, is one of our main goals as MEs!

Your gut cannot do this, not on its own. Remember what Warren Buffett said about the tide going out? Well, the tide goes out many times during an entrepreneurial career, with recessions, pandemics, industry consolidations, etc. And as we well know, we learn a lot more—and really quickly—when we go through a crisis. Smooth sailing is nowhere near as good a teacher. It's the data, when combined with intuition, that best sees us through the ups and downs of our businesses and the economy in general.

Now that the company has baselined its customers at the size level that makes the most sense, the critical question for the ME becomes this: *Where should we be in three years?* When the Revenue Lever Strategy Tool works most effectively to set strategies for the future, the Truth and Trends of the data combined with the intuition of the ME, along with deep knowledge of the industry, both customers and company will yield "full potential" answers for each lever. When we ask ourselves, "Where should we be?" we are looking at the future in terms of its full potential.

Where should we be in three years with each lever?

New customers?	New features?
New offerings?	New models?
New experiences?	New processes?

Here's a success story that drives the full-potential point once again. When the pandemic hit, Pfizer CEO Albert Bourla set out to make the impossible possible—developing the world's first COVID-19 vaccine with breakneck speed. As we know today, he was wildly successful, and the world is a better place because of his big bet. But when he was asked why he took the bet, he said something that all of us should highlight when thinking about your own full-potential bets:

"If not us, then who?"[44]

If you are indeed the best at what you do, then I would challenge you to keep asking that question during the Revenue Lever exercise. Think of it whenever you're seeking to answer the key question— Where should we be in three years?

Yes indeed, if not you, then who?

Now it's time to connect each Revenue Lever to the future and begin considering it as a strategy going forward. For this exercise to work, we have to focus on each Revenue Lever separately, one at a time. Full focus includes answering some questions: Where should we be in three years? What is our true potential? What does full potential look like *for the company* when we have given 100 percent focus to expanding *each lever* to its full potential? These questions require us to consider each one in light of the X to Y to Z model. This step takes the customers and revenue per customer and forecasts these out three years using the "Where should we be?" question. Do we want to continue to grow *all* levels of customers? Or do we want to grow our larger customers—and their spending—at a faster pace?

When you get to this point in the exercise, where you're deciding "where you should be" with each lever, this is when broad, strategic discussions should occur, taking into account the following:

- Your SWOT analysis—strengths, weaknesses, opportunities, and threats

---

44 "Pfizer CEO Albert Bourla Reflects on Unprecedented Vaccine Development," Fortune On Demand, February 1, 2021, updated March 9, 2021, https://fortune.com/videos/watch/Pfizer-CEO-Albert-Bourla-reflects-on-unprecedented-vaccine-development/e1bcef8e-9fb3-444a-9c16-e1a99f50331b?activePlaylistName=Fortune%20Magazine%20Features.

- The trends in your industry and the economy, and what is driving them

- Any further changes you expect to see in your competitive landscape, and why

- How to establish and build on your clear, defendable differentiators in the market (where your job is to educate your clients, not just sell them), and why

- What your product and service portfolio will look like in the future, how that's different from today's portfolio, and why

- The trends visible in your customer base—whether they're adding or consolidating vendors or looking for partners who can do full service for them. And of course, why this is

- How your sandbox is likely to change—where you'll choose to operate and dominate, how many offices or locations you will maintain, and where, and the reasons behind these choices

- How the structure and makeup of your organization will change in the years ahead, and why

- Whether your future vision includes only organic growth, or whether you're committing to M&A and/or seeking outside investment, and why

- What trends, positive or negative, you're seeing in areas such as finance, customer growth, productivity, employee and customer satisfaction, and so on, and why

Add to your consideration two of my favorite questions asked by Amazon's Jeff Bezos:
- What will stay exactly the same in the next ten years (three years for the Revenue Lever exercise) that we can dominate?

- What will change in the next ten years (three years) that will move us toward innovation versus disruption (and what) decisions need to be made to remain an innovative industry leader?

Back to the chapter's example, our friends at MaxCo. Should they reduce their focus on smaller customers? Here is what the company decided:

	2017	2018	2019	2020	2021	2024
Number of large customers	10	12	14	15	20	40
Number of medium customers	50	75	80	80	90	120
Number of small customers	190	313	406	605	690	400

	2017	2018	2019	2020	2021	2024
Revenue per customer, large	$100,000	$116,667	$142,857	$160,000	$140,000	$200,000
Revenue per customer, medium	$30,000	$26,667	$31,250	$36,250	$35,556	$50,000
Revenue per customer, small	$10,526	$9,904	$8,621	$6,116	$5,797	$10,000

	2017	2018	2019	2020	2021	2024
Large customer revenue	$1 million	$1.4 million	$2 million	$2.4 million	$2.8 million	$8 million
Medium customer revenue	$1.5 million	$2 million	$2.5 million	$2.9 million	$3.2 million	$6 million
Small customer revenue	$2 million	$3.1 million	$3.5 million	$3.7 million	$4 million	$4 million

By 2024, MaxCo will actually have fewer customers (reduced from 800 to 560) with overall revenue per customer slated to increase from $12,500 to $32,143. The company decided to shift away from smaller, less profitable customers that were taking more and more of its time to service, instead focusing on building its large- and medium-customer base. The potential Strategic Rock for customers becomes this:

- Grow large customers from twenty to forty and increase revenue per customer from $140K to $200K.

- Grow medium customers from 90 to 120 and increase revenue per customer from $35K to $50K.

- Decrease small customers from 690 to 400 and increase revenue per customer from $5.7K to $10K.

Next step(s): Baseline the additional levers in the business with the same rules in place. For every lever there will be a quantity that is baselined (i.e., number of products) and a second measurement (revenue per product) that when multiplied together will equal the overall company revenue for the lever. Each lever should be looked at individually as though it would be the only strategic play the company would pursue, answering the question "Where should we be in three years?" for each lever. By focusing on each lever, one at a time, company leadership can fully discuss what the Full Potential Growth Model would look like for each lever.

Be advised: It is *critically important* to remain focused on the "Where should we be?" question and not allow yourself to get caught up in the wrong question, which is "How will we get this done?" I love what one of my long-term clients did to ensure this did not happen. Aaron Marcus, one of the company's leaders with a particularly strong entrepreneurial mindset, was appointed to be the "not how" leader. Anytime he started to see the discussion go from the "where" to the "how" question, he stepped in and got things back on track. I highly recommend that you do the same in your organization.

Once each lever has been baselined and the X (Truth and Trends) to Y (current budget target) to Z (Strategic Rock) strategy is set in place, then MaxCo develops a chart that allows leaders to analyze everything together, side by side. Remember, this model is an organic growth-only model. M&A is separate. And we're not talking about any buildout of new products and services for new customers. By identifying all of the levers in your organization and conducting a three-year projection for each, you should see which levers offer the greatest future opportunities, and also where your growth is not as strong.

As I hope you now see, the revenue levers are the starting point, the pure gold in your organization. They clearly identify how you operate today. When you add your intuition and decide where you should be headed with each lever, well, that's how you mine real diamonds for the future. Below is the example that MaxCo would review at the end of its exercise with the Revenue Lever Strategy Tool. Once the numbers are compared for all levers, the company can start to decide which of the levers demand more focus. From there it's a small step to determine which ones will be chosen as Strategic Rocks, and which ones will not. Of course, the discussions of levers cannot be done completely in serial fashion; you will have overlap and parallel discussions when discussing your various levers. But remember, the key is to focus 100 percent on each lever, one at a time. You are not committing to your rocks yet, just to developing full potential for your levers.

Revenue Lever	Where should we be in three years? Company revenue—growth from $10 million to ?
Customers	18 million
Products	18.1 million
Geographies/offices	22.6 million
Method of sales	14.3 million
Industries	15 million

When you have set your Strategic Rocks with the help of the Revenue Lever Strategy Tool, then and only then can you begin thinking about how you're going to achieve them. Looking back at the Productive Growth Pyramid, ask yourself and your leadership team the following: What people, infrastructure, etc., are you missing? What will you need to change or add to ensure you'll reach your goals? What are the right incentive plans to put into place for your team? Once you have settled on your Strategic Rocks, the next step is to set the One-Year Rocks that move your organization one year closer to its Three-Year Strategic Rocks. Then, set the Quarterly Rocks that show how you will move, quarter by quarter, toward the Annual Rocks.

The Revenue Lever Strategy Tool's process connects back from three years to one year at the full-potential point, with a controlled risk approach instead of the default position of entrepreneurial risk-taking. It also reduces the tendency to simply underpromise and overdeliver as a model for dealing with projections relating to big companies. Will the entrepreneur's gut still be involved? Absolutely!

Before we move on to the next chapter, let's go through a second revenue tool example: MaxCo's products:

	2017	2018	2019	2020	2021	2024
Revenue	4,500,000	6,500,000	7,000,000	9,000,000	10,000,000	18,100,000
Number of products	10	14	16	18	20	30
Revenue/product	450,000	464,286	437,500	500,000	500,000	603,333
Number of large products	3	3	3	3	3	5
Number of medium products	4	6	8	8	10	10
Number of small products	3	5	5	7	7	15
Total revenue— large product	3,000,000	4,300,000	4,400,000	6,100,000	6,500,000	12,500,000
Total revenue— medium product	1,000,000	1,350,000	1,700,000	1,600,000	2,100,000	1,850,000
Total revenue— small product	500,000	850,000	900,000	1,300,000	1,400,000	3,750,000
Revenue/large product	1,000,000	1,433,333	1,466,667	2,033,333	2,166,667	2,500,000
Revenue/medium product	250,000	225,000	212,500	200,000	210,000	185,000
Revenue/small product	166,667	170,000	180,000	185,714	200,000	250,000

What do you see? What jumps out at you, raises questions for you?

Let's look at MaxCo's large product. (I'll let you come up with the right names or categories for your company's products, so the exercise works productively for you.) Revenue here is increasing nicely, so company leaders decided to build two more large products by 2024 and to keep working to increase their revenue per product target. Interestingly, the medium products have stalled, but they continue to be a cash cow for MaxCo, so the company will keep them. Their real time and energy, however, will be devoted to building more of the small products, which are showing consistent growth. The thought is that the smalls may eventually replace the existing mediums—creating a newly constituted small category.

TOOL: THE DECISION SERIES "FULL POTENTIAL" GROWTH MODEL

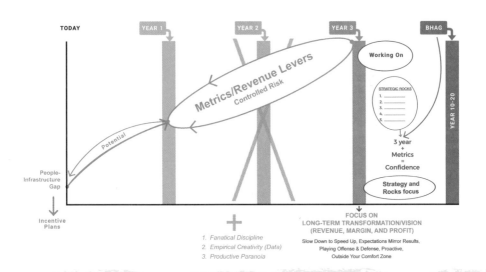

Set MaxCo aside now. Where should *you* be in three years? What are *your* revenue levers?

If I had to summarize the evolution of an entrepreneurial leader, it would be as follows:

Entrepreneurs start off by making decisions with their gut, their intuition. Successful entrepreneurs learn that it is better to combine their intuition and their data to ensure they are not flying blind when they make decisions. *Maximized* entrepreneurs take it a step further—utilizing their gut and their metrics/data to (say it with me now) *make better-calculated decisions faster and with more confidence.*

All it takes to get there is a commitment to regularly and periodically baseline your organization—namely, establishing your Truth and Trends and using other Decision Series tools, including this chapter's Revenue Lever Strategy Tool, to understand how data points the way toward achieving full potential. *But that's not all.* By committing ourselves to a continuing and rigorous examination of where our growth comes from and putting our companies in the best possible position to reach full potential, we also scale company leadership beyond ourselves. We create a cadre of Qual-E-Gaged leaders—each of whom is capable and ready to make better decisions.

So there you have it, the Revenue Lever Strategy Tool—a potent method by which you position yourself to really understand the strategic decisions you're making. If you want to quit fooling yourself that you're being strategic when you're really not, this chapter should have taken the blinders from your eyes.

MEQC—What's Next?!

Learn. Think. Decide. Implement.

Initials

1. Develop a customized qual card for your organization to qualify leaders on the Revenue Lever Strategy Tool to increase the number of leaders capable of setting strategy within the organization.

   _____

2. Identify all of the revenue levers for your organization(s), categorizing them in ways that make sense for careful apples-to-apples analysis and comparison.

   _____

3. Utilizing the Truth and Trends Tool, baseline your data/metrics for all revenue levers.

   _____

4. Conduct the exercise using the Revenue Lever Strategy Tool on each category of customer, and then each customer, asking "Where should we be in three years?"

   _____

5. Discuss in detail how you set your Three-Year Strategic Rocks utilizing the Revenue Lever Strategy Tool.

   _____

Signature: _____

Date: _____

Now you're ready to go back and complete the chapter 7 MEQC I asked you to skip until you finished this one!

CHAPTER 9

Three+ Business and Personal Decision-Making Models

What got you here won't get you there.

—DR. MARSHALL GOLDSMITH, MEMBER
OF THINKERS50 HALL OF FAME

Let's start this chapter with some questions:

What prevents us from just saying no *in our business and in our life?*

What prevents us from truly being present *(when we are present) in our business and in our life?*

I heard a former Navy SEAL, Alden Mills, speak a few years ago, and I have never forgotten one of his phrases:

"It ain't complicated, but it's hard."

You're right, Alden. It ain't complicated. And it's hard. And that's true both in life and in business.

Looking from the inside of the company, as we did in chapter 6, "The Audit-Ready Question and Decision Tool," you'll recall that the Growth and Busy Pyramids yield opposing business models. It's very easy to tell them apart. From the outside, however, it can be hard to distinguish between the two pyramids when all you see is the hustle and bustle of an entrepreneurial culture. Yes, tons of activity going on, but is that outfit just busy or is it productive?

The Productive Growth Pyramid guides what we should be doing, and, with the Audit-Ready Decision Tool, we set our organization in motion to make positive progress on a consistent basis. But *how do we, as entrepreneurs and leaders, stay organized and remain focused on our priorities?*

Here's a reminder of what I said back in chapter 6: when Core Values and Core Purpose are established, a strong corporate identity can't help but follow. This makes it easier for the organization to know which opportunities to say *yes* to and which require a firm *no*. That, of course, makes everything about running a company easier.

The lack of the ability to say *no* can infuse "busyness" into a culture that is otherwise ready to do the right things right, with the right qualified people in place. As long as that ability to say *no* is missing, achieving full potential remains a goal out of reach—for both the ME and his or her business(es).

It's by no means an uncommon problem. When most of us look back at our past, there are a few "badges of honor" that we tend to wear and share:

- Missing or coming close to not funding a payroll.
- Failing but getting off the mat and moving forward.
- Saying *yes* to basically everything!

My hope is that your days of almost missing payroll are over. (If not, consider taking a refresher from the cash chapter in *The Second Decision*.) As for the second bullet, about failing and moving forward—well, failure's okay. Without it, as entrepreneurship addicts, we're probably not venturing far enough beyond our comfort zone.

But this chapter is about that third "badge of honor" on the bulleted list—that tendency to say *yes* to every possibility or opportunity:

The ME fully embraces that to become *maximized*, we entrepreneurs must learn to work differently, not just harder. This begins with learning to say *no* proactively.

Disclaimer: I will never advise anyone to accomplish less, especially when we are talking about maximizing. The real benefit of this chapter will be to give you two different tools—one on the business side and another on the personal side—to help you build your business *and* enjoy your life more. After all, reaching full potential isn't a one-sided deal. It requires a blend (not a balance, remember) of both work and life.

Our first target should be that ever-present to-do list. I often ask entrepreneurs and leaders this question: How many items are on your to-do list? Answers range from fifteen to more than fifty, with many answers on the higher side.

So, reader, how many things would you say you have on your list today?

_____

How many would you say are critically important?

_____

Okay, with these answers in mind, let's see if we can break the to-do list into three categories:

Must: *You're obliged to do these things, maybe required to.* Just as we refer to our highest priorities in business as Rocks, I think we can do the same with the personal and professional things on our to-do lists.

Should: *Ought to, but you are not required to do it.*

Could: *If you say that someone "could" do something, all you really mean is that they have the ability to do it.*

Back in chapter 7, we discussed the three business models, along with a fourth that explained the reason that so many companies end up lacking in strategy, despite their best efforts and intentions. I called it the Subjective Strategy Growth Model—*busy risk*.

Here, instead of business models, we will be exploring the three different *decision-making* models that are typically used by entrepreneurial companies for the purpose of developing strategy. Once again, I'll add a fourth, but this chapter's fourth model will point toward success instead of failure.

By the end of this chapter, you will

- learn to just say *no* in your business and in your life, and

- position yourself to truly be present when you are present—in your business and in your life.

Let's lay the groundwork by looking at three very different models for the entrepreneur's to-do list:

1. The SC Model (should and could)

2. The MSC Model (must, should, and could)

3. The Revised MSC Model (prioritizing must)

TOOL: THE SC MODEL

SHOULD DO	***COULD DO***
• • •	• • •
• • •	• • •
• • •	• • •
• • •	• • •
• • •	• • •

The Decision Series™

The SC Model

This model clearly lacks the must-do's, which would be located in the upper half of the block in the figure. In this model, the entrepreneurial organization lacks Rocks and operates according to the Busy Pyramid model. The entrepreneur mentally categorizes new ideas as either *should do* (ought to) or *could do* (we have the ability to do it). Since entrepreneurs are driven by activity and speed, the rule is often "the more ideas the better," and teams are challenged to come up with new ideas to bring to customers or the market as a whole. Fail early and often—it's the most basic of entrepreneurial mottoes, right?

Under the SC Model, the entrepreneur is in the mode of saying *yes* to almost everything, regardless of the number of ideas he or she may be trying to put into motion. More is better. Faster is better. Without the guide of the must-do's (Rocks), the fast-paced entrepreneurial culture in the SC Model looks productive, but in reality, it's anything but. Everyone will be working long and hard—what is this thing you call a weekend? But with so many ideas to work on, and the glass nine-tenths full of optimism, it's just a matter of time before something hits big and makes it all worth it. Right?

Imagine a start-up, or fast-growing entrepreneurial company, with its highly energized team sitting around a conference table shouting:

"We should do this!" Fire away, in other words, because we're on it!

"We could do this!" Here, there's no "should," but with the ultimate entrepreneurial self-confidence (read *cockiness*) underlying the words, the team truly believes it's capable of doing just about anything. So why wouldn't they do it if they could or can? The assumption becomes, "Why would we *not* do this?"

Without the Rocks, the must-do's, clearly in place and prioritized, the entrepreneur has every reason to say *yes* to everything because anything could work. Ideas lead to activity, activity leads to potential revenue, and revenue leads to growth! So the more ideas, the more growth!

"I had an idea in the shower this morning that I think can work. Can I work on it?" *Yes!*

"I just thought of another idea while I was telling you that idea. Can I work on it?" *Yes!*

The organization becomes addicted to the adrenalin of saying *yes* to more and more ideas that should or could work, creating a reactive culture that continually rewards itself for reacting. It's a syndrome that's hard to recognize from the inside, where people (happily?) accept the shifting priorities and fast-paced change. Nobody wants to be the one to say *no* and interrupt that flow of adrenalin. Nobody wants to reject the shoulds and coulds, slowing all that forward momentum. Especially when, from the outside, people see this organization as incredibly productive, just given its high level of activity. With its boundless positivity, the company looks tremendously vibrant.

None of this is bad—for a start-up. It's where everybody begins their entrepreneurial journey. But if becoming proactive in decision-making and priority-setting is the organization's goal—which it should be—this SC Model will prolong the effort to get there. Those ideas keep flowing, and leadership keeps welcoming them.

TOOL: THE SC MODEL

PROACTIVE

SHOULD DO (YES!!)	COULD DO (YES!!)

REACTIVE

Saying YES to Everything!

The Decision Series™

RANDYH
NELSON

While the SC Model can feel like the very definition of entrepreneurship, it's like the Entrepreneurial Growth Model we considered in chapter 7. If the SC Model resonates with you, unfortunately it's the Busy Growth Pyramid that will end up being the operating model for your organization. Your daily/weekly priorities will shift like the wind as new ideas pop up, leaving you with a busy-but-energized, capable-but-unbalanced organization.

TOOL: THE "BUSY" GROWTH PYRAMID

The MSC Model

As you are a successful entrepreneur, my guess is that you've learned along the way that the SC Model is not sustainable. You've seen how the frenetic pace of the SC mentality can lead to very long working hours, with sometimes average-to-minimal return and, consequently, limited productive growth. I would also assume that you have learned how important it is to set some priorities for yourself along the way, even as you hang on to the entrepreneurial creativity and freedom that you so desire. So most likely you've added some *must-do's*—your Rocks—and these have become your top priorities. In your meetings, the *should-do* and *could-do* ideas still flow, but there is some proactive planning getting done to set and address the top priorities.

Unfortunately, the MSC Model keeps the entrepreneurial leader from definitively answering the following questions, which are absolutely critical when you seek to become an ME.

What prevents us from just saying *no*—in our business and in our life?

What prevents us from truly being present when we are present—in our business and in our life?

TOOL: MSC MODEL

PROACTIVE

MUST DO (YES!!)

ROCKS

SHOULD DO (YES!!)

COULD DO (YES!!)

REACTIVE

Saying YES... a lot!

Quantity is what drives the MSC Model—more of everything—with some prioritization. Saying *no* is not happening much, if at all. With this model, the successful entrepreneur may not understand that saying *yes* to everything is a problem. This model becomes a busy/productive model because, even though priorities are set, the activity level remains high, work hours are long, and there's lots of hiring going on. The entrepreneur feels good about maintaining the entrepreneurial culture's willingness to consider the should-do and could-do ideas that will keep them relevant with customers well into the future. But the brutal reality is that by always saying *yes*, more work is always necessary. That's certainly true at the end of each workday, but also on the weekends and even when one is supposed to be on vacation.

Because the MSC Model doesn't allow for enough time to get working on all the ideas on the table, one of two things happens:

- Either we work on a ton of ideas, giving them far less focus than they deserve, endlessly multitasking to try to get more accomplished, *or*

- We work longer and harder trying to give the ever-growing workload of implemented *yes* ideas the attention they require.

The law of the jungle here in the MSC Model is *the overall to-do list always grows.*

When finally the frazzled and frustrated entrepreneur is forced to take a few days of vacation, you know what happens: It takes a few days to even feel like it's a vacation, because at this point, slowing down is simply an unnatural state of being. Then you start enjoying the downtime. That is, until you start thinking about how much longer your to-do list has grown during your absence.

Ask yourself, "Is this sustainable?" In a word, *no*, and that's the word that you'll want to make your best friend as an ME.

The *Revised* MSC Model

Back in the "Three+ Business Models" chapter, I described in detail the Full Potential Growth Model, and then, with the Subjective Strategy Growth Model, I revealed the strategic breakdown that occurs in many organizations that think they're on the right track. Let's review a bit before I describe my fourth—and this time, my preferred version of a business and professional decision-making model:

First, there's not just one kind of Strategic Rock—there are two:

- **Objective Rocks**: should be stated in quantifiable terms, as outcomes, not processes, and should specify the result of an activity.

- **Subjective Rocks**: lacking quantifiable terms, stated as processes or activities, not outcomes.

Any time the Rocks are subjective instead of objective, no matter which of the three business growth models we're talking about, the risk of strategic failure escalates. Therefore, for any of the decision-making models we're talking about in this chapter to work well, the various to-do lists will need to be driven as much as possible by *quantifiable and specific Rocks with identified outcomes, not* activities undertaken to try to achieve the Rocks.

Here are a few examples to illustrate my point:

Objective and outcome-based:

- Grow large customers from fifteen to twenty-five and grow revenue/customer from $50,000 to $74,000

- Grow net promoter score from 4.25 to 4.5 for greater than 85 percent of customers

Subjective and activity-based:

- Focus on building our customer base

- Improve on our customer services scores

For those of you who have added discipline to your organization via an MSC Model, I am happy for the progress you have made. But there is a better decision-making model to follow for MEs. I would like to give a shout-out to Morten Hansen for assisting me in moving to the *Revised* MSC Model. Morten cowrote *Great by Choice* with Jim Collins, then wrote his own book, *Great at Work*, both of which I highly recommend adding to your reading list. Two of his ideas popped out quickly to me:

- Do less, then obsess.

- Say *no* to things that you can make money at.

Do less, then obsess was another way of saying that we should have fewer priorities and serve them well. For those of us, including myself, who have added operational excellence to our organizations, it rapidly became clear that we had to restrict the number of things we said *yes* to, freeing us to focus/obsess on fewer things.

Learning to separate your to-do list into must, should, and could is a good first step. But learning to restrict the number of yesses in each block is also an important step in reaching full potential for both you and your business(es). By building the audit-ready mindset, and setting the Strategic, Annual, and Quarterly Rocks properly, you set yourself up to productively build your organization. By focusing first on your top Rocks, the must-do's, and then being willing to work fully focused on them before moving on to the should-do and could-do lists, you're setting yourself up for more success.

Regardless of how many you decide is *the right number of Rocks for you (but fewer)*, I am going to suggest that you move forward with the 5 x 4 mentality:

- Develop five Rocks four times a year (Quarterly Rocks).

- In the last quarter of the year, also develop your Strategic and Annual Rocks.

- Start with developing the company Rocks, then everyone in the organization should set their respective 5 x 4 Rocks to align with the company Rocks, starting with top leadership setting their own Rocks. Please note: The CEO must also have his or her own Rocks; they are not the same as the company Rocks!

The First Revision to the MSC Model:
Reducing Your Must-Do List

In addition to doing too much, one of the elephants in the room when it comes to organizational planning is that we treat everything equally. You've got seventy-five to-do's, all needing immediate attention? Wrong.

The greatest inequity is the equal treatment of unequals.

Remember, the must-do's are your Rocks, and the fewer the better—think 5 x 4. Recall that with the Productive Growth Pyramid, goal-setting starts with getting your baseline in place, your Truth and Trends, followed by the organization setting its BHAG, and then its Strategic, Annual, and Quarterly Rocks.

Do less, then obsess.

If you think of the Revised MSC Model as a Value Decision-Making Model, *the must-do list is all about building organizational value,* focusing on the right priorities, the ones that will move the organization to reach its full potential.

The Second Revision to the MSC Model:
Redefining the Should-Do List

In the Revised MSC Model, the should-do list becomes your *maybe* list. It is 100 percent focused on your customers, both external and internal, and its only goal is building customer value. While we can find ourselves wanting to *push* items onto this list by asking ourselves what we should be doing for the customer, we should be focused on the *pull*.

Where are we getting pulled, by our customers or their industry, to create new solutions? What valuable products and services should we be considering offering for the future they foresee?

Obviously, for your redefined should-do list to work as a *pull* rather than a *push*, it's imperative to stay close to your customers. The list should be built and maintained through conversations and surveys, teamed with your intimate understanding of customer wants, needs, and business or industry trends. The higher the growth rate in your environment, the more often the should-do's should be reviewed and updated (and I'll say more about this in chapter 10).

The should-do list is where your ideas go, and as an ME you will never be lacking for those! By having them start in the should (and could) section, and part of the *maybe* list, you don't react immediately to every thought that pops into your head. Rather, you capture them, and then utilize the must/should/could process to help you make better decisions as to what to do with them and when.

The Third Revision to the MSC Model:
Redefining the Could-Do List

Rather than habitually saying *yes* to the could-do's, as we perennially can-do entrepreneurs prefer, this list now needs to become a list of mostly *no*s. In this revision, I'm asking you to stop pushing all of your ideas into the organization and onto your customers. Just *stop*.

Some of your ideas can stay on the could-do list, but most should earn a *no*. Otherwise, you've changed nothing. You're still saying *yes* to everything; the only question is how soon you'll try to get to them.

As I learned from Morten Hansen, the *no*s on your current could-do list are almost certainly ideas that you can make money from now and also in the future. But under this revision of mine, they're still *no*s. Yes, you heard me right—I'm advocating that you not only learn how to say *no*, but to say *no* to things that are surefire generators of revenue. That raises the stakes, doesn't it?

TOOL: REVISED MSC MODEL

PROACTIVE		
MUST DO (YES!!)		
1.		
2.		
3.		
4.		
5.	***ROCKS***	

SHOULD DO (MAYBE??)	*COULD DO (LEARN TO SAY NO!)*
• •	• • •
• •	• • •
• •	• • •
• •	• • •
• •	• • •
PULLED BY CUSTOMER/INDUSTRY	*CAN MAKE $$ AT/PUSH*

REACTIVE

Saying *no* to things that can make us money is contradictory to the "abundance mentality" we entrepreneurs know so well. But it is an absolute qualifier for any ME, and it's critical to your long-term success as one. Here's how I see it: if you're confident in what your must-do's are, and you have the discipline in place to build a produc-

Saying *no* to things that can make us money is contradictory to the "abundance mentality" we entrepreneurs know so well.

tive organization and create a fluid list of should-do's that are focused on your customers, then the next step is learning to say *no*, even to ideas that will make you money. Back when the must-do's were missing in the SC Model, saying *yes* made all the sense in the world. Under the prerevision MSC Model, saying *yes* also made sense. But to move from successful to maximized, the ME must learn to treat priorities differently. Remember:

The greatest inequity is the equal treatment of unequals.

Saying *yes* to all ideas is entrepreneurial. On the other hand, saying *no* to some or many ideas is transformational. It furthers the journey from entrepreneur to ME. It builds what I call *work-life blending value* into our efforts to achieve an entrepreneurial life that's appropriate for each of us.

Let's put these revisions in proper context:

Your evolution from entrepreneur to successful entrepreneur and, ultimately, to *maximized* entrepreneur includes becoming qualified in the following:

- Saying **yes** (Rocks) and building organizational value.

- Saying **maybe** to ideas where you sense a *pull* from the customer—building customer value.

- Saying *no* to money-making ideas that require you to *push* them into your organization or onto a customer. By proactively saying *no* to these, you will be building work-life blending value. (More on this at the end of the chapter.)

Let's look more closely, now, at your range of decision-making under the Revised MSC Model:

1. *Yes.* **Your must-do priorities—your Rocks.** *You are obliged to—something that has to be done.* Your goals, your Rocks, become the things you say *yes* to. These ideas become your top priorities, the areas you choose to spend the majority of your time on. Stay focused on saying *yes* to fewer things, and then obsess about them to get them accomplished. The definition remains the same as it was before our revision— each of these is what *you are obliged to do—something that has to be done.*

2. *Maybe.* **Your should-do's, your *pull* priorities.** *You ought to do but are not required to do.* To become a *maximized* entrepreneur, you need to shift your thinking to ensure that you are paying due attention to both external and internal customer considerations. The older companies get, the more internally focused they become—spending time on people, processes, and infrastructure and overlooking or ignoring the external customer, who is the key to the success of any business, anywhere in the world. So **the new definition of should-do is this**: *You ought to do it because you are feeling the customer's pull to do it, but you are not required to do it until you make it a must-do.* There's a big difference between being pulled by your customers and pushing them to buy something they don't want or need. Steve Jobs was the very

best at telling us what we wanted and needed to buy, but unfortunately most of us aren't Steve Jobs; we haven't built companies that can tell customers what to buy. As part of the Revised MSC Model, we need to truly listen to determine where the market and our customers want to take us. Here's something to keep in mind, though: if you do add more items to your must-do's, then either add more people to support the additional work (assuming your current people are fully utilized with musts) or get more productivity out of your current employees. If that's a step you're unwilling or unable to take, keep saying *no*—lest you end up back in the "saying *yes* to everything" mode.

3. ***No*. Your could-do *push* priorities**. *You could do something because you have the ability to do it, but you don't have to do it if you choose not to.* Now comes the second of our new definitions. We now recognize the could-do's as a customer *push* instead of a *pull*. We've established the discipline necessary to know that just because we have new ideas doesn't mean we will act on them. In fact, under the Revised MSC Model, we learn to say *no* to pursuits we're sure we can make plenty of money at. This makes a *no* more than just a *no*, because it leads us to say *no* for the express purpose of being able to say *yes* to a *must-do* and focus on accomplishing it. **The *new could-do definition* is this**: *If you say that someone could do something, you mean that they have the ability to do it, but that doesn't mean they will do it. In fact, the ME says no proactively to areas that the organization can and does make good money at, for two purposes: to focus better on fewer must-do's, and to provide time to properly compile and evaluate the organization's should-do's.*

Please take a minute to digest these changes.

This Revised MCS Model represents a significant shift in thinking. Our mindset as entrepreneurs is to say *yes* to everything, and that is how we have built our entrepreneurial careers, all the way from wannabe to entrepreneurial success. But to ensure that our entire ME career is productive and enjoyable, we must learn to work differently. We must learn to say *no*. Now would be a good time to go back to the "Entrepreneurial Life Stages" chapter (chapter 3) and review the differences between ages thirty-five to fifty-one and fifty-two to sixty-eight.

It sounds easy, but it isn't. "It ain't complicated, but it's hard."

And this is where the fourth model enters our discussion. Unlike the Subjective Strategy Growth Model, which absolutely *broke* the Full Potential Growth Model in chapter 7, this is a model that will firm up even the best-implemented Revised MSC Model. It's the necessary enhancement that fulfills the promises I made at the beginning of the chapter:

You will learn to just say no—*in your business and in your life!*

You will position yourself to truly being present when you are present—*in your business and in your life!*

The fourth model adds two critical factors: the N and the T.

The Fourth Model — the N-MSC-T Model

So what exactly is the N? Well, remember that *intentional* entrepreneur? No regrets, no alibis?

The N stands for *nonnegotiables*, and they take their place in our model *above* the must-do's. They have to, or everything in your personal life will be negotiable, and you'll always allow work to take priority over the rest of your life. If you've set your nonnegotiables for the next twelve months, as I recommended in *The Third Decision*, and they are truly nonnegotiable, then the rest of the Revised MSC Model will fall more neatly into place.

The T? It stands for the *things-to-do list* that each of us keeps—the yellow sticky notes, the list from Evernote, the list that changes daily as plans are made and adjusted to accommodate fires that need to be put out. In order to move forward effectively as an ME, your things-to-do list today/this week/this month (or whatever) will need to align to your Revised MSC Model list. Sure, you'll always need to respond to urgent and important matters during the day/week/month, but when your time becomes your time again to focus on your priorities, that daily/weekly/monthly things-to-do list should align with and support the MSC list. What happens if it doesn't? You'll be adding "busyness" to the model and, just as the Subjective Strategy Growth Model broke the Full Potential Growth Model, a lack of discipline with your daily/weekly/monthly things-to-do lists will break down the effectiveness of the N-MSC-T Model. There you have it—the reason for the addition and alignment of the T.

Take a look at the evolution of the decision-making models, from the SC/MSC/Revised MSC, in preparation for seeing how the N-MSC-T tool differs.

TOOL: THE SC MODEL

SHOULD DO	**_COULD DO_**
• • •	• • •
• • •	• • •
• • •	• • •
• • •	• • •
• • •	• • •

TOOL: MSC MODEL

PROACTIVE

MUST DO (YES!!)

• • •
• • •
• • •
• • •

ROCKS

SHOULD DO (YES!!)	**_COULD DO (YES!!)_**
• •	• •
• •	• •
• •	• •
• •	• •
• •	• •

REACTIVE

Saying YES... a lot!

TOOL: REVISED MSC MODEL

PROACTIVE
MUST DO (YES!!)

1.
2.
3.
4.
5.

ROCKS

SHOULD DO (MAYBE??)	COULD DO (LEARN TO SAY NO!)
PULLED BY CUSTOMER/INDUSTRY	CAN MAKE $$ AT/PUSH

REACTIVE

© 2021 Gold Dolphins LLC   The Decision Series™   RANDYH NELSON.COM

Now, back to those two questions I asked at the beginning of the chapter:

What prevents us from just saying no—*in our business and in our life?*

What prevents us from truly being present when we are present—in our business and in our life?

Well, I hope this entire chapter, capped by the N-MSC-T Model, has helped set you up to better say *no* in your business. But we still need to address the life portion of the first question and the meaning of being present when present in the second question.

That's where the N-MSC-T alignment tool comes in again, this time to offer us frameworks from both the business and personal life perspectives. The must-do's are the same, because you are still striving to reach your full potential, and the nonnegotiables are the same as well. The should-do's and could-do's, however, are different.

TOOL: N-MSC-T BUSINESS MODEL

**Productive
Work/Life
Blending**

NON - NEGOTIABLES

-
-
-

ALIGNED ↓

MUST DO (ROCKS) (YES!!)

1.
2.
3.
4.
5.

BUILDING ORGANIZATION VALUE

SHOULD DO (PULL) (MAYBE??)	COULD DO (PUSH) (NO!!) ·
·	·
·	·
·	·
·	·

BUILDING CUSTOMER VALUE

↑ ALIGNED

DAILY/WEEKLY/MONTHLY TO DO's

-
-
-

"Busy" Work Focus

Just as you saw the difference made when the SC Model lacked the must-do's, the absence of nonnegotiables in the Revised MSC Model yields a similar effect: without nonnegotiables clearly in place and objectively written, you don't have higher priorities driving your overall model in business. But with nonnegotiables included, the must-do's become commitments that are fully aligned for a better work-life blend, which is a critical objective for the ME.

Please don't doubt the value of nonnegotiables. One of my clients (CG) was woefully late to the party when it came to setting his nonnegotiables. His wife had needled him on several occasions, wondering when he was going to slow down and enjoy life more. Rather than slowing down, he'd chosen to speed up again—without telling his wife! He'd accepted a new business partnership, out of state, and only mumbled his way out the door when asked what the trip was for, hoping she might not catch enough detail to call him on it. Had he set some nonnegotiables for himself, the conflict could have been avoided—and in bugging him to get off the dime and git 'er done, I promised that, even better late than never, he'd never regret the exercise. Well, he hasn't. In fact, he's told me that he's grateful to have saved himself a future regret. How can he be sure he has? He's learned that, as hard as it is for an entrepreneur to learn to say *no*, it gets significantly easier once your nonnegotiables are in place.

Now that we've looked at the business version of the N-MSC-T Model, let's shift to the personal life side, so we can address that be-present-when-you're-present stuff.

TOOL: N-MSC-T PERSONAL LIFE MODEL

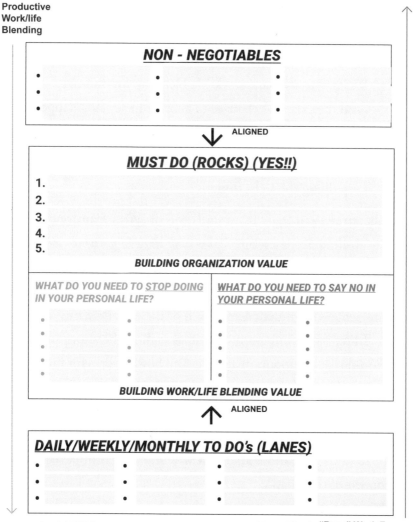

Productive
Work/life
Blending

NON - NEGOTIABLES

-
-
-

ALIGNED

MUST DO (ROCKS) (YES!!)

1.
2.
3.
4.
5.

BUILDING ORGANIZATION VALUE

WHAT DO YOU NEED TO STOP DOING IN YOUR PERSONAL LIFE?	WHAT DO YOU NEED TO SAY NO IN YOUR PERSONAL LIFE?
• •	• •
• •	• •
• •	• •
• •	• •
• •	• •

BUILDING WORK/LIFE BLENDING VALUE

ALIGNED

DAILY/WEEKLY/MONTHLY TO DO's (LANES)

-
-
-

"Busy" Work Focus

In this tool, you will see two different questions in the should-do and could-do blocks. Just as we can-do entrepreneurs tend to automatically say *yes* to new possibilities in business, we also bring that

"Sure, why not?" attitude to our personal lives. And that's how we become overloaded, virtually to the breaking point, both personally and professionally.

Here's what we all know is true (or ought to be):

- We want to say *yes*, but we need to learn to say *no*.

- We may really want work-life blending for ourselves, but we need to make real changes to allow it to actually happen.

- We may want to reach our full potential and blend our work and life, but to make it happen, we need to start, stop, and keep doing the right things.

The struggle is real. It reminds me of lyrics from one of my favorite Rolling Stones songs: *"You can't always get what you want, but if you try sometimes, well, you might find, you get what you need."*

That "trying" part is absolutely key. It takes genuine and sustained effort to achieve alignment across both of these models, business and personal life, with your nonnegotiables calling the shots and your things-to-do list in support of all of it. And how it works for me or you as an ME is likely to differ from other MEs—we're not all the same.

Earlier I mentioned that your company's growth rate is a factor in how you handle your must-do's, should-do's, and could-do's. Now I want to say a little more about growth and how it impacts you in the context of this chapter.

I have always followed a planning rule of thumb that I learned from Verne Harnish, founder of EO and Gazelles/Scaling Up:

- Company is growing 15 percent or less—business plan is good for a year.

- Higher rate of growth 20–100 percent—business plan is good for a quarter.

- Highest rate of growth >100 percent—business plan may only be good for a month.

To this point, I've let you assume that the models I'm talking about apply to each of you in the same way, but it's not true. Remember: *the greatest inequity is the equal treatment of unequals.*

So let me show you how your company's growth rate may affect how you approach these models. Your N-MSC-T Models, both business and personal life, need to be filled out at least annually. But depending on your company's or companies' growth rate, the frequency may need to be quarterly, or even monthly. Just like the Self-Awareness Decision Tool introduced in a previous chapter, the tools that I have created are only as good as the practical uses you put them to. The higher the rate of change, the more you need to evaluate your MSC list. The higher the rate of change, the more frequently you review your nonnegotiables to ensure they haven't changed. The higher the rate of change, the larger your things-to-do list can get. And the longer the list gets, the more you risk backsliding into working busily instead of productively.

Let's summarize:

1. Until an entrepreneur learns to say *no*, he or she will continue to lead a "busy" organization that has the feel of a successful business but the results of an unproductive one, leaving tons of potential on the table. Learn to say *no* to areas where you know you can make money. Learn to say *no* in your personal life too.

2. Until an entrepreneur and his or her organization has in-depth conversations with their customers about their needs, the temptation to *push* ideas on customers and provide unrequested solutions will remain. By understanding customers'

strategies and needs, along with the markets they serve, the ME will begin to feel an appropriate *pull* to address areas where the company can win and dominate by meeting and exceeding the needs of the customer.

3. Until an entrepreneur learns to say *yes* to fewer things, and to reprioritize some of the yeses to maybes and noes, the company will underperform.

So how exactly does all this help you become more likely to "be present when you are present"?

To answer, allow me to circle back to that hypothetical vacation I mentioned earlier in the chapter. After you've qualified yourself on the N-MSC-T tool, this is what your vacation could look like:

*   You are focused on your must-dos and have set a plan in motion to keep them moving while you're on the beach or in the mountains. You've provided an emergency contact number, but you've left town fully expecting your team to do their jobs so you can enjoy some well-deserved time off (just like they will in the future).

*   Your should-do list will be there when you get back. You've set a rhythm for reviewing that list with your team, but it most certainly won't happen while you're on vacation. If you're thinking about adding items to the list during your vacation, just write down the ideas and consider them when you get home.

*   As far as your could-do list, they've either become noes, or they've risen to the level of must-dos.

*   Your daily/weekly/monthly to-do list is in complete alignment with your MSC list, and the fires are being extinguished by

people back at the office, so you don't need to worry about the list growing while you're away. Noes are noes.

• You have transitioned to the practice of doing fewer things better. By worrying less about the clutter that used to be the overall MSC yes list, you can focus on fewer things and put yourself in a position to be truly "present when you are present."

Is it complicated? No. Is it hard to do, this N-MSC-T Model? Yes.

But the transition is necessary. Remember, what got you here (being an entrepreneur) won't get you there (becoming an ME).

MEQC — What's Next?!

Learn. Think. Decide. Implement.

Initials

1. Describe the SC, MSC, and Revised MSC Models in detail. _____

2. Describe the N-MSC-T Model in detail. _____

3. Describe the changes necessary to move the organization from the SC, MSC, and Revised MSC Model to the N-MSC-T Model. _____

4. Implement the meeting routine to decide when changes will be reviewed with the N-MSC-T Model. _____

5. Explain how you will accomplish the following: *You will learn to just say no — in your business and in your life!* _____

6. Explain how you will accomplish the following: *You will position yourself to truly being present when you are present — in your business and in your life!* _____

7. Fill out the N-MSC-T Model for your business life and review it with your coach, peer, etc. _____

8. Fill out the N-MSC-T Model for your personal life and review it with your coach, peer, perhaps your family as well! _____

Signature: _____

Date: _____

CHAPTER 10

Customer Awareness—Crossing the Customer Diamond Bridge

Everything starts with the customer.
—ATTRIBUTED TO LOUIS XIV

It seems even the "Sun King" was keenly aware, back in the 1600s, of the importance of clients. But not everybody is.

I'll never forget asking officials of a leading product supplier, known within the industries the company serves as the "cool-product company," how often they engage with customers seeking feedback. Annually? Quarterly?

After a brief pause, the leaders all looked at each other and agreed that, well, they just didn't.

Wow. Now you know why I'm not naming the company! Here's a leading product supplier, known for its cool products, admitting that customers are never asked for feedback.

Up until now, *The Fourth Decision* has focused on you as the *maximized* entrepreneur—*your* self-awareness, *your* ability to build your organization to its full potential. But the MEQC wouldn't be complete without a section on your customer and your very necessary focus on *customer awareness.*

So let's make the shift to customer awareness, which is a form of leadership. It won't require a lot of contortion, because everything you've learned so far can be applied to the customer. All it takes is a slight shift in mindset, and what I'm calling **The Four Customer C's**, which we'll get to in a minute.

My story above is not atypical. As organizations age, one of the classic mistakes they make is to become too focused on their internal processes and procedures at the expense of the entrepreneurial savvy and customer attention that made them entrepreneurial successes to begin with. With growth, they start to have conversations that are more internal than external. Unfortunately, the story gets worse for this product supplier, which had been operating successfully in an industry that it had served with a high level of intuition/gut feel for more than twenty years. When we sat down and conducted a Truth and Trends analysis of the customer data, it quickly became apparent that

- 70 percent of the company's customers produced 7 percent of its revenue, and

- 70 percent of the company's products produced the very same 7 percent of its revenue.

The leaders found this stunning, but I wasn't surprised. I had seen these "ahas" before in Truth and Trends sessions I've had with many clients over the past decade. I fully expect to keep seeing them well into the future.

Remember, Cubic Zirconia decisions are led almost entirely by your intuition/gut feel and include little in the way of metrics/data. But numbers don't lie, as my friends in the product supplier company have learned!

Now let's set the anecdote aside. Let me trace for you the shift in perspective I'm advocating in this chapter:

Know thyself.
Know thy customer.

Improve thyself.
Improve thy customer.

Complement thyself.
Complement thy customer.

So the shift in mindset is from *self-awareness* to *customer awareness*, which is the lifeblood of any organization. Let's also shift a now-familiar definition just a bit:

Customer awareness = Know thy customer / complement thy customer / add value to and improve thy customer

But the shift in mindset doesn't end there. There's a second shift necessary here, and it's captured in **The Four Customer C's**:

- Connection

- Conversation

- Capability

- Capacity

Let's take a brief look at each:

Connection—In order to work with customers, we have to establish, maintain, and then hopefully expand our connections with them, and these connections can happen at various levels or departments of the two organizations, from the salespeople to the CEO.

Conversation—How many different conversations are you capable of, given the connections you have with your customer/client?

Can you help them meet their immediate needs? Most likely you can. But can you have a productive conversation with them about *their Productive Growth Pyramid* blocks? This is what adds value to them beyond simply your capabilities for providing products and services. It's a different conversation, and most of the time, it requires a higher-level connection. Just as I said about different connections (above), different conversations will happen between people at the sales level all the way up to the CEO, and *listening with the intent to understand* applies up and down the chain.

Capability—This refers to the products and services that you provide to the customer, along with the customer service that you provide before, during, and after the sale. This is what they pay you for—your ability to deliver what they need.

Capacity—This defines the extent to which you can support your customer. You may have the connection and the capability but be limited in your capacity to deliver. If this is the case, two things will likely happen: your organization will fall short of reaching its full potential, and your customers will need to rely on your competitors to help them reach their full potential.

Let's add another component to the mix, using the matrix below. I see four different combinations with customers, and three of them are not so good. A lose/lose sale should never happen. When the customer wins and we lose, typically the concessions we make to close that sale will be a hit to our bottom line in the form of lower margins and profitability. If we are able to close a sale where we win and the customer loses, it may look good in the short term. But long term, there is nothing sustainable. The only value you're adding is to your own organization, not the customer's. We're left with just the win/win block, which is the focus of this chapter.

Using the matrix, I'd like you to come up with live examples in your own organization of these types of customer transactions or relationships:

Lose/Lose: _____

_____

_____

Customer Wins/You Lose: _____

_____

_____

You Win/Your Customer Loses: _____

_____

_____

Win/Win: _____

_____

_____

After finishing your work, take it an extra step. Ask yourself, "What do I need to do to make more of my relationships the win/win type?" Make some notes above on this too.

To continue shifting your focus to the customer, let's zero in on three common terms used to describe the various relationships we have with our customers: *vendor, partner, strategic partner.*

Now, this is not a sales book per se, so if you are looking for a more in-depth analysis of the vendor/partner/strategic partner relationships with customers, you'll have to go elsewhere. But these are my guides to those terms:

Vendor Relationship

Vendor: *a person or company offering something for sale.*

In any organization, we need to establish vendor relationships with our customers in order to grow our business. The initial *connection* to the customer can come from multiple places in your organization, but once started, it tends to stay at the lower levels of your company.

In this relationship, the customer will select vendors (i.e., us) that have the *capability* to support their needs, and typically, customers will work with multiple vendors to get their needs met. The *conversation* in this type of relationship will be based more on the *capabilities and capacity* of the vendor. Because the customer is using multiple vendors, the customer will most likely be looking for lower prices. The higher the *capacity* we have to support our customers, the more business we will close. We hope. Customers don't particularly need to like the organizations they work with, but so long as the organization is capable of supporting their needs, both sides can work together toward a win/win scenario. If price becomes too much of a factor in the vendor relationship, and we decide to work with the customer regardless of the profitability of the relationship, then we risk going into a win/lose situation, especially if our business model is not built to succeed in a low-priced/low-margin environment. We risk becoming *commoditized,* which is defined as *the act of making a process, good, or service easy to obtain by making it as uniform, plentiful, and affordable as possible. Something becomes commoditized when one offering is nearly indistinguishable from another.*[45]

Partner Relationship

Partner: *a person who shares or is associated with another in some action or endeavor.*[46]

The *connection* can come from multiple levels at both the customer and the partner companies, and the connection in a partner relationship carries more weight than does a vendor relationship. Typically, the customer has a good relationship with one or more of your organization's salespeople, and potentially with higher-level connections as well. Under this scenario the customer will still work with more than one vendor but not the multiple vendors of the straight vendor relationship. This lends the relationship a feeling of partnership. Due to the enhanced value of the connection in this partner relationship, issues of *capability and capacity* become

---

45 "Glossary of Terms," Capital Trading Group, accessed November 3, 2021, https://capitaltradinggroup.com/managed-futures/glossary-of-terms/.

46 "Partner," Dictionary.com, accessed November 3, 2021, https://www.dictionary.com/browse/partner.

even more important, as the customer is selecting fewer vendors to meet their needs. As a partner, we should be aiming for a win/win scenario with our customers and to structure our *conversation* accordingly. That conversation will stay focused on the overall needs of the customer, but it may become more detailed in data and more strategically intimate. As a result, the partner conversation tends to feature more sharing back and forth, as opposed to the mostly one-way interaction from customer to vendor.

Strategic Partnership Relationship

Strategic partnership: *an agreement between two distinct business entities to share expertise, resources, or competencies for mutual benefit.*[47]

A partner-type relationship can morph fairly easily into a strategic partnership. *Conversation* and *capacity* take front and center in the strategic partner relationship, as the customer has already gained confidence in the *capability* and would have the right *connection* with the partner company in place as well. Typically, the customer will work either exclusively with one strategic partner or with a very small number of strategic partners. In this type of relationship, the customer is putting "more of their eggs in one basket," and thus the stakes are raised significantly, for both the customer and the strategic partner. There's definite win/win potential here, since so much of the relationship focuses on mutual benefit. However, the stakes are higher. In order to remain a strategic partner, our companies must be able to consistently deliver what the customer needs, dovetailing our own *capabilities, capacity,* and *conversation* with those needs.

---

47   Melanie J. Martin, "What Are the Basic Elements to a Strategic Partnership?" *Chron,* accessed November 3, 2021, https://smallbusiness.chron.com/basic-elements-strategic-partnership-35782.html.

For the remainder of this chapter, we'll set aside the vendor relationship and zero in on the *partner* and *strategic partner* relationships. We'll look at our *capabilities*, *capacity*, and *conversation* from the point of view of a customer organization that wants to reach its full potential. Here are the questions I want to answer for you:

How can we take what we have learned in the Decision Series and apply it to our customers, as their partner or strategic partner, to consistently bring value to the relationship? How can we use the relationship to help the customer reach full potential, just as we are striving to do?

Here's the quote that begins to provide the answers:

The customer will create the most value for you at the point they think you are creating the most value for them.
—DON PEPPERS

So let's accept Peppers's framing. Let's focus on building value for our customers by building or enhancing our own *connections*, *capabilities*, *capacity*, and *conversations* with customers. There are three things we need to consider when attempting to significantly increase our customer awareness:

1. The Diamond Bridge to your customers' Productive Growth Pyramid

2. Your Defendable Differentiators

3. The Diamond Review System Tool

NUMBER 1—THE CUSTOMER DIAMOND BRIDGE

Let's start with the Growth Pyramid. The figure shows a comparison of your organization's Growth Pyramid with one representing a customer's.

TOOL: CUSTOMER DIAMOND BRIDGE

Know Thy Customer - Complement Thy Customer - Improve Thy Customer

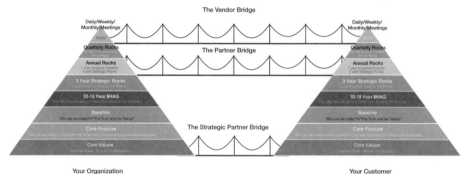

The Decision Series™

As I have often said, the hardest thing to discover is the most obvious. So I'll give you a shortcut for how to better *know, complement, and improve* your customer: *you just need to stop thinking like a vendor and start thinking like a partner or strategic partner.* It doesn't require any special set of skills. You use the same tools you've been taught throughout the Decision Series, which begins with how you operate your own organization:

- Choosing the Full Potential Growth Model

- Asking Diamond Level questions

- Becoming Qual-E-Gaged

- Staying audit ready

- Remaining committed to the Truth and Trends

- Using the Revenue Lever Strategy Tool to help you set the right Strategic Rocks

- Reaching clarity around your must/should/could-do models

- Using the N-MSC-T Alignment Tool to align your nonnegotiables, goals, and priorities with your daily actions

- Arriving at the necessary prerequisite for reaching full potential as an organization, achieving unconscious competence

With all of these models, tools, and skills shaping your mindset and helping you identify your goals, you'll be putting yourself in the best position for crossing the Diamond Bridge to your customer's Productive Growth Pyramid. That's where you need to be if you want to ask your customers Diamond Level questions about their organization. The answers you receive will help you find ways to assist your customers in making better-calculated decisions faster and with more confidence. That's the key: *you bring value to your customer by having higher-level conversations and asking Diamond Level questions.*

Think about what this means. It's a game changer, given the advantage you'll have with customers if you know their Productive Growth Pyramid as well as you know your own, including their Core Purpose, BHAG, and Strategic Rocks. Wouldn't this knowledge put you in a dramatically better position for asking those Diamond Level questions? The answer is emphatically yes.

> That's the key: *you bring value to your customer by having higher-level conversations and asking Diamond Level questions.*

When I talk about "crossing the Diamond Bridge," which is illustrated between the pyramids, it's much more than just a connection between your way of looking at the world and your customer's. It's an actual transfer. It illustrates your ability to cross over from your own vision to a new vision—one that incorporates the vision of your customers into your vendor, partner, and/or *strategic partner* discussions at various levels of the customer's Productive Growth Pyramid. The vendor bridge takes you to their shorter-term needs. The partner bridge gets deeper into their Productive Growth Pyramid but does not approach the full pyramid access that the strategic partner bridge allows.

Strategic partner discussions such as these follow the same Four Customer C's pattern we looked at earlier.

Connection and conversation—After you have crossed the bridge, there is not a level in your customer's organization that you cannot have a connection with, or a conversation regarding. But you must match the right connections with the right conversations in your two organizations.

Capability and capacity—Once you've had the higher-level conversations, it will become readily apparent whether you need to add new capabilities and capacity in order to fully support the customer as a partner or strategic partner.

But hey—to this point, I've been making a very big assumption about your customers. I've been taking it as a given that your customers, no matter how big or small, are operating under a Productive Growth Pyramid Model, not a Busy Growth Pyramid. In reality, that's a too-big assumption. But while it may be that way at first, it certainly doesn't have to stay that way. I see no reason why your organization, which is capable of crossing the Diamond Bridge and engaging in higher-level conversations for the benefit of the customer, couldn't also teach that customer a thing or two. What would prevent you from bringing value to them by sharing with them what you've learned about operating a highly efficient company that's well on its way to reaching full potential? Absolutely nothing, as long as the motivation is strictly to allow your partner or strategic partner to level up in a way that enhances the relationship.

Well, actually, there is one thing that prevents us from passing along our learning. Just as we've seen within our own organizations, we can get stuck at Gold or Cubic Zirconia Levels with our customers too. The Gold Level equivalent here is becoming aware of customer data but remaining relatively blind to their Productive Growth Pyramid status. And the Cubic Zirconia Level in this context is like the unnamed company I mentioned previously, where it looks like everything's going great until we dig into the details—or somebody asks just the right question.

TOOL: THE GOLD-DIAMOND MINE

MAKE BETTER, CALCULATED DECISIONS FASTER, AND WITH MORE CONFIDENCE

Now that we've adjusted our full-potential mindset to include our customers, and *their* pursuit of full potential as well, we can make some adjustments to our Customer Awareness definition.

Know thy customer by crossing the Diamond Bridge and having higher-level, more productive conversations regarding their own Productive Growth Pyramid.

Complement thy customer to help them reach their full potential, gaining an understanding of their Truth and Trends, listening with the intent to understand, and then asking better Diamond Level questions.

Improve thy customer by adding capabilities and capacity that are mutually beneficial via the Diamond Review Process.

A critical aspect to crossing the Diamond Bridge is to match up the right people in meetings, with an eye toward the time frames they're concerned about. Your account executive (AE) has quotas to meet, and your customer has employees who have similar shorter-term goals. Like your organization, the customer has higher-level leaders who are thinking much further out, as they are responsible for the vision in their organization. It's up to you to bring the right people to the conversation with your customers, so that the person with the strategic vision in your organization can ask his or her counterpart the appropriate Diamond Level questions. In reality, your AE could ask the questions, but the answers might serve only to tee up a short-term sale to help meet a quota.

Another way to say it: ensure that you match the connections and conversations across the various Diamond Bridges to accelerate your partnership and enhance the chances of both sides reaching full potential.

NUMBER 2—YOUR DEFENDABLE DIFFERENTIATORS

Once we've proven capable of crossing the Diamond Bridge to our customer's Productive Growth Pyramid, the *connections* and *conversations* we engage in will lead us to a better understanding of the *capabilities* and *capacity* we will need to fully support our customers, both now and in the future. But knowledge alone is not enough. We need to actually put the capabilities and capacity in place. If we don't, we'll fall short in the eyes of the customer and give them reasons to go back to the market in search of either new or additional partners.

For this section, let's assume that you have built a capable sales force to meet with and sell to your customer. Ultimately, though, the customer has choices and wants to build a longer-term relationship with someone who not only is capable of connection and conversation but truly has a differentiated solution—something different from what their competitors offer, something that is of special value. So what's your differentiator, your unique selling proposition (USP), your market positioning strategy? Whatever the term(s) you choose to use, the question is basically this: What makes your company the best, with the capabilities and capacity you bring forth in the markets you serve? What separates you from your competitors? What makes the business a success today? What will keep it successful as the years go by, both in sales tallied and customer loyalty shown?

A lot hinges on the verdict your prospective customer delivers after you've made your sales pitch. You know the scene—you're pitching, your VP of sales is joining you, and the third chair belongs to the company from which

> Once we've proven capable of crossing the Diamond Bridge to our customer's Productive Growth Pyramid, the *connections* and *conversations* we engage in will lead us to a better understanding of the *capabilities* and *capacity* we will need to fully support our customers, both now and in the future.

you hope to win a multiyear products or services contract. But when you get there, you find that the seats on your side of the table are already warm. Turns out your number one and number two competitors have been in those same chairs, making *their* pitch. It's not really a surprise. For any suitor-company, snaring this business would be the biggest win of the year.

What key thing do you say or demonstrate to land this important contract?

Or maybe it's a different pitching situation. Let's say you're halfway through your year, your July meeting with your board of directors/advisors is a week or so away, and—like higher-rank Navy officers with signature authority on your qual card, or the captain administering Oral Boards to determine whether you get to drive the submarine or not—your board members have asked you to come prepared to discuss your company's USP. Basically, the board wants to know how well you've built your company for the marketplace, and all eyes will be on you as you attempt to impress your audience. Your pass-fail grade will depend less on how well you sell the board on your company's ability to compete than it will on how the industry's most knowledgeable participants would grade your company's ability to sell against any competitor and win.

I challenge you to take this on as a real exercise. If you don't have a board of directors/advisors, ask a coach, a mentor, or some peer CEOs to test you. Pretend it's the biggest pitch you and your VP of sales will make all year, and here's that question again:

What key thing do you say or demonstrate to land this important contract?

I sincerely hope you've got something specific and original in mind. Having been in the prospective customer's chair more than a few times myself, I can assure you that most pitches sound like records skipping—the same words over and over again. A lot of the time, the words pitched are so general and overused that they convey almost no meaning at all.

As an example, let me take you back twenty-five years. Our company was selecting an IT firm to help us implement a new software solution. The contract was to include the purchase of the software itself, plus implementation and training. We had done our research. At the point we called in the vendors, we were well immersed in trying to understand the real differences between them. Which vendor would provide value, the best overall solution for the price? How would the vendors differentiate themselves from their longtime competitors?

I will never forget it. When I asked vendor number one's lead spokesman what sets their product and service apart, and why we should choose them, he said, "In the end, we will distinguish ourselves from our competitors with our unparalleled customer service." I thanked them for their time, and on we went to number two. When asked the same question, the lead spokesman of the second company said, "In the final analysis, we will distinguish ourselves from our competitors with our world-class customer service." When we got to number three, I didn't even want to ask the question, because I was certain it would be a similar response, and guess what? I was not disappointed. Yep, the answer was similarly vague and customer-service oriented. (And no, the one company that could truly stand on its unparalleled, world-class customer service—Nordstrom—wasn't selling software solutions that day.)

So I ask you: When is the last time you took a good, hard look at your PowerPoint presentation (or whatever you use to make your pitches)? Does it give your prospective customer their "why?" Does it tell them why they should buy from you? Does it say what your company does that makes it different? Is the description specific and detailed? More importantly, when you read it, *do you buy what it says?* Or is it, frankly, a load of BS?

I hope I've made you take a step back and question yourself and your organization. Is this an(other) area in need of attention? Is it going to take some work to earn your MEQC signature in this area of responsibility? Let me be more specific: *Is your company working its vision and plans? Is it setting and hitting goals?*

You may be thinking, *Why does that stuff matter when we're talking about making pitches for new business?* Well, it's another example of *beginning with the end in mind.*

Here's another question for you: *Does your company's collection of vision, plans, and goals include building upon your differentiators, so as to make your company more valuable to your customers and the market?*

This is the thing: As much as your sales prospect wants to hear the right stuff said about what your company can do for theirs, your company's future is also a key concern. Your would-be customer wants reassurance that you'll be around in a couple of years, and that the company will be a bigger and better version of itself by then. I can't guess at what precisely the decision-makers of that target company of yours are looking for. But I can guarantee that your company is being evaluated for its ability to excel—to build on its differentiator and continually improve its performance. No doubt there are lots of companies that can solve this prospective customer's pain, or any customer's. Why should yours get the nod if the next company can do the job just as well and at a similar price?

Take a moment now to think about what you currently claim as your company's defendable differentiator(s). Yes, there may be more than one. Which of these can be quickly exposed as *not defendable*, simply by the fact that your competitors are making the very same claims?

- *We have the best quality.* Unless you can prove this with awards or other specific measurements, this is too general to truly be differentiated. It sounds like it means something, but it probably doesn't!

- *We have the best people.* Where exactly do you find these "best" people, and who's measuring?

- *We have been in business for __ years.* Meaning? Unclear. Yes, I said earlier

Take a moment now to think about what you currently claim as your company's defendable differentiator(s).

that your customer wants to know you are going to be around years from now, but be careful; you also have to ensure that you are communicating clearly. What does this claim do for the customer, except perhaps offer them some confidence that you won't be out of business soon? What value does this claim actually bring to the customer? A competitor with a much more valuable solution will win out most of the time, no matter how new or established.

- *We have the best customer service.* Ritz-Carlton can say this. Most of the rest of us can't—though we will want to claim the mantle for whatever industry ours may be. It's getting to be quite a bandwagon, this particular claim, especially as the world's major economies shift from manufacturing to services. *Everybody* wants to be customer intimate now.

- *We care more about our customers!* Ah, I bet you do this with your "best" people giving the "best" customer service, right? See the bullet preceding this one. This is but another over-crowded section of the same bandwagon.

- *We have the lowest prices.* Well, the internet will quickly prove or disprove this selling point.

- *We are a global (or national) company.* Yes, I was guilty of this too! After being purchased by a large multinational with over fifty offices worldwide, I immediately started touting our global capabilities. But I had to take a step back quickly, because there was a big difference in saying "we're global (or national)," and actually being able to supply services globally (or nationally) right after the deal was done. Another lesson learned! We were differentiated, with great conversations and connections to our customers now that we had a global footprint, but the reality was that we were lacking on global capabilities and capacity.

If you see yourself in the above statements, it's time to find a differentiator that really *is* defendable. And as technological change continues to accelerate, you will most likely need to review your defendable differentiators more often to ensure they really are defendable. Companies back in the 1950s lasted, on average, sixty to sixty-five years. The data today varies with who's surveying, but currently corporate longevity is more like fifteen to eighteen years!

Start by taking a stroll down memory lane, recalling the earliest motivations that led to your company being established. *When you started the business, why did you do it?* Or if you aren't the original entrepreneur, think about the aims of the original founder. Then write down why this business began, using just a few words:

_____

_____

_____

_____

_____

I can guess at what you wrote. You (or the original founder) saw something to create, or a way to do something better than how it was currently being done. Or maybe it was about meeting needs in the marketplace that weren't currently being met. There is some variety in the possible responses, but the list really isn't very long. New ideas. Identified opportunities. Unmet needs.

Going at it from a different angle, did you (or the original founder) understand your competitors—who they were and what they offered? Were they part of the calculation? Probably not at first, I'd guess. I don't think many of us deeply considered the competition until later in the process—I know my companies didn't. *Did you come into the market intending to me-too something already out there, or did you set out to build something different—and presumably better?*

Indeed, succeeding in business is always going to be easier, even in the roughest market conditions, when you've got a defendable differentiator working for you:

With defendable differentiators, you have the opportunity to *distance yourself from your competition* with a strategic plan, competent salespeople, and operational excellence.

With*out* defendable differentiators, you have the opportunity to *keep up with your competition* by relying on a strategic plan, competent salespeople, and operational excellence—in other words, your success will come as the result of running a highly efficient organization, along with sheer willpower.

With defendable differentiators, *but* without the plan, the sales force, or the operational excellence, you may well succeed to an extent. But in the end, you will be just another company that *didn't live up to its potential*; in short, it's the undisciplined entrepreneur's approach!

**With*out* defendable differentiators *and* without the other

attributes, your only choice is to rely on what I would call "the hope-and-prayer strategy."

It was ever thus: No matter how hard you work or how good you think you are, the decision is the customer's, and it will be based on a variety of factors—some that you control, and some that you don't. *But with clearly defendable differentiators, you're not really selling. You're educating.* You're asking for the business, yes, but you're also explaining why you should have it. You're showing the prospective customer how uniquely positioned your company is to address their pain by providing the solutions they need. And that's something your competition can't fight. If you truly have a defendable differentiator, nothing the opposing salesperson can say or do will give him or her the upper hand. Your potential customer is too smart to fall for it, and too much in need of what your company is demonstrably best equipped to offer.

> But with clearly defendable differentiators, you're not really selling. You're educating.

To sum up, all of the *connections* and *conversations* won't help you have long-term success in your partnerships if you can't demonstrate that you not only have the *capabilities* and *capacity* to help them but that you are a step ahead of the competition with some *defendable differentiators*. I know that we built our organizations to either be the vendor/partner/strategic partner of choice for our customers or to be on their doorstep waiting for our competition to fail in their capabilities and capacity. With defendable differentiation, you give yourself an extra layer of protection for keeping that door shut to your competition for as long as possible. And at the very least, if your partnership with a customer is shared with competitors, your defendable differentiator should always ensure that you come out on top as the number one supplier to that customer. Because when that door opens, you don't want it to be so that they can kick you out!

NUMBER 3—THE DIAMOND REVIEW SYSTEM TOOL

We have talked about *connections* and *conversations*, and *capacity* and *capabilities*. Now is the time to give you another new tool to ensure that you are proactively building capabilities and capacity by having the right connection and conversation strategies—by creating Diamond Value for both your organization and your customer's organization through the Diamond Review System. I'm confident that this will become one of your most important leading indicators in your business.

The Diamond Review System has proven itself through uses in many different companies, of various sizes and in varied industries. The Diamond Review System can and should be customized to work with what you're already doing, if in fact you have a sales system in place in your organization. Remember, all my Decision Series content is meant to be collaborative with any system, not competitive.

In a nutshell, the Diamond Review System is the tool used by MEs to traverse from the Numbers Growth Model to the Full Potential Growth Model via your sales plan. Let's assume that you've done a great job understanding the customer's Productive Growth Pyramid, including their Strategic Rocks, and that you've also made a commitment to improve your capabilities and capacity. That's great progress! But have you reached your organization's full potential yet? Probably not, though not for the reasons that you might be thinking. So let's dig into a tool that will reveal more about what's holding you back—the Diamond Review System.

I created this system over two decades ago to ensure that our organization was built to reach its full potential by proactively building out our capabilities and capacity in alignment with our customers.

The system I devised is intended to *maximize* our conversations and connections with the customer, along with our ability to meet their present and future needs.

Let me take you back to where it all began. As you'll recall, General Electric (GE) was led by Jack Welch as its chairman and CEO from 1981 to 2001. Jack was a big fan of hiring ex-military officers and enlisted members, people known for their work ethic, maturity, loyalty, leadership, etc.—all the intangible skills that the military is famous for producing and enhancing in its people. I was leading my first company, Orion International, when GE began its focus on military hiring back in the mid-1990s. GE decided that it wanted to build up its ranks with high-quality military talent, and it chose various recruiting agencies to support that goal. Luckily, we were one of the company's major partners, and for many years we provided it with great military-trained and seasoned talent. GE hired a lot of people from us.

As part of our business review process, I conducted quarterly reviews with our sales reps—we called them account executives, or AEs—to review their sales production, client list, and overall business plans. The aim was to ensure that they were reaching their goals and objectives in alignment with the company's mission of helping GE with its military hiring.

As I dug into details, I noticed that most of our AEs were indeed working on GE accounts, and they had GE on their lists of second, third, and home base customers. Many had made multiple "placements" with GE, helping the giant recruit former military personnel into the various divisions of GE across the US. When I asked my AEs about their future forecasts, they were very optimistic that they could continue to grow their business with GE.

A typical review would look something like this:

Annual placements with GE: 5

Average hiring fee: $10,000

Annual billings with GE: $50,000

Projected billings the following year: 8 placements x $10K fee = $80,000

Success! And when I added up the GE projections across all my AEs, it was clear that GE was going to be one of our largest clients in the following year. The AEs' commissions would grow, we would grow, and GE would grow as well, a win/win/win.

But then I asked some different questions.

"What division of GE are you working with?" (At the time, GE had multiple divisions such as aircraft, appliances, plastics, etc.)

I am working with GE Aircraft.

"Excellent, at which location? Cincinnati, you say? Great. What other locations does GE Aircraft operate out of?"

I don't know.

Hmmm. "Who are you working with at GE Aircraft in Cincinnati? Shelly Smith? Excellent. Who else would hire military talent at GE Aircraft in Cincinnati?"

I don't know.

Hmmm. "What other divisions of GE are you calling?"

None.

Now, as we've said, *the hardest thing to discover is the most obvious.* We were very successful with placing military talent at GE, and we'd become one of its top providers, but we were not even close to supplying them with what they really needed. How could we be? We had no idea of the height, width, or breadth of the company's needs. No, we were satisfied with what we could readily see—the short-term needs we could meet for the company, and how we could use these opportunities to help GE's business growth in terms of numbers. But we were nowhere close to identifying what full potential looked like in our relationship with the company. We were missing out on scads of connections and conversations at GE that would have proven mutually beneficial.

> Now, as we've said, the hardest thing to discover is the most obvious.

And this was the critical question that we were not answering: *How much money is GE going to spend on military recruiting overall in the next year?*

Think about this one for a minute. Think about your own company and your customers. Do you know how much they have budgeted to spend on your products and services this year, with not just your company but all of the vendors that support them?

Take a few minutes. Think about the year ahead. Write down your current understanding of what's known, from information derived from your customers, regarding their plans to purchase products and services that you—and a host of other vendors—are ready to sell them.

_____

_____

_____

_____

_____

In the case of Orion International, my company at the time, we had a sense of what GE's Quarterly Rocks for military hiring were, and that was a good start. But when it came to One-Year and Three-Year Strategic Rocks, we had a disconnect in our business, one that was going to prevent us from supporting them with higher-level capabilities and significantly more capacity.

The issue was our AEs were satisfied with growing their individual business with the client incrementally, say from $50,000 to $80,000 in the following year—whether or not the true growth potential was greater. We were leaving huge potential on the table, and for many different reasons:

- Our AEs were very satisfied with their growth in billings. They were content to underpromise and overdeliver on their projections. Sound familiar? Most of them had a target much higher than $80K in their minds, but no, they weren't going to commit to that. In other words, they were following the Numbers Growth Model! The growth was there, consistent and steady, but not at all what it was capable of becoming. There was, indeed, *a potential gap forming* for the GE account, one that was going to get bigger with every AE's Diamond Review. And had I not asked them the right questions, we would have never been able to identify the overall gap, which I call the Diamond Gap.

- The AEs didn't want to look greedy and ask for too much business, even though the client was going to spend lots of money with other vendors/partners such as us if we didn't ask for it. Yes, crazy as it sounds (though also familiar), even though GE was pulling us to help it do more military hiring, we didn't want to push it. If we had been following the must/should/could system at that point, we would have seen that the greatest opportunity that *we should have been building* on was GE. GE was *pulling us to build up our capabilities and capacity, but at the executive levels we were unaware of truly how much potential was on the table from them.* Our customers wanted more from us, but our AEs were satisfied!

347

- Because we hadn't identified what GE's full potential looked like, we couldn't build out the systems and processes to capture it.

- The AEs (sales) did not have confidence that operations (production) could keep up with the demand for military talent, so they underpromised in the hope of overdelivering later. This is a classic in organizations, the we/they problem. Production doesn't trust sales to do its job well, and vice versa. Be on the lookout for this in your own organization and, if it exists, fix it by implementing the Full Potential Growth Model.

After conducting quarterly reviews with our thirty-plus AEs, the "ahas" were, for me, unmistakable. Essentially, the AEs had chosen to forecast with the Numbers Growth Model, comfortable with growing their individual AE businesses by an increment each year, fully content but still hopeful that they could overdeliver at some point. They were doubtful that the company could support more capacity anyway, and that left them reluctant to promise their clients they could support them because they truly didn't believe they could.

TOOL: THE DECISION SERIES "NUMBERS" GROWTH MODEL

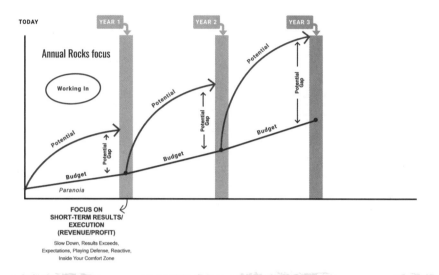

As the CEO looking down and across the organization, the disconnects were clear. Let's look back at the Full Potential Growth Model below and focus on identifying the people and infrastructure gap and implementing the right incentives.

TOOL: THE DECISION SERIES "FULL POTENTIAL" GROWTH MODEL

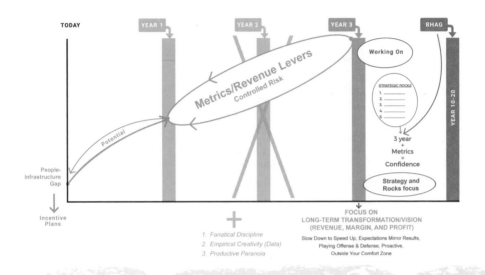

Because I wanted to implement the Full Potential Growth Model and the AEs were operating under the Numbers Growth Model, we were at risk of doing two things:

- Internally, we were setting our organization up to grow, but not at a level reflecting our full potential.

- Externally, we were underperforming for GE, necessitating the need for it to add other vendors.

When I completed that AE quarterly review process twenty-plus years ago, the Diamond Review Process was born. When I finished the model, the process it suggested allowed me to clearly see and demonstrate the difference between what the AEs had committed to and what the customer was willing to spend (which, in turn, was tied to what it actually needed). I call this the **Diamond Gap**.

Moving forward, rather than having my sales and production staff limit their projections for the reasons listed above, *I focused on the goal of reaching full potential and on identifying what full potential would look like, for the AE, for our organization, and for the customer.* This is **Diamond Value.**

During the review, it became clear that the AEs, with their self-limited forecasts, were also placing unwarranted limits on the growth of our capabilities and capacity. By coming up with forecasts based almost entirely on a belief that production couldn't meet the demand for increased orders, they were preventing the organization from identifying a need for growth and acting on it. This was something that only I, as CEO, and my VP of sales were in the position to discover, and it was my/our job to do so. If my goal was for us to meet our full potential, I needed to understand the nature of the Diamond Gap in people and infrastructure that would be exposed by fully supporting GE's needs. Only then would we be able to make the proper investments in people, infrastructure, and incentive plans necessary for meeting all Four Customer C's for our customers—increased *connections* and *conversations*, and improved *capabilities* and *capacity.*

It is now time to define the terms in the Diamond Review System, and especially that new term I just threw at you—Diamond Value.

Let's start with a visual representation of the system, using a photo of Yankee Stadium for reference. You'll notice that in the infield, where players are spread out around the dirt, there are four bases, and the resulting shape is what makes it a baseball diamond.

Source: John Dalton, CC BY-SA 2.0

As the vast majority of us know, the four bases are first base, second base, third base, and home (base). Nobody scores in baseball without working their way home one, two, or three bases at a time, or by hitting a home run to touch all four on a single time at bat. The Diamond Review System has four bases as well, each with a customer-related definition:

Definitions

1. First Base account—a customer that has not been called yet. This is a prospect. You can't score in baseball until you reach base, and you can't get a new customer without a list of prospects!

2. Second Base account—a customer that has had a presentation given to it by a sales rep in your organization, and it has expressed an interest in working with your company in the future. By building up the Second Base "Diamond Value," the organization is building up its future sales potential.

3. Third Base account—a customer who has "activity" with us currently. It is in the process of potentially buying our products or services. We can't close a sale unless we have one in the process, so third base activity includes everything that you are trying to close in your sales pipeline.

4. Home (Base) account—a customer that has purchased our products and/or services.

Before we dig into the detail, let me pull back and provide more context for the review process I'm about to describe.

Purpose. The Diamond Review is a tool by which the AE develops a comprehensive sales plan for his or her portfolio of companies, along with an indication or forecast of where the account activity will take place in the upcoming quarter. The diamond is essentially the equivalent of a business plan, and for each AE, the diamond will be different based on the AE's time with the company, as well as his or her Home account development, sales skills, and overall skill set. During the Diamond Review, it's up to you to set targets that make sense. It's also important that you help everyone remember why you're creating the diamond: it's not just a numbers review; it's a business plan for expanding the business the company already has and identifying new business to target and develop.

Overall philosophy. Your aim as a company should be to cover all the ground, blocking out your competitors. If you can't do that, then at least cover all the ground that could become available to you in the future. You want to be standing right at the proverbial door when your competitor blows it, and you absolutely know it's gonna happen. Just like they are hoping you will! Especially during recessionary times, when others may be slacking because things have become too hard, your organization needs to be the one that's positioning itself behind as many doors as possible. When business picks up again and those doors start to open, you want to be first in line.

Frequency. The complete Diamond Review Process occurs once a quarter, though a condensed monthly Diamond Review can be done as well. In between, your Diamond functions as a living, breathing document that summarizes your account activity and, most importantly, prioritizes your sales efforts—if you've sorted your prospects correctly. To ensure that proper sorting, the Diamond should be updated whenever there are changes in activity that affect your strategic and tactical business plan. Maintain your data! That's how you derive maximum value from the business plan your Diamond creates.

Uses and implications. Whenever we complete a Diamond Review, we have essentially created not just a sales strategy and revenue expectations, but we've also drawn up a production plan. With it, production teams can proactively build inventory to support the currently projected needs for inventory. More broadly, a properly done Diamond Review can reveal a significant amount of information that is critical to the overall success of the company. It can enhance our ability to predict what type of business conditions we're going to see in the future (i.e., recession, semiconductor is hot, manufacturing is booming, etc.).

Now that you know basically what the Diamond Review is and what it offers your company, let's go a bit deeper into the how-to:

Evaluating customers and choosing bases. To know who's on first, so to speak, and who your Home Base customers are, requires gathering some basic information. You probably don't need a new system for this, because I'd assume anybody reading this book has some means of tracking your sales funnels and customers. So rest assured, the Diamond Review System doesn't require you to build a new structure or double your effort in any way. This is meant to be a value-added process. Almost all of the information you need to gather to start your Diamond Review is obvious, and you undoubtedly have most of it. But in the list below, there are a few that should be new, and I'll elaborate on the ones I've italicized.

- Name of client

- Company name

- Division of company

- Location of client

- Sales history of client (five years' Truth and Trends data)

- Relationship—vendor/partner/strategic partner (remember, our goals are to expand our Ps and SPs)

- Base—choose Second, Third, or Home, because targets (First Base) will have their own tab on the spreadsheet

- *Annual Diamond Value potential*

- *AE annual forecast*

- *The Diamond Gap*

- *Ninety-Day Forecast*

- *Target list / client development*

- *Game plan—next steps*

The critical success factor for a Diamond Review is for the reviewer to evaluate every client entry with the AE, asking Diamond Level questions about the numbers the AE is reporting in the last six bullets. This is important, because to reach full potential both internally and externally, we need confidence in the Diamond Values we establish. That confidence comes only through conversations with our customers—ones that identify their future needs and the shorter- and longer-term capabilities and capacity we will need to fully support them.

Annual Diamond Value potential—This is the critical entry for the Diamond Review System. The AE estimates what the client's annual spending will be for the products and services in our categories—and not just what they'll spend with us but with *all* of their vendors and partners. In order to come up with a reasonable and educated guess at this number, the AE must be in direct conversation with the customer. Ideally, the AE has obtained enough information about the customer's short- and long-term goals to cross the Diamond Bridge, as we discussed earlier. If you have only crossed the vendor bridge, then getting the data will be much harder to do. The resulting Diamond Value will vary greatly among customers, depending on the type of relationship (V/P/SP). Some customers will be forecast to do the minimum, while others will have expansive Diamond Value Potential. For each of the entries in the bulleted list, start with an Excel spreadsheet or combine with your existing CRM system—customize what works best for you.

AE annual forecast—This is very different from the Diamond entry, the base chosen for each customer. The AE is going to input a number that represents the share of the Diamond Value that the AE thinks your organization will get from the customer's overall Diamond Value Potential. The number may be lower than may be expected and for various reasons. During the Diamond Review Process, it will be critically important to understand *why* the AE is projecting a difference.

The Diamond Gap—This is the difference between the Annual Diamond Value Potential and the AE's annual forecast. The reviewer must fully understand the reasons for this difference. They could include the following: the customer works with multiple vendors, the AE lacks confidence that the production side will keep up with customer demand, or the AE is simply underpromising. With achieving full potential as the goal, the CEO or top leadership will need to use this process to identify what internal omissions, oversights, or problems exist, and then design and implement a plan for solution.

Ninety-Day Forecast—The Diamond Review takes place on a quarterly basis. Each quarter the AE will forecast what customers they project to spend money in the next quarter, thus with which they expect to close a sale. In order to project these billings, the AE must be in contact with his or her customer frequently and has to have seen buying signals that provide optimism that sales activity will occur. We would expect that the Ninety-Day Forecast will eventually make its way to the organization's sales system that tracks their Third Base activity (CRM). This tool doesn't substitute for your existing system; it's just another tool that management can use to enhance predictions. It is another leading indicator for your organization, and a very important one in your journey toward reaching full potential.

Target list / client development—Remember, First Base is where you put your prospects, the list of customers that you are going to call and have a conversation with. This list should be populated from various sources, but the critical addition to this list is the Home account expansion targets. Back when I was devising this tool, it became very clear, very fast, as I talked to AEs that the answers I was getting mostly told me how satisfied they were with their existing clients, and how we could grow our business with them over the next twelve months. I wasn't hearing anything, really, about how they could use significantly increased connections, conversations, and capabilities to expand their Home account list. The mistakes began with the most basic one: listing our client as GE when it should have been broken down as follows:

- GE

- GE Divisions—there were eleven at the time!

- GE Location by division—there were hundreds!

- GE Hiring authorities by location—there were multiple!

My first request to every AE was for them to produce a Home account expansion plan, showing me their sales expansion plan just for GE. What divisions, locations, and hiring authorities were they targeting to connect with, and have conversations with, regarding our capabilities and capacity?

As you might imagine, this approach expanded our list greatly. AEs who are merely successful grow their numbers every year, but *maximized* AEs and organizations reach for *full Diamond potential.*

Game plan / next steps—The Diamond Review System is built to help an organization get its arms around what full potential looks like for each customer, allowing the organization to build a game plan that ensures that we deliver on that potential. The first step in the Diamond Review—data sorting the information by Annual Diamond Value, from highest to lowest, and then going line by line in conversation with the AE regarding their relationships, forecasts, and ultimately their overall game plan. Remember, this can be done via a spreadsheet or with your existing CRM system. That plan is as follows: identifying the next steps necessary to move the sales toward closure and determining how to do so with a sense of urgency.

Whereas the Numbers Growth Model has a defensive stance to it, the Full Potential Growth Model, teamed with the Diamond Review System, has us going on offense to build business with our customers. These questions must be part and parcel of the process: What does the AE, himself or herself, need to do? What help does the AE need from others? Where and how might we be at risk of losing the customer's business? Ask Diamond Level questions like these to ensure that you have fully brainstormed the next steps. Where does our organization need to add people, infrastructure, and processes to build our capabilities and capacity to support full-potential growth? This is what positions AEs and the organization to win, and more importantly, for the customer to win! As ever, it's a matter of asking the key question: *What's Next?!*

Putting it all together—The metrics—they are the pure gold—lead to the Diamonds. So let's run the bases of our Diamond:

- *First Base*: Your prospects, which can come from anywhere. These are your Home account expansion targets. They can be competitors, leads from your marketing department, etc. There is no Diamond Value associated with First Base. It's all prospective until you can begin moving them off First.

- *Second Base:* These are interested customers who haven't done business with you yet. Their overall Diamond Value is an indication of the latent potential in your business.

- *Third Base:* These accounts transition into your company's existing sales system, whichever one you use to indicate your pipeline, your sales orders, etc. Each of you should be tracking every potential sale in the company already, and as I've said, I'm not asking you to duplicate that work with the Diamond System. Since a Diamond Review is done every ninety days, you simply change the base for any company with existing sales activity to Third Base for that quarter. If the sale is closed, they become a Home account; if not, they go back to Second Base.

To make the Diamond Review Process work most effectively, your company needs to track, with high confidence, your conversions of Diamond potential to actual sales. This is how it works: we take the overall Diamond Value and multiply it by the conversion metric—a number you trust because it's proven accurate over time and continual checking. Let's consider an example:

Overall Diamond Value (from Second, Third, and Home Base accounts) = $32,500,000

Conversion = 6 percent

$32,500,000 x 6 percent = $1,950,000

The only way a company can make a sale is to have interested companies who eventually place orders. Every year, a portion of those interested companies in your Diamond System will buy, and the rate at which the conversion occurs makes a huge difference. Let's look at the Diamond Value at a conversion of 11 percent and see what happens to sales—it's an increase of over $1.6 million!

$32,500,000 x 11 percent = $3,575,000

So when the Diamond Review happens every ninety days, we will want to be looking for ways to not only increase our Diamond Value levels but also to *improve our conversion rate.* We do this through better game-planning.

The Ninety-Day Forecast works the same way. We assume here that what is forecast will make it into your sales system. Since we are only looking out ninety days, we should be able to make better educated guesses as to how much the customer will be spending, which should result in a conversion number that's higher than the annual target we discussed above.

Now, if you've been following closely, you may have noticed that I've been assuming that your AEs are experienced and knowledgeable, as I'm sure many of them are. But let me give you another example of the Diamond, this time for a brand-new salesperson. When we hire new AEs, we most likely start them out with an annual sales target to hit, let's say, $250,000 in billings. We hold them accountable for that number, along with the number of calls they make and other activities that we know are necessary for them to build up their database of interested customers.

Well, remember when I said earlier that the Diamond would become one of your most important leading indicators? Let me prove that to you now. That annual sales target of $250,000 in billings we set for a newbie AE is a lagging indicator—each month they're either on track or not. But the Diamond offers us a better prediction of success, as *it provides us a leading indicator of what they will eventually sell.*

Consider a reasonable goal for a new AE: make ten new presentations per day to prospects. We expect (based on previous AE experience) that the ten presentations will produce two companies that are interested. We expect our AE to work fifty weeks per year, and yes, we want them to hit our target—$250,000 in billings per year.

So with the Diamond Review Process, this is what our new AE looks like, from the Diamond Value standpoint:

1. Ten presentations per day will yield two interested customers per day, ones that can be added to Second Base.

2. For example, let's assume that the Diamond Value of a new Second Base entry is $10,000, although some can be worth significantly more if we've identified them as a customer who has the potential to do much higher levels of business with us. Your numbers will most likely be very different, but all concepts apply the same, regardless of your typical Diamond Value.

3. The AE will work five days per week during their fifty-week year.

4. We will convert on average 8 percent of their Diamond throughout the year.

So before I give you the answer, how much do you predict the AE will bill in his or her second year with the company, assuming they don't add even one more prospect to their Diamond in the second year?

10 presentations/day = 2 interested companies/day x 5 days/week = 10 interested companies per week added to their Diamond as Second Base entries

10 companies x 50 weeks = 500 interested companies added in the first year to the AE's Diamond

500 x $10,000 (minimum Diamond potential of each entry) = $5 million in Diamond Value

$5,000,000 x 8 percent conversion = $400,000 projected billings in year two!

Now which is better: pounding on the new AE every day to make a sale, or asking him or her how many presentations and interested companies they logged today? Your quarterly Diamond Review should also check the quality and quantity of the Diamond entries that the AE has added. Believe me when I say it: this is a great *leading indicator* that every business should be taking advantage of!

What's more, the Four Customer C's will be *maximized*.

Connections and *conversations*—These are increased by adding to your First Base prospects, expanding your Second, Third, and Home Base accounts, and expanding opportunities in your customer's organization after crossing the Vendor, Partner, and Strategic Partner Diamond Bridges.

Capabilities and *capacity*—By thoroughly understanding your customers' needs via improved conversations and expanded connections, we can then identify what the Diamond Value is and proactively build our capabilities and capacity to fully support our mutual goal—reaching full potential.

As we finish the chapter on customer awareness, let's review the revised definition.

Know thy customer *by crossing the various bridges and having higher-level, productive conversations regarding their own Productive Growth Pyramid.*

Complement thy customer *by helping them reach their full potential—namely, gaining an understanding of their Productive Growth Pyramid, listening with the intent to understand, with all of your conversations and connections, and then asking better Diamond Level questions.*

Improve thy customer *by adding capabilities and capacity that are mutually beneficial, via the Diamond Review Process.*

Take a look at this chapter's qual card, then on to the ME Bridge and *reset*!

MEQC—What's Next?!

Learn. Think. Decide. Implement.

Initials

1. Discuss in detail the purpose of crossing the Diamond Bridge to your customer's Productive Growth Pyramid. Ask yourself "What's Next?!" to move your customer relationships toward higher-level win/win relationships (Vendor, Partner, and Strategic Partner). _____

2. Segment your customers into Vendor, Partner, and Strategic Partner relationships. _____

3. Complete a SWOTT analysis (explain your strengths, weaknesses, opportunities, threats, and trends) with regard to each current customer, focusing on conversations, connections, capabilities, and capacity. Start with Strategic Partner first, then Partner, then Vendor. _____

4. Discuss in detail your Defendable Differentiators. _____

5. Explain where your organization is set up for potential failure because of its lack of differentiation. _____

6. Discuss in detail the Diamond Review System and the use of "What's Next?!" to implement the Diamond Full Potential Tool in your organization. Define Diamond Value Potential, the Diamond Gap, the annual AE forecast, and Ninety-Day Diamond Forecast. _____

7. Develop a Diamond Review Process for your organization, to include the steps necessary to forecast company annual Diamond potential, and Ninety-Day Forecasts for individual AEs and the company.   _____

8. Develop a Diamond plan for new salespeople (AEs).   _____

Signature: _____

Date: _____

CHAPTER 11

Reset—Four Questions and the ME Bridge

This is happiness—savoring the journey in the middle of living it.
—ROXANNE BLACK

Each book in the Decision Series has a "Reset" chapter, and *The Fourth Decision* continues the tradition. After all you've read and considered, it's time now to spend some time thinking about the route you're mapping out for your future, and to consider what sort of adjustments might need to be made. What will your *reset* look like? And how often will you need a *reset*?

Let's jump right into it. This book's journey has taken you from success as a *qualified* and *intentional* entrepreneur to one that's *maximized*. You've gained perspective. You've picked up some new tools to help both you and your company reach full potential. Now, what is it you want and need during this ME phase of your career? In the short run, what nonnegotiables in your blended life will you establish to structure your choices? (More on the blended nonnegotiables coming up in this chapter.) To borrow from Roxanne Black above, what do you need to ensure that you'll savor the remaining peaks in your entrepreneurial climb while you may be very much in the midst of climbing them?

Unlike a true mountaineer, who is more likely to most savor the climb upon reaching the top, our goal as MEs is to truly enjoy the whole journey, not just the picture-taking at the summits. That's so key for us. We entrepreneurs don't linger long at moments of success. We're already headed—at least in our minds—for the next mountain. It's important, then, to enjoy the climb. It's most of what we do.

Nothing against summits, of course. You'll savor the moment for all it's worth, knowing the hard work and perseverance it took to climb your personal mountain. Then, after taking many pictures and soaking in the moment, your thoughts will turn to what's next because no achiever of any stripe expects to stay at the peak forever. It just doesn't work that way. You will always come back down from the summit, and most of us will have already begun looking toward the horizon.

What summiting really does is add fuel to the entrepreneurial fire, adding accomplishment to desire, and proving that your drive for autonomy has paid off big-time—you're forever able to do absolutely what you want to, and only what you want to, for as long as you want to. The possibilities seem endless, and they just might be.

Maybe you won't tackle another mountain right away. Or maybe you will. Climbers set their own targets, and so do entrepreneurs. The only thing that's fairly certain is that your first mountain won't be your last.

So yes, in this chapter as in the rest of the book, I'm assuming that your entrepreneurial lifetime career will include multiple summits, whatever their shape or form. In one particular way, they're guaranteed to be different experiences than the first climb. For many of us, the exciting but scary drive to start our first business was the kind of experience so well described in Reid Hoffman's famous quote: *"An entrepreneur is someone who will jump off a cliff and assemble an airplane on the way down."*

Summiting mountains is dangerous. Building businesses is also high risk; we only need to look at the statistics to see that 70 percent of companies failed by the ten-year point.

We did it before. There's little doubt we can do it again. But having gone from successful to *maximized,* we don't need—or even necessarily want—to head off on the next expedition without due preparation and planning anymore. We've probably got a different definition of what's fun by now. Maybe we've also learned enough to know that there are much better ways to complete a climb than what we did before. There won't be any running shoes on the trail this time. We've got the equipment, the tools. And while we feel confident of handling whatever dicey situations we might encounter, we have a much better eye for spotting crevasses. We pause, we consider. We don't just tromp across any old bridge.

No, we set up the bridge we trust. I call it the **ME Bridge**, the one that completes the journey from entrepreneur to *maximized* entrepreneur. Unlike the Diamond Bridge of the last chapter, which was a customer-centered, company-focused bridge, this bridge is yours personally. With tools stowed in your pack for any climb you might choose to undertake, the ME Bridge is something you undertake on your own terms, when you're ready. And I'd bet plenty that you're ready. Not for jumping out of the figurative plane, or starting the climb in running shoes, but for embarking on *"What's Next?!"* the ME way.

In *The Second Decision* and in this book, we've considered the difference between being an entrepreneur and becoming a CEO and compared the characteristics of each. Now, I want to offer you another list of comparison words—from entrepreneur to ME. The question is, what traits, tendencies, and characteristics do you want to carry across the bridge with you to the *maximized* side? What will you need for the rest of your career as a *maximized* entrepreneur? What might you prefer to leave on the entrepreneur side?

On each line, check the appropriate box to indicate what you desire to become qualified in and those areas where you consider yourself qualified now. Please remember that to become maximized, the audit-ready mindset remains front and center, and it will once again with the ME Bridge. In addition, make note of the time frame that you would like to move your desired items to qualified in the next three months, twelve months, three years.

TOOL: THE ME BRIDGE

Entrepreneur	Desire to Cross Yes/No		Audit-Ready/Qualified Yes/No	Maximized Entrepreneur
Saying Yes	_____	⋀⋀⋀⋀⋀⋀	_____	...and Saying NO
Entrepreneur	_____	⋀⋀⋀⋀⋀⋀	_____	and QE/IE/ME
In a hurry	_____	⋀⋀⋀⋀⋀⋀	_____	or not always in a hurry?
Negotiables	_____	⋀⋀⋀⋀⋀⋀	_____	and non-negotiables
Reactive decisions	_____	⋀⋀⋀⋀⋀⋀	_____	or proactive decisions?
Do what you love to do	_____	⋀⋀⋀⋀⋀⋀	_____	and love the people you work with
Self Confident	_____	⋀⋀⋀⋀⋀⋀	_____	and ...ME Level Self-Awareness
Do everything	_____	⋀⋀⋀⋀⋀⋀	_____	or Work in your genius/excellence?
Speed up	_____	⋀⋀⋀⋀⋀⋀	_____	or learn to slow down to speed up?
Work long hours	_____	⋀⋀⋀⋀⋀⋀	_____	and/or work smart hours
Work with brute force	_____	⋀⋀⋀⋀⋀⋀	_____	or work with finesse/priorities?
Perfection	_____	⋀⋀⋀⋀⋀⋀	_____	or Progress?
Quantity mindset	_____	⋀⋀⋀⋀⋀⋀	_____	or quality and quantity mindset?
Bore-E-Gaged	_____	⋀⋀⋀⋀⋀⋀	_____	or Qual-E-Gaged?
Successsful	_____	⋀⋀⋀⋀⋀⋀	_____	and Full-Potential
Growing the company	_____	⋀⋀⋀⋀⋀⋀	_____	and taking more time truly off
Ego	_____	⋀⋀⋀⋀⋀⋀	_____	and Humility
Little to no strategy	_____	⋀⋀⋀⋀⋀⋀	_____	or Strategic rocks fully in place?

The Decision Series™

Entrepreneur	Desire to Cross Yes/No		Audit-Ready/Qualified Yes/No	Maximized Entrepreneur
Setbacks	_____	⋀⋀⋀⋀⋀⋀	_____	and Learnings
Learning	_____	⋀⋀⋀⋀⋀⋀	_____	or learning and implementing?
Want focus	_____	⋀⋀⋀⋀⋀⋀	_____	and need focus
Delegate	_____	⋀⋀⋀⋀⋀⋀	_____	and verify with qual cards
Push	_____	⋀⋀⋀⋀⋀⋀	_____	and Pull mentalities
Checking blocks	_____	⋀⋀⋀⋀⋀⋀	_____	or maximizing focus?
SC model	_____	⋀⋀⋀⋀⋀⋀	_____	or N-MSC-T Model?
?????? Model	_____	⋀⋀⋀⋀⋀⋀	_____	or Full-Potential Growth Model?
??????? Mindset	_____	⋀⋀⋀⋀⋀⋀	_____	or Audit-Ready Mindset?
Work Hard	_____	⋀⋀⋀⋀⋀⋀	_____	and Work different
30-60 minutes-quick	_____	⋀⋀⋀⋀⋀⋀	_____	or 2 hours focused?
Risk	_____	⋀⋀⋀⋀⋀⋀	_____	and/or Controlled risk
Know all the answers	_____	⋀⋀⋀⋀⋀⋀	_____	or ask all the right questions?
Make all decisions	_____	⋀⋀⋀⋀⋀⋀	_____	or develop qualified leaders?
Internal focus	_____	⋀⋀⋀⋀⋀⋀	_____	and customer awareness
Rushed thinking	_____	⋀⋀⋀⋀⋀⋀	_____	or think days/hours?

The Decision Series™ RANDYH.COM NELSON

You have seen my list above, so now add a customized section for you, with the words that describe your trip across your own ME Bridge.

Currently	Desire to Cross Yes/No	Audit Ready/ Qualified Yes/No	Future Time Frame

You get one shot at this entrepreneurial life, one shot to accomplish your entrepreneurial goals without any regrets or alibis. Well, actually you get 27,375-plus shots during your lifetime.

27,375?

Okay, your reaction was the same as mine when I heard it from John O'Leary, one of the most inspirational speakers you will ever hear in your life—check him out!

John assumes a life span of seventy-five years. We all desire more than seventy-five, but I'm okay with his number if we look at it as the minimum number of years we'll live healthily, without disability. Multiply his seventy-five years by 365 days, and that's how he gets to 27,375 (healthy/nondisabled) days in our lives. Consider the following:

- If you've graduated from high school, you are down to 20,000.

- If you are in your early thirties, you've got about 15,000 left. If you are sixty, my age in 2021, then you're looking at a bit more than 5,000.

John views the exercise as much more inspiring than depressing. In his own life, it prodded him to live in a way that is congruent with his personal values, passions, and sense of vocation. That's a lesson we can all stand to learn, for the meter is running for each and every one of us. Every single day matters.

> *Yesterday's the past, tomorrow's the future, but today is a gift. That's why it's called the present.*
> **—BILL KEANE**

How will we choose to accept that gift and make best use of it? How will we *reset* to live deeply into our ME careers, knowing that each and every day matters?

As the tables above are designed to illustrate, our future is about choices. Each day we decide whether we're going to live the life we want to live. To stay the same, or change. And to improve what could be working better. All of this—and so much more—can sometimes feel like a monumental challenge, but basically it's just a choice or a set of them.

In a *Bloomberg* article by Arianne Cohen titled "The Psychological Formula for Success After Age 50," the author highlighted what psychologists have long known—that success is fueled by grit, passion, and a growth mindset.[48] Now, the "growth mindset" described here is

---

48   Arianne Cohen, "The Psychological Formula for Success After Age 50," *Bloomberg Businessweek*, December 8, 2020, https://www.bloomberg.com/news/articles/2020-12-08/tips-for-finding-career-success-even-as-you-approach-retirement.

one of personal growth, but what is an entrepreneur's growth mindset but a personal one harnessed to a business setting, right? The critical factor is one that entrepreneurs and all leaders share: a deep-seated belief that there is success to be found in a new pursuit.

Interestingly, Norwegian psychologist Hermundur Sigmundsson—quoted in Cohen's article—concluded that while passion is by far the most important psychological factor in success, it peaks early in life. Unfortunately, that's true of the growth mindset as well, though to a lesser extent. So by the time we're in build-a-company phase two (or whatever), two of the three most important ingredients in the recipe for achievement are waning. As Sigmundsson puts it, "You lose the thinking that maybe you can do this."[49]

But don't count out the importance of that third factor, grit—which is generally defined as a combination of perseverance and determination. Grit rises through middle age and peaks in our seventies, as do several other intellectual traits that I covered earlier in this book, such as crystallized intelligence. Critically, the mind's accumulation of facts and knowledge doesn't peak until around retirement age, and that's great—because it's also when your mind is best suited to dominate on the job, thanks to grit. It's that abundance of grit that helps us overcome passions that flag and a growth mindset that has perhaps begun to trail off. Of course, our experience as entrepreneurs fuels the fire particularly well for us when we consider new possibilities. We know we can climb mountains, because we've already done it—maybe not just once but several times!

What this research tells us is that we entrepreneurs can be driven to success for a long, long time, at least until seventy-five and probably well beyond. We can come up with ideas forever, and even if our passion and growth mindset is on the wane, the combination of grit,

---

49   Ibid.

crystallized intelligence, self-awareness, and our ever-present desire to change the world should keep us energized, especially when we are in the right seat in our own bus.

Or maybe not? Sometimes, for some of us, the can-do spirit is overwhelmed by a sense of "been there, done that, bought the T-shirt." Yes, for some of us, the *reset* we actually yearn for could include a key component—*rest*. Perhaps there's a need to recharge before we can consider resuming. *That is more than okay.*

I credit Dan Sullivan of Strategic Coach for impressing on me the importance of taking time off—completely—to really build some cranking power into that battery. It's not weakness or laziness to recognize that need. Nor does it mean you're not really an entrepreneur if you (or I) decide to work harder at blending than building. For many of us "experienced" entrepreneurs, a key factor in becoming *maximized* is learning that it's really possible to have both a growing company and more time off. Identify and establish the right nonnegotiables to guide your must/should/could decisions, and you'll achieve that blend. That is also why we will be adjusting nonnegotiables later in the chapter to become blended, taking into account both our work and life—more on that in a few pages.

> Yes, for some of us, the *reset* we actually yearn for could include a key component—*rest.* Perhaps there's a need to recharge before we can consider resuming. *That is more than okay.*

Reset: to set again, or differently.

Remember, the point of the *reset* in each of my Decision Series books has been about exactly this: using newly gained self-awareness to make better choices, ones that will help you live out the entrepreneurial life of your dreams—without regrets or alibis.

Rest: to cease work, or movement, in order to relax, refresh oneself, or recover strength.

To recover strength—that's the part I'd draw to the attention of anyone who feels sheepish about wanting to have his or her *reset* include some *rest*. It's that slowing-down-to-speed-up stuff again, that's all. It's not a failing; it's a virtue to be self-aware enough to see a need and address it, right?

That's everybody's idea of what a *reset* button looks like. But what the word means when you push the button, that's different for each of us. Maybe your *reset* will involve just a few tweaks to include *rest* at this stage, perhaps with bigger changes to come. Maybe it will be the opposite—big changes now, to be followed by little ones, and after that, small steps back to an entrepreneurial future. Or maybe you're nowhere near ready to see the possibility of *rest* in a *reset*. Your mileage may—and should—vary! It's *your reset*; you need to make it truly yours.

Of course, that's easier said than done. Remember that Alden Mills quote I've referred to a few times in this book? That "it ain't complicated, but it's hard"? Well, let's try a few exercises aimed at teasing out the factors and issues that will guide your *reset*. It's my hope that these step-by-step opportunities for additional self-awareness will take some of the "hard" out of identifying your choices, at least.

I'll start with three questions covering different time horizons. One or two of them may resonate more strongly with you, depending on your age and entrepreneurial status, but each of them should help you answer questions pertaining to your *reset*.

QUESTION 1—PART ONE: WHAT ARE YOUR TOP TWENTY-FIVE GOALS?

The first question is credited to Warren Buffett, one of the most successful businesspeople on earth, though Buffett himself has said it's not his! Whatever its origin, it offers us a great exercise. The question is a two-parter, and the time frame is the next ten to twenty-five years, but you're in charge of determining the time span you're working with.

TOOL: WARREN BUFFETT TOP 5 EXERCISE, PART ONE

Write down your top 25 goals for both your life and career.
These can be both personal and professional.

1.
2.
3.
4.
5.
6.
7.
8.
9.
10.
11.
12.
13.
14.
15.
16.
17.
18.
19.
20.
21.
22.
23.
24.
25.

The Decision Series™

RANDYH NELSON .COM

Take some time with this—an hour at least, preferably two, possibly more. Slow down and really think: What *are* your goals for the next ten to twenty-five years, or possibly the rest of your life?

Do you want to climb Mt. Everest?

Do you want to build a highly profitable $1 billion company that changes the world?

Do you want to spend more time with family and friends?

Or do you want to do something entirely different? Or perhaps some combination of these sorts of things?

Once you start thinking, many possibilities will come to you, including some that may surprise you. Tune out the distractions and let them flow. Try not to have something scheduled that will limit your time. This thought process may run long, and that's more than fine!

You may be thinking, "How on earth can I block off *two hours— or more*—for this?" If that's you, you probably already noticed, with skepticism, the ME Bridge list, where I'm inviting you to move from "thirty to sixty minutes quick" to "two hours focused." Let's deal with that "I don't have time" issue here and now.

To cross the ME Bridge, you *must* put "think time" into your calendar. While he was still heading up Microsoft, Bill Gates would take an entire week off, twice a year, and escape alone to a secret cabin in the Pacific Northwest. He called it his Think Week. Gates used the time to read papers that pitched him on new innovations or investments. We're told he spent up to eighteen hours a day reading these internal documents and information from other fields, related and unrelated to Microsoft.

No, I haven't just turned two hours of thinking into an entire Think Week. I'm just trying to show that time to think is valuable and valued by some very notable people.

As part of your ME *reset*, I want you to take a serious look at when and even how you think. Said another way, I want you to consider whether you're giving yourself a sufficient amount of focused time to think like an ME—or if you're still mired in the belief that you don't have time to do anything but think quickly, make your decisions, and move on.

A psychologist who's thought a lot about thinking has something to offer here. His name is Daniel Kahneman, and he's the author of *Thinking, Fast and Slow*, a best-selling book from a few years ago. The book is dense with information, but the takeaway is clear: there are two kinds of thinking, fast and slow, and they differ. Fast thinking, which Kahneman calls System 1, is unconscious, emotional, and instinctive. It results in snap judgments, even prejudice. In a business setting, it can lead to overconfidence and improper judgments regarding risk. This kind of thinking is very familiar to entrepreneurs. It's what gets us through a busy day. But slow thinking, System 2, takes longer (obviously), and because it's more logical, it takes more work. It weighs alternatives, considers data and metrics, and holds intuition at bay until the time's right for it. It's what gets us through a career.[50]

My point is this: you're going to find that to cross the ME Bridge, you need to learn to work differently by first thinking differently—that is, if you're going to become *maximized* **and** enjoy the journey getting and staying there.

---

50 Daniel Kahneman, *Thinking, Fast and Slow* (New York: Farrar, Straus, and Giroux, 2013).

One of my recommendations, along with putting think hours or days on your calendar for reflection and idea generation, is to up your game when it comes to the two-hour company-wide or divisional brainstorming session. If you're really wanting to pick the brains of those who work with and for you, then two hours is just a guideline. Why not keep the session open for as long as it stays productive? When you think it through as I do below, you see that (a) it takes more time than you think to get anything done, and (b) setting any length of time is arbitrary:

- Thirty minutes—you've hardly started. You're just checking the blocks and writing down answers, and not necessarily the right answers. You might say you finished in a half-hour's time, but how well did you finish?

- One hour—not enough time, especially if you've got another meeting after this one. Around the forty-five-minute mark, you and everyone else are starting to think about the next meeting instead of this one. Focus is lost. Great thoughts, answers, and decisions just don't happen.

- Two hours—the recommended time frame, especially if there's no firmly scheduled end point to distract from the tasks at hand.

- Four hours—scheduling this much time can work, but you've got to put breaks into the meeting and keep engagement levels high with various "change it up" techniques.

For entrepreneurial or CEO think time, my recommendations are more extravagant:

- **Two-hour private think time.** Sure, put it on the calendar for tasks that are somewhat targeted. You can also give it a go for the sort of thinking/prioritizing I suggested previously in part one of the Buffett exercise. I predict that one of your conclusions, however, will be that it's not enough time, even when the only thinker is you. Dispensing with distractions and steering your thoughts away from domestic tasks or intra-company drama gets a bit easier over time, but basically, two hours rarely proves to be sufficient for getting as deep and wide with your thinking as you need to.

- **Four-hour private think time.** Better, definitely. With my clients, I recommend starting out small. Calendar just one four-hour block of think time in a single month. And be like Bill Gates—pick a time and a place that's going to be yours for doing nothing but thinking. Trust me—once you prove to yourself that you can do this, you'll be wanting more. Soon, it will become a habit, especially if you've taken the time to figure out what time of day you think most productively. For me, the best thinking time is seven-thirty to eleven-thirty in the morning. When I'm starting to write a book chapter or handling some client-related issue, I'm up at six to get administrative work done and eat breakfast. By the time I'm pouring my first cup of coffee, my four-hour session begins. Like clockwork, I can feel my energy and focus start to wane as noon approaches, so that's when I end the session. I could keep going, but not nearly as productively. Beyond the four hours, I'm not making positive thinking progress; I'm just checking the blocks.

Before we go on, I challenge you to put your first four-hour block of think time on your calendar right now. Write here why this is a good time for you:

_____

_____

_____

Choosing your goals has been the main task for what we're calling the Buffett exercise. The habit we're trying to instill to get us there (and beyond) is setting aside dedicated "think time." I know that if you work to provide yourself thinking time and use it diligently and with focus, it will become an invaluable tool for making better-calculated decisions faster and with more confidence—which is definitely a worthy goal for each and every one of us.

If you're sure you've slowed down and focused sufficiently on your twenty-five goals, you're ready to move on to part two of the Buffett exercise's question 1. If you haven't, go back and finish the work. Don't move on until you're satisfied that you're done.

QUESTION 1—PART TWO: WHAT ARE YOUR TOP FIVE GOALS?

Okay, now that you have made the list of your top twenty-five goals, I would like you to take that list and break it down into your top five. This is where it gets a bit tougher, and I know this from personal experience. When I do this exercise, and I do it every year, I find that some of my answers go into the same "bucket" so I can combine them, because they're all similar in content. As an example, I might have multiple goals related to spending more quality time with family, but in the end, I write that goal as a certain number of days I will block off each year to accomplish all my family goals. Good luck as you begin homing in on your own top five!

TOOL: WARREN BUFFETT TOP 5 EXERCISE, PART TWO

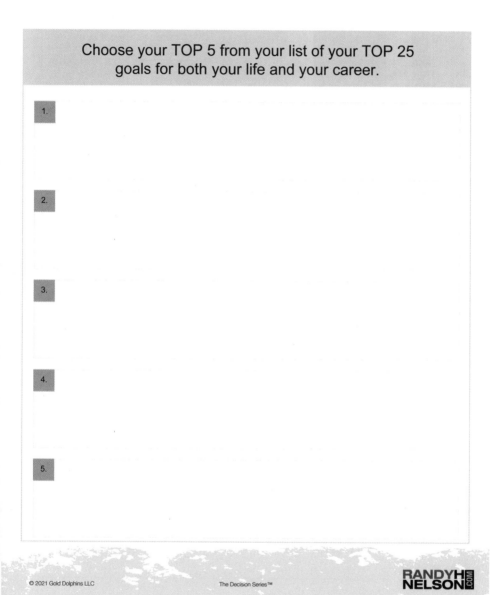

Choose your TOP 5 from your list of your TOP 25 goals for both your life and your career.

1.

2.

3.

4.

5.

The Decision Series™

RANDYH
NELSON

Thanks to your hard work of thinking and focusing, you've made good progress on the first two parts of question 1. Part three of that first question packs a surprise punch, and it's time to get to that now.

Look back on the twenty items that didn't make the cut for your top five. Nice goals, I'm sure, so it might seem a head-scratcher when you encounter what comes next. Those twenty items don't get relegated to some sort of secondary or "if I have time" list; no, they become your "avoid at all costs" list. The fact that they're perfectly fine goals is the reason you must set them aside. Don't let them distract you from achieving your top five!

Another one of Buffett's famous quotes supports this perhaps perplexing part of the exercise: "The difference between successful and really successful people is that really successful people say no to just about everything."

Sound familiar?

On to question 2 and a different time frame—ten years. You'll recognize the question from earlier in this book.

QUESTION 2—WHAT WOULD YOUR TEN-YEAR-OLDER VERSION OF YOURSELF TELL YOU TO START, STOP, AND KEEP DOING?

We're switching focus here. Question 1's three parts pertained to your long-term goals as a maximized entrepreneur. Now I'm asking you to look into your future and consider what advice your older self would give you regarding what you should be considering important at this phase of your life.

What would your decade-older self tell you to start doing?

_____

_____

_____

_____

_____

What would your decade-older self tell you to stop doing?

_____

_____

_____

_____

_____

What would your decade-older self tell you to keep doing?

_____

_____

_____

_____

_____

Now that we have some momentum, let's not lose it. Let's get right to question 3.

QUESTION 3—WHAT DOES SUCCESS LOOK LIKE IN YOUR LIFE AND YOUR ENTREPRENEURIAL CAREER THREE YEARS FROM TODAY?

Note the shorter time frame. We're only looking out three years now. Take the time necessary to answer with clarity and focus, because the effectiveness of your answers to question 4 depends on the work you have done in the first three questions.

_____

_____

_____

_____

_____

_____

_____

QUESTION 4—WHAT ARE YOUR NONNEGOTIABLES FOR THE NEXT TWELVE MONTHS?

In an earlier chapter, I introduced you to the N-MSC-T personal and business models, and in it the starting point was your nonnegotiables. Now in this chapter, I am going to give you an opportunity to *reset* your nonnegotiables, taking into account your answers to the three Buffett questions I just asked you, as well as a summary from *The Third Decision: The Intentional Entrepreneur* checklist below.

TOOL: INTENTIONAL ENTREPRENEUR CHECKLIST

	In what areas of my life am I creating or accepting alibis as they pertain to my happiness?	In what areas of my nonbusiness life am I feeling regrets, or forecasting regrets in the future?	Based on the alibis and the potential regrets, what nonnegotiables am I willing to commit to?
My educational achievement and skill building			
My career or current job description			
Love and marriage			
Family life			
Money			
Leisure and fun			
Friendship			
Physical health and fitness			
Mental health and well-being			
Spirituality and finding meaning			
Community involvement			
RESET			

The Decision Series™

As a reminder, the Intentional Entrepreneur Checklist outlines all the typical areas of regret that people have in their lives. So when you are answering question 4, you will be using your answers to the three questions posed previously, along with your overall thoughts on nonnegotiables, but with one significant adjustment: *instead of looking at your nonnegotiables strictly from the perspective of your personal life, we're now shifting to a* blended *perspective, taking into account both your business and your personal life.*

We have spent a great deal of time ensuring that you put focus to nonnegotiables in your personal life to minimize future regrets as you are building your business. But look back to the first question that I posed to you in this chapter: What are your top five life and career goals?

> *Instead of looking at your nonnego-tiables strictly from the perspective of your personal life, we're now shifting to a* blended *perspective, taking into account both your business and your personal life.*

Yes, all along in the Decision Series, we have spoken about work-life blending, and if all you focused on was your personal life nonnegotiables, you would be missing out on your business nonnegotiables. So the answer for nonnegotiables moving forward will be a blend between business and life.

To help you come up with this answer, I have combined the previous questions into the form below:

TOOL: NONNEGOTIABLE TOOL FOR ENTREPRENEURS

Warren Buffet Top 5 Goals List

1.
2.
3.
4.
5.

What would your *Ten-Year older version* of yourself tell you to start, stop and keep doing?

START	STOP	KEEP

What does success look like in your business and life three years from today?

Non-Negotiables (Blended Life) Next 12 Months

As you think about your decision on *reset*, I would be remiss not to highlight the certainty of future recessions in your ME career. They will happen, it is just a matter of when, and the history I have shown in the Entrepreneurial Life Stages will repeat itself.

TOOL: ENTREPRENEURIAL LIFE STAGES

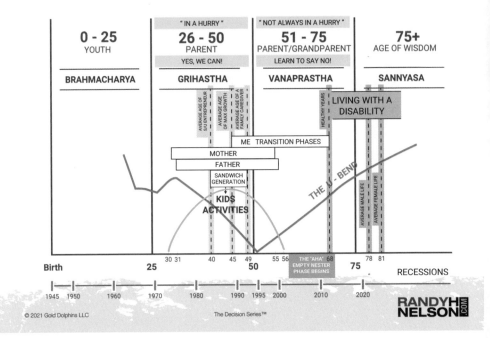

Personally, having started and led multiple businesses during recessions, I know that leading through difficult economic times is challenging, to say the least. The COVID-19 pandemic in 2020 was devastating for so many different reasons, but primarily because it affected the entire world's economy, and for a long period of time. Recessions highlight the absolute need for the entrepreneurial mindset, as all of us who have lived through them understand that we have choices, either to complain or to create. We choose to create, and to be resilient, albeit not without pain. In an *Entrepreneur* article from the early months of the pandemic, editor-in-chief Jason Feifer eloquently described us during the most difficult of times:[51]

> *Think of it: For entrepreneurs—all of us who work for ourselves in some capacity—this can feel like the moment we're least prepared for. Most entrepreneurs are underfunded, unsupported, and far too emotionally tied to our businesses to face it alone. But then I realized something. This is also the moment we're most prepared for—because we have always been self-directed and forced to survive by being resourceful. We can work from home with children dangling off our arms, in sweatpants, and find opportunity where others see none.*

- You know that failure is possible, but you're not a pessimist.

- You know that danger is lurking, but you're not risk averse.

- You know that the world is uncontrollable, but you'll control what you can.

- You know you have to lead, but you also have to serve.

- You know that you're a visionary, but that you also have limitations.

- You confidently say "I can do that" even when you have absolutely no idea how to do that. Doesn't matter! You know you can figure it out!

- Entrepreneurship has always required a little craziness, and a lot of contradictions. And now, during a global crisis, as our lives and businesses are upended, these contradictions are the things that will save us.

---

51 Jason Feifer, "Entrepreneurs Are Prepared for Crisis, Whether They Know It or Not," *Entrepreneur*, May 13, 2020, https://www.entrepreneur.com/article/350577.

So where do you want to be during the next recession? Ready for another round of that? As you consider your *reset*, consider that eventuality too.

As always, I hope I've given you a lot of ways to figure out what it is you want next. I firmly believe that the *reset* button is one of the greatest tools in your toolbox. For some, the exploration will reveal that what's really needed, at least for the near term, is more of a *rest* than a *reset*. But for others, all the arrows will be pointing to a clear next-phase entrepreneurial destination, and the best course of action is to push that *reset* button firmly and cross the ME Bridge. If that's you, good luck and safe travels! How you proceed is your route to map. Your advantage is your experience. Like any decade-long experience in life—be it business, love, marriage, raising kids, whatever—you'll be coming into your *"What's Next?!"* with a baseline from which to shape your plan in ways that are different, subtly or wildly, from what you've done before.

That baseline includes the strategic planning you should be doing annually, yielding your business goals. It also includes the new tools you've added to your decision-making repertoire, courtesy of the second half of this book. As of this chapter, you've completed the so-called Buffett question, along with two more questions, all spanning different time frames. You've also updated the nonnegotiables for your blended life.

If you now feel equipped to reach full potential as an ME and ensure that full potential also lies ahead for your business(es), and if you're confident of being able to savor the journey ahead, however you may shape it, that's great! If you're less than certain of either of these, might your first step be a period of *rest* instead of a *reset*? Or could you benefit from the help of a peer group or coach?

If you're feeling less than clear, I've got one more opportunity for you to drill down into what's important to you. Go back up to the ME Bridge list. Write down the items you identified as ones you want to take across the ME Bridge and get qualified in over the next twelve months. I've given you ten lines for ten bridge crossings—if you need more space, you may need to reconsider your choices and prioritize, because the aim here is to distill the list into one that's more useful in setting route goals for your *reset*. This new list, when considered in light of your updated list from the Nonnegotiables Decision Tool in this chapter, may not give you everything you need to know about your *reset* down to one-hundred-foot topographical detail. But it will show you where the trail leads and how you'll choose to get there.

Currently	Desire to Cross Yes/No	Audit Ready/ Qualified Yes/No	Next Twelve Months

I hope that both of your lists look different from how they would have ten years ago. As Muhammad Ali put it, in one of my favorite quotes: *"A man/woman who views the world the same at fifty as he did at twenty has wasted thirty years of his life."*

What's next?! Only you can know. What *I* know is that the *reset* button is a necessary exercise for anyone who's serious about finding out.

MEQC—What's Next?!

Learn. Think. Decide. Implement.

Initials

1. Complete the ME Bridge exercise and determine (1) in which tools you desire to be qualified, (2) in which tools you are already qualified at an audit-ready level, and (3) the career time frame in which you intend to get qualified. _____

2. Complete the Nonnegotiables Decision Tool exercise, including both parts of the Warren Buffett question, the start/stop/keep "What would your decade-older self advise?" question, and the question "What does success look like three years from now?" Repeat on an annual basis, or sooner if there are significant changes in your business and life. _____

3. Complete the Intentional Entrepreneur Checklist. Repeat on an annual basis, or sooner if significant changes occur in your business and life. _____

4. Decide on your blended nonnegotiables and reconsider them on an annual basis, or sooner if significant change dictates. _____

5. Determine what your *reset* button looks like, identifying the specific changes you will make to ensure you savor the ME journey that you have mapped out. Reconsider on an annual basis, or sooner if significant change dictates. _____

Signature: _____

Date: _____

CHAPTER 12

The Fourth Decision and the Clarity Leadership Decision System

*I have been impressed with the urgency of
doing. Knowing is not enough; we must apply.
Being willing is not enough; we must do.*

—LEONARDO DA VINCI

So you have made it to graduation day for the Decision Series books. You are now reading the last chapter of either a set of three books (the Second, Third, and Fourth Decisions) or the entire four-book series.

It has been my pleasure to lead you on your journey and evolution from a start-up entrepreneur to an ME. *The Fourth Decision* and all the books of the Decision Series apply a unique qualification process that helps entrepreneurs (and business leaders who think like them) to continually answer the question *"What's Next?!"* as they shift their mindset and make decisions that *transform the individual, qualify the team, and scale leadership across the organization.*

Like any new graduate, you're not really done. You've reached commencement, which is a new beginning. You are now equipped with the knowledge and tools necessary for you to move forward, and

I can imagine that you have a heightened sense of purpose with which to put your learnings to work. It is indeed a new beginning, and not just for you but for your entire organization!

You are now uniquely qualified for the role of *maximized* entrepreneur, and ready to move forward with your

- significant *successful* experience,

- energy,

- curiosity,

- self-knowledge,

- innate drive toward self-improvement,

- focus, which has widened beyond "entrepreneurship" to "entrepreneurial leadership,"

- bias toward creative discipline,

- sense of limits or preferred parameters, and

- commitment to continuing your entrepreneurial "calling."

You are also ready to commit to making the Fourth Decision. Here's how I presented this book's challenge to you, back when I first introduced it—with a little updating to reflect the work you've done:

*Maximized entrepreneurs are those who commit proactively to a career as an ME. They fully embrace their drive toward full potential, both for themselves and their companies, to achieve true entrepreneurial leadership. Through a new application of discipline in both your personal and professional lives, you, as ME, are now ready to continue your work to strategically **align** every axis of your entrepreneurial life.*

The Decision Series books have been built on the Five Pillars, now known as Challenges, throughout. I have consistently challenged you, and now the leaders in your organization, to do the following:

1. Grow your leadership skills as fast as your company (or companies or portfolio) is growing. Why?

   "The growth of a company is limited by the growth of its leaders."

2. Grow your self-awareness. Why?

   "The lack of self-awareness is the fatal flaw of a leader."

3. Double your personal capacity every two to three years. Why?

   "Always be qualifying for your next role, for what is coming next."

4. Become more intentional and set your nonnegotiables. Why?

   "To live a life with work-life blending as a focus, with no regrets and no alibis."

5. Grow your financial leadership skills, including your ability to plan for contingencies and crises, by mining for gold and diamonds. Why?

   "To help you make better-calculated decisions faster and with more confidence."

Remember, you get one life to live, and by adding these Five Challenges to your life, you can design the entrepreneurial career that you want to live and lead.

So it's time to gain some *clarity* on the key question of "What's next?!" In other words:

What's next to unlock and maximize your inner entrepreneurial leader ... to get you right ... first ... at every stage of your entrepreneurial career?

What's next to set your organization(s) up for reaching full potential?

What's next in terms of new applications of discipline, in both your personal and professional life?

It is my pleasure to introduce you to the **Clarity Leadership Decision System** (CLDS), a system/checklist you can implement and utilize to guide you in your pursuit of "What's next?!"

The CLDS is designed to

- guide entrepreneurs to embrace leadership and discipline through qualification, and
- guide leaders to embrace entrepreneurship and creativity through qualification.

The CLDS challenges the leader(s) to live and lead outside their comfort zone. It also challenges their existing mindset, to rethink their business growth / leadership development and work-life blending by slowing down first, and then speeding up, and always focusing on the question—"What's Next?!"

Our focus for the CLDS is on five areas, in alignment with the Five Challenges (formerly Pillars) of the Decision Series.

The Five Challenges

1. **Work-life blending**—This is about how to live a life with no regrets and no alibis while also growing your business to its full potential, by consistently setting and adjusting your nonnegotiables.

2. **Leadership development and qualification/self-awareness**—Three focus areas: the leader, the leadership team(s), and emerging leaders. The qualification system is unique, built around the successful military system of "qual cards." This system gets the company's leaders to "rethink delega-

tion"—by verifying that potential leaders are qualified, rather than simply promoting them.

3. **Baseline everything**—This includes financials, leadership assessments, the company, etc. By combining data and metrics with intuition and your "gut feel," the leader(s) can achieve one of the main goals of the Decision Series, which is to *make better-calcu-lated decisions faster and with more confidence.*

> This system gets the company's leaders to "rethink delegation"—by verifying that potential leaders are qualified, rather than simply promoting them.

4. **Decision-making organizational models**—Saying *yes* to every idea you have is entrepreneurial. Learning to say *no* to many of your ideas to instead focus on the right ideas is transformational. The CLDS guides you to say *no*, proactively, in both life and business as well as to set priorities that align to full-potential growth.

5. **Business growth/goals**—Core Values, Core Purpose, Baseline, BHAG, Three-Year Strategic Rocks, Annual Rocks, Quarterly Rocks, and daily/weekly/monthly focus. An important addition to this challenge for the ME is careful crisis and contingency planning. For your organization(s) to reach full potential, all planning and goal-setting must be tempered with the knowledge you've gained regarding how much can go wrong—and how quickly! This hope-for-the-best-but-plan-for-the-worst ethos is deeply embedded in the military. It's critical that we develop customized approaches

to this kind of thinking and make them foundational in our entrepreneurial company or companies.

You might notice on the Five Challenges list above that I have listed your business growth/goals last, behind other goals, and yes, this was on purpose. Throughout the Decision Series, we have spoken about leading and lagging indicators and knowing the difference between the two.

Leading indicators—you have influence over them, and they will predict the future.

Lagging indicators—they tell you what happened in the past.

Growing *maximized* businesses doesn't just happen. Prior to setting growth goals—much less celebrating achieving them—we need certain prerequisites in place. To be specific, we need numbers one through four in the Five Challenges list above. These are your leading indicators. The fifth, which includes everything on the Growth Pyramid, are all lagging indicators once they are set in place, except for the crisis/contingency planning part of it, and the leading activities you are involved with on a daily basis. Doubt me? Think you can do everything concurrently? Below are some thought experiments to illustrate the value of doing first things first:

- If you're lacking in establishing or updating your personal nonnegotiables, then you're likely to be setting yourself up for a busywork-focused entrepreneurial career. You might very well meet and even exceed your business growth goals, but at what personal cost?

- If you've aligned everything except what you do on a daily basis—leaving you to fight fires instead of focusing on the important activities that will lead you toward achieving your

Rocks—then, once again, you've set yourself up for an entrepreneurial life focused on busywork.

- If you don't establish your baselines, you will still make decisions throughout your career, but you also might regret the haste with which you made some of them, especially when you realize you could have slowed down to speed up, using both data/metrics and intuition/gut feel to make better decisions.

- If you set your business growth goals without developing the right leaders and qualifying them with the leadership development plans you've put in place, you'll definitely work harder, longer, and faster—but only to keep up with the pace of hiring, promoting, firing, and replacing ineffectual leaders.

- If you don't learn to say *no* to the wrong things, and *yes* only to the right things, both your personal and your professional life will remain too cluttered to allow for transformation—*maximization*—to occur. Reorganizing your musts, shoulds, and coulds is the key to jump-starting your work-life blending and powering your company's efforts to reach full potential.

To sum up, by simply setting aggressive growth goals and expecting everything else to fall into place (work-life blending, baselining, leadership development, and decision-making), *you will **lead** your competition in terms of your goals—but **lag** your competition when it comes to long-term results.*

"Slowing down to speed up"—it's just another way of talking about preparation, the kind any specialized individual in an elite environment builds into his or her program. Athletes can't guarantee that they're going to win every game, but they can focus each day on improving their skills and focusing on the right aspects of their technique. That puts them in a position to win when game day arrives, because they've done the work that's required to win. For an athlete, winning equals reaching full potential. They'd be the first to tell us that just wanting to win won't do it. Of course, it's no different for us as entrepreneurs: we don't grow the business just by saying we will. We grow by putting the building blocks in place to grow.

Are your building blocks in place—not just for growth, but for *maximizing* and reaching full potential? You don't know unless you're conducting the kind of annual checkup my Clarity Leadership Decision System calls for. It's designed to establish your mindset and engage it to consider all the various aspects of *"What's Next?!"*

Annual checkups are important, both personally and professionally. If you think back to *The Third Decision*, you'll recall that I encouraged you to prioritize your health, because that's the basis for everything else in life. We exercise and eat well. On an annual basis, we also should be visiting the doctor to figure out what's working and what's not. We do this with our car, and with our HVAC system, and we absolutely should be doing it with our mental and physical condition. In a busy life, it might seem selfish to make ourselves a priority in this way, but is it selfish to deal with a car that won't start or an AC unit that won't cool? Of course not. It should be no different for us or our companies—we need to know that something isn't working so we can do something about it. With the Clarity Leadership Decision System in place, you'll establish an annual checkup regimen. You'll take the measure of the leading indicators in your organization(s) and your lives.

Before you can begin working with the Five Challenges, however, you need to adopt an audit-ready mindset. Remember what that means? It's based on the financial world's three levels of compliance:

1. **The compilation**—The outside accountant converts the client's data into financial statements *without providing any assurances or auditing services.*

2. **The review**—*The accountant obtains limited assurance.*

3. **The audit**—An audited financial statement refers to a provider's financial statement *that has been taken to the highest level of detail and rigor.*

Audit-ready MEs get their annual checkups, proactively and eagerly. They're willing to face the truth, whatever that might be, *learning what they don't know they don't know,* and then moving forward with planning and determination. That's very different from the other two types. Those who lead by the compilation mindset never visit the doctor, uninterested in knowing more than what they know right now. And those with a review mindset will visit the doctor when they're sick and for some preventive

> Audit-ready MEs get their annual checkups, proactively and eagerly. They're willing to face the truth, whatever that might be, *learning what they don't know they don't know,* and then moving forward with planning and determination.

checkups, but they realize that there is another level for their checkups that they could rise to.

The degree to which a person (or organization) can grow is directly proportional to the amount of truth he/she can accept about themselves without running away.
— @IAMOLIVIACARLI

Now, let's start. Are you going to do this alone or assisted by others? Establish your accountability method or partner for your CLDS, checking one (or more) of the options you see below:

- Self-discipline _____

- Business partners _____

- Peer group _____

- Business coach / life coach / mentor / advisor _____

- Board of directors / board of advisors _____

- Other _____

Those of you who can form a duo or small team will more easily establish accountability for your checkup, but those who want or need to proceed solo will get plenty of guidance on what to address from the checklists coming up in this final chapter. The checklists help in two ways: First, I outline the annual checkup needs for your organization and for your various leadership positions, *starting with yourself,* and then proceeding to your leadership team and your emerging leaders' checkups. Second, I separate the tools by the five practice areas of the CLDS to make it easier to focus on one practice area at a time, if you choose to. In addition, the fully compiled MEQC, found in appendix A, which covers all the MEQCs throughout the book, is a useful component of your annual checkup.

Remember, everything starts with you, the entrepreneur. Just as you needed to become qualified to lead, you need to stay qualified to lead throughout your career. As you are a dedicated reader of the Decision Series books, I can assume that you deeply know this. And that means you understand that you have to keep earning people's respect. Where gaining knowledge and insight is concerned, they don't go first—you do. Before you ask anybody else to do an annual checkup, make sure you do yours.

It's your company, and your entrepreneurial life. As much as you want to succeed in business, you also want to live a life without regrets. So if you are committed to building a productive (not busy) company, one that will reach full potential, you will need to regularly assess your company's

> As you are a dedicated reader of the Decision Series books, I can assume that you deeply know this. And that means you understand that you have to keep earning people's respect. Where gaining knowledge and insight is concerned, they don't go first—you do. Before you ask anybody else to do an annual checkup, make sure you do yours.

current needs for leadership and seek out whose leadership will complement yours. That means looking for people who, like you, are aligned with the Five Challenges and feel tested by them. You may think there are other ways to create the work-life blend you imagine when you consider your *"What's Next?!"* But you'd be fooling yourself. The success of your qualified people determines the heights your company will reach. They also determine how much freedom you will have to continue living the entrepreneurial life you love in the evolving way you want to live it. And they take their cues, every one of them, from you.

> Once you've taken yourself through an annual checkup of the CLDS process, you'll know you're ready to move forward with your leaders' checkups. But get ready for some rigor—this isn't a base-touching exercise. It requires your full embrace of *accountability, discipline, and qualification.*

And once again, I am asking you to slow down to speed up in this chapter. As an entrepreneur, you need answers now. As an ME and a graduate of the Decision Series, this is an additional test—can you indeed embrace slowing down to get the building blocks of the chapter in place so that you can speed up at the end?

ACCOUNTABILITY
Know Thyself, Accept Thyself

It's critical to approach CLDS with a sense of true accountability to yourself and to others. This requires objective self-awareness, the kind you've been developing across the Decision Series books. The CLDS helps you continue learning how to balance your entrepreneur's intuition with a leader's objectivity so you can make informed decisions, confidently and quickly.

DISCIPLINE
Improve Thyself—First

From organization-building to setting your own nonnegotiable boundaries in life and work, living the entrepreneurial life you dream of requires a disciplined approach that starts at the top. The Clarity Leadership Decision System offers you another opportunity to hone your ability to say *no* to the things that don't serve your desired outcome, so you can focus your energy on the things that do.

QUALIFICATION

Accept Others, Complement Thyself

In order to know where you need to go, you must know where you are. Decide what kind of leader you are, then get clarity on whether you're in the right role. No matter which leadership role you choose for yourself, you must qualify yourself and others, full stop.

Which Role Is Yours?

The leader: *single company-focused entrepreneur, exited entrepreneur*

The role-player: *portfolio entrepreneur, intrapreneur, investor/angel and venture capitalist, consultant, coach, advisor, mentor, teacher*

The creator: *serial entrepreneur, start-up/buildup entrepreneur, habitual entrepreneur*

My hunch is that when my own creator role pushes me to write the last book in this series, "The First Decision," I'll find many of you right there with me, also launching another enterprise. That's because we can, and should, if the entrepreneurial fire inside still burns and the ideas still flow. But how can you know your "What's Next?!" if your annual checkup hasn't yet gotten you there? How can you complete that checkup without taking that initial step that you've learned to take with your own business and now need to apply to yourself?

It's crucial for each of us to establish our new baseline as the first part of any annual checkup. Then, and only then, can any of us do the same with our leadership team(s) and organization(s).

Transforming the Individual

Here now are the checklists for the various annual checkup components that are part of the CLDS. They tell you what to review.

Let me get ahead of a potential complaint here. Is this a long list? Yes, it's long and absolutely inclusive, because I don't want anybody accusing me of holding things back. It's all here. You can work through the list on your own, or if you need guidance, the Decision Center coaches stand ready to develop a process for and with you. Those of you who opt to do the work on your own have options—of course! You can follow the bullets to the letter or customize them to better suit where you are in your ME journey. What's more important than the precise detail of your review is that you truly "slow down to speed up"—that you give yourself and your organization time to conduct a review that isn't slap-dash but thorough.

A critical success factor will be this: Create a baseline for each area you review, so that you can compare your progress from checkup to checkup, with each new one establishing your current baseline. By looking back on previous checkups, you can decide *"What's Next?!"* to ensure continued improvement.

BASELINE—ENTREPRENEUR / TOP LEADER(S) CHECKUP: *WHAT'S NEXT?!* (ONE TO TWO DAYS)
Goal: Set a new baseline annually and review quarterly.

- Review Entrepreneurial Qual Card from *The Second Decision*, appendix B

- Review MEQC from *The Fourth Decision*

- Entrepreneurial Life Stages

- Lifeline/Timeline from *The Second Decision*, page 33

- ME Transition Phase(s)

- ME Bridge

- Nonnegotiables tool for entrepreneurs/leaders

- Warren Buffett exercise—top twenty-five / top five

- N-MSC-T tools

- Must/should/could tools

- Core Values / performance

- Mental Health Checklist from *The Third Decision*, chapter 11

- Intentional Entrepreneur Checklist from *The Third Decision*, page 17

- Family Life Survival Kit from *The Third Decision*, page 112

- Marriage to an Entrepreneur Survival Kit from *The Third Decision*, page 96

- Self-Awareness Decision Tool

- The Qual Card (present and future role)

- Leadership Quiz (Randyhnelson.com website)

- QE Notebook from *The Second Decision*, pages 252–254

- Qual-E-Gaged/Bore-E-Gaged mentalities from *The Fourth Decision* and *The Second Decision* chapter 12, respectively

- "The Elephant in the Room" exercise

- Definitions of Qualified, Intentional, and Maximized Entrepreneurs, *The Second Decision*, pages 2–3, *The Third Decision*, page 10

Qualify the Team and Scale Leadership

Before you are a leader, success is all about growing yourself.
—JACK WELCH

BASELINE—LEADERSHIP DEVELOPMENT PROGRESS CHECKUP—QUAL CARDS: *WHAT'S NEXT?!* (ONE TO TWO DAYS)
Goal: Set new baseline annually and review quarterly. Create new qual cards as often as necessary.

One of the critical differences between an entrepreneur and a successful and ultimately *maximized* entrepreneur is the focus on quality versus quantity. Said another way, it's not just the number of businesses you start; it is—or ought to be—the number of great businesses you build that also achieve their full potential *and assist employees in meeting theirs.*

A Qual-E-Gaged ME embraces the need to have qualified leaders in his or her organization, ones who can position the organization to reach its full potential. By making the effort to ensure that would-be leaders are qualified to move up, MEs provide them the opportunity to take on responsibility and, potentially, relieve themselves of burdens they're no longer interested in shouldering.

The trick to qualifying your leaders is identifying and establishing the right knowledge requirements for each qual card, then stepping back to let the process work as it was designed. Qual card in hand, each person getting qualified seeks out the experts necessary for attaining each of the knowledge requirements. It becomes their job to get that line on the qual card signed off. When all of the signoffs have occurred, you'll have a new leader who's earned the right to be considered *qualified*. They'll have earned their promotion instead of simply asking for it or having the seniority to get it.

There are four qual cards that every Qual-E-Gaged ME should be willing to introduce into their organizations, along with any customized qual cards the organization may require for its specific needs. The design of a customized qual card takes time and focus, but it's worth it—for no two organizations are alike, as follows:

1. **The CEO Qual Card**—Prior to replacing themselves or placing a CEO in charge of one of the companies they own, an ME ensures that any replacement will have proven himself or herself qualified to take over the day-to-day leadership of the organization, rather than simply assuming they can due to experience or tenure. As part of filling out the CEO Qual Card, the potential CEO successor should also fill out the EQC, which was developed for *The Second Decision*, and the complete MEQC, developed for *The Fourth Decision* (see appendix A).

2. **The Leadership Development Qual Card**—This qual card can be used for the top leadership, second-tier leaders, etc., in your organization. To scale properly, you need to build a cadre of qualified leaders in the company who can take on more responsibility when needed.

3. **The Emerging Leader Qual Card**—Any organization has high-potential employees, and the Emerging Leader Qual Card gives them the opportunity to proactively prove,

through their own initiative, that they not only want to take on more responsibility, but that they are willing to get qualified to do so.

4. **The Senior Leader Qual Card (Outside Hire)**—Outside hires fail, unfortunately. A lot. This qual card is necessary for the senior leaders you may hire from outside your organization. Many have all the experience and expertise you seek, but they are still newcomers to your culture and the entrepreneurial way you build and run your businesses. Ensure that they become qualified in your culture, and in the specific ways your organization works that may be different from there they came from, and you'll increase the long-term potential for great impact and success from these hires.

BASELINE—LEADERSHIP DEVELOPMENT PROJECTS "UNDER INSTRUCTION": *WHAT'S NEXT?!* (ONE TO TWO DAYS)

Goal: Set new project lists annually and review quarterly. Create new projects as often as necessary.

By implementing qual cards, the organization shows that it is "rethinking delegation" by qualifying people and verifying knowledge and skills rather than just promoting people. Part of any good effort in this regard should be creating "under instruction" time for upcoming leaders to work with leaders who are already qualified. This type of mentorship provides significant acceleration of growth opportunities for leaders who are deemed to be under development. *The Fourth Decision* offers a variety of areas for leadership development, listed below. Each is a possible topic for a project team to explore with leadership candidates:

- Audit-Ready Growth Pyramid

- Top reasons for great performance and underperformance

- Defendable Differentiators

- Truth and Trends

- Revenue Levers

- Three+ Business Models—Full Potential Growth Model

- Must/should/could

- Start/stop/keep

- Projects specific to your organization

_____

_____

_____

_____

_____

For each project, the accountable leader sets up the goals to include deliverables and timelines. As an example, consider the Audit-Ready Growth Pyramid Project:

- An audit should be completed annually. Establish the baseline percentages for each block of the pyramid, and, on a quarterly basis, review progress with your leadership team and establish the new percentages. A great time to do this is during your quarterly leadership offsites.

- The leadership team must commit to build the business with the audit-ready mindset and to be aware/wary of the busy mindset.

- The project should include giving responsibility to the members "under instruction" so that they gain invaluable leadership experience under the guidance of qualified leaders.

Another project would be to give a team the start/stop/keep survey to complete. It's as straightforward as it sounds: annually or quarterly, ask the question "What should we start, stop, and keep doing?" The critical success factor for this project is getting people to fully provide their input. It can be done at the company level, at the divisional level—any level that makes sense in your organization and where you're looking to get great ideas from your employees. In the end, the project team will be accountable for summarizing the ideas and recommending which ones to move forward by when. Have this project led by a leadership development candidate who is "under instruction," and when they do a great job, sign that line of their qual card!

The Decision Center Coaching Organization can assist with setting up any or all of the aspects of the CLDS. For more information on the Decision Center and its services, please read appendix B.

BASELINE—ANNUAL BUSINESS GROWTH CHECKUP: *WHAT'S NEXT?!* (THREE TO FIVE DAYS)

Goal: Establish the environment necessary for your organization to make better-calculated decisions faster and with more confidence.

For the overall business checkup, you should give yourself dedicated time to establish a new baseline around all of the components below. Yes, it's another long list, and my comment is the same as above—you can either do this work yourself, or you can seek help from the coaches at the Decision Center. But each of these touch points is important, so don't skip around. Just as you give yourself a week of vacation to pause and refresh, this series of exercises does the same for your organization. The critical success factor is slowing down long enough to do a thorough review of each bulleted item below. Your aim should be to achieve a level of comfort with your knowledge of what's really happening—the brutal facts, yes, but also a productive plan for moving forward:

- Compilation/review/audit baseline

- Audit—Growth Pyramid (review Busy Growth Pyramid)

- Audit—Full Potential Growth Model (review all growth models) and the gaps

- Audit—The "ands"

- Review of current operating systems to align for future collaboration—consider using the Vision and Execution Checklist from *The Second Decision*, page 72

- The Truth and Trends

- The Gold-Diamond Mine

- Top reasons for great performance/underperformance, *The Second Decision*, pages 250–252

- Core Values / Performance Tool

- Defendable Differentiation

- Leadership assessments

- Competition

- Revenue Lever Strategy Tool

- Customer Diamond Bridge

- Market penetration percentage

- Qual card tool

- N-MSC-T Business

- Must/should/could business

- Strengths/weaknesses/opportunities/threats/trends (SWOTT)

- QE Notebook, *The Second Decision*, pages 252–254

- The Diamond Review System

References and Tools

The remainder of the chapter is your reference section for the Clarity Leadership Decision System and the tools that go with each practice area. Think of this as your ongoing guide to utilizing the right tools at the right time to help you make your next most important decisions.

PRACTICE AREA 1 — WORK-LIFE BLENDING

How to live a life with no regrets and no alibis while also growing your business to full potential by setting your nonnegotiables.

Tools/PDFs

1. Entrepreneurial Life Stages PDF (Full Entrepreneurial Career)

2. Entrepreneurial Life Stages PDF (ages thirty-five to sixty-eight)

3. Lifeline/timeline from *The Second Decision*, page 33

4. ME exit and transition phase from *The Fourth Decision*, chapter 4

5. Intentional Entrepreneur Checklist from *The Third Decision*

6. Mental Health Checklist from *The Third Decision*, chapter 11

7. Marriage to an Entrepreneur Survival Kit, *The Third Decision*, page 96

8. Family Life Survival Kit, pages 112–113

9. Warren Buffett exercise—top twenty-five / top five from *The Fourth Decision*, chapter 11

10. Nonnegotiable Decision Tool from *The Fourth Decision*

11. N-MSC-T Business and Personal Tools from *The Fourth Decision*, chapter 9

TOOL: ENTREPRENEURIAL LIFE STAGES

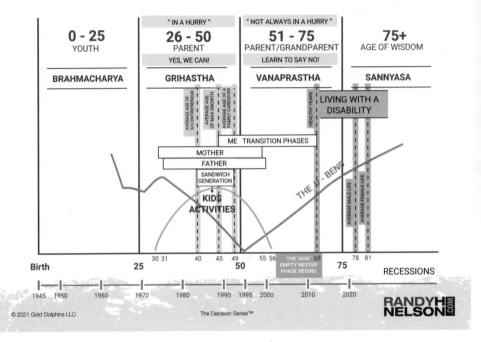

TOOL: ENTREPRENEURIAL LIFE STAGES

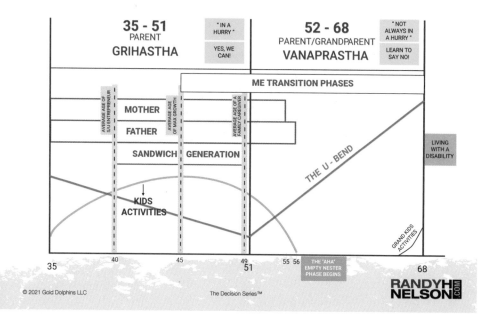

LIFELINE/TIMELINE FROM *THE SECOND DECISION*

BUSINESS TIMELINE/LIFELINE

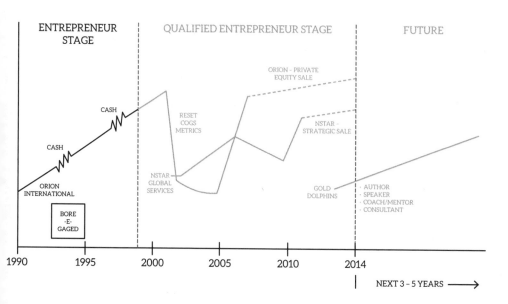

TOOL: ME EXIT AND TRANSITION PHASE™

(5 + 5 = 10)

SECTORS

PREP WORK	SALES PROCESS	INTRAPRENEURSHIP PHASE
Getting the business ready to sell	Target and Qualify potential buyers & select ultimate buyer	

Non - Entrepreneurial

→ Entrepreneurial

Intrapreneurial

- Define Owners Goals / Potential Exit Strategies

- Enhancing Value Prior to the Sale

- Compile all Information Required for Due Diligence and Complete the Purchase Process

- Employment Agreement

- Earnout

- Working for a Boss

- Choose Your Role
  • Leader
  • Role Player
  • Creator

- Work in Your Unique Strengths

- Find Your New Core Purpose

The Decision Series™

TOOL: INTENTIONAL ENTREPRENEUR CHECKLIST

	In what areas of my life am I creating or accepting alibis as they pertain to my happiness?	In what areas of my nonbusiness life am I feeling regrets, or forecasting regrets in the future?	Based on the alibis and the potential regrets, what nonnegotiables am I willing to commit to?
My educational achievement and skill building			
My career or current job description			
Love and marriage			
Family life			
Money			
Leisure and fun			
Friendship			
Physical health and fitness			
Mental health and well-being			
Spirituality and finding meaning			
Community involvement			
RESET			

The Decision Series™

TOOL: MENTAL HEALTH CHECKLIST

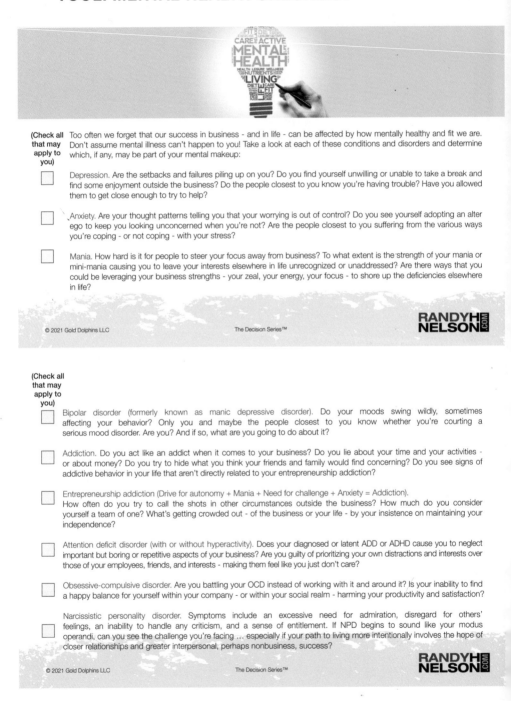

(Check all that may apply to you) Too often we forget that our success in business - and in life - can be affected by how mentally healthy and fit we are. Don't assume mental illness can't happen to you! Take a look at each of these conditions and disorders and determine which, if any, may be part of your mental makeup:

☐ Depression. Are the setbacks and failures piling up on you? Do you find yourself unwilling or unable to take a break and find some enjoyment outside the business? Do the people closest to you know you're having trouble? Have you allowed them to get close enough to try to help?

☐ Anxiety. Are your thought patterns telling you that your worrying is out of control? Do you see yourself adopting an alter ego to keep you looking unconcerned when you're not? Are the people closest to you suffering from the various ways you're coping - or not coping - with your stress?

☐ Mania. How hard is it for people to steer your focus away from business? To what extent is the strength of your mania or mini-mania causing you to leave your interests elsewhere in life unrecognized or unaddressed? Are there ways that you could be leveraging your business strengths - your zeal, your energy, your focus - to shore up the deficiencies elsewhere in life?

The Decision Series™   RANDYH NELSON

(Check all that may apply to you)

☐ Bipolar disorder (formerly known as manic depressive disorder). Do your moods swing wildly, sometimes affecting your behavior? Only you and maybe the people closest to you know whether you're courting a serious mood disorder. Are you? And if so, what are you going to do about it?

☐ Addiction. Do you act like an addict when it comes to your business? Do you lie about your time and your activities - or about money? Do you try to hide what you think your friends and family would find concerning? Do you see signs of addictive behavior in your life that aren't directly related to your entrepreneurship addiction?

☐ Entrepreneurship addiction (Drive for autonomy + Mania + Need for challenge + Anxiety = Addiction). How often do you try to call the shots in other circumstances outside the business? How much do you consider yourself a team of one? What's getting crowded out - of the business or your life - by your insistence on maintaining your independence?

☐ Attention deficit disorder (with or without hyperactivity). Does your diagnosed or latent ADD or ADHD cause you to neglect important but boring or repetitive aspects of your business? Are you guilty of prioritizing your own distractions and interests over those of your employees, friends, and interests - making them feel like you just don't care?

☐ Obsessive-compulsive disorder. Are you battling your OCD instead of working with it and around it? Is your inability to find a happy balance for yourself within your company - or within your social realm - harming your productivity and satisfaction?

☐ Narcissistic personality disorder. Symptoms include an excessive need for admiration, disregard for others' feelings, an inability to handle any criticism, and a sense of entitlement. If NPD begins to sound like your modus operandi, can you see the challenge you're facing … especially if your path to living more intentionally involves the hope of closer relationships and greater interpersonal, perhaps nonbusiness, success?

The Decision Series™   RANDYH NELSON

TOOL: MARRIAGE TO AN ENTREPRENEUR SURVIVAL KIT

My husband and I have the twenty-year badge. Yep, the coveted badge showing we made it through twenty years of start-ups, successes, failures, and paycheck roulette. The badge is not shiny; it is worn, tattered, and singed, more a well-earned badge of honor than a showpiece. But we got it. Here are some of the tools we both used along the way that helped us earn this elusive prize.
Kristi Nelson

1. Appreciation - Entrepreneurs, never ever, ever underestimate what your passion and obsession is costing your partner. People like you are driven by forces alien to the rest of us. You can be a difficult, preoccupied, emotionally distant partner.

2. Understanding - Make sure to occasionally attempt to put yourself in your partner's shoes. Try to get a sense of how it feels to always come in second to an unbeatable rival—the business.

3. Be realistic -A good partner in an entrepreneurial relationship or marriage is one who can enjoy a fairly full life on his or her own. Your laser-sharp focus on your business makes this a necessity for spousal survival. Embrace this. Expect your partner to look forward to the time you do get to spend together, but do not expect him or her to be ecstatic when your attention comes in the form of leftover crumbs that you dole out after your work has completely consumed the best of you. We deserve better

The Decision Series™

4. Watch your ego - A certain level of arrogance is necessary for the successful entrepreneur. Confidence in yourself is endemic for success. However, be mindful of how this plays out with your partner. Make it a habit to control how much you talk about work and yourself. Your partner loves to discuss your latest ideas, but he or she also desires a partner who brings more to the table than a passionate obsession for the business. Strive to make yourself an interesting person outside of your business—one who can hold a conversation that doesn't center on the company. There is a big world outside your company. Notice it.

5. Constant reflection - Entrepreneurial marriages fail. A lot. Listen to that inner voice of yours (and your partner's) for clues to when you are in a danger zone. Heed warnings. Give more. Take less. Many partners simply get tired of taking a back seat to your business. They move on to someone who is not so consumed and is therefore capable of the give-and-take necessary for a good partnership.

6. Join a group - Join one of the many entrepreneurial peer networking groups available. Spending time with like-minded people will help give you an outlet for your fantastic ideas (the ones your partner is tired of hearing about). You'll learn from your peers both professionally and personally, and you'll be held account able by them.

As my husband and I look forward to the next twenty years, both of us hope for the same thing: a life filled with passion, joy, and mutual respect. We will continue to rely on our "tools" to keep our relationship finely tuned. We both know that the ups and downs of an entrepreneurial marriage bring unique joys and challenges. But our marriage is worth the work.

> **Both of us know that a wildly successful business is no solace for a regretful soul.**

The Decision Series™

TOOL: FAMILY LIFE SURVIVAL KIT

My husband and I have the twenty-year badge. Yep, the coveted badge showing we made it through twenty years of start-ups, successes, failures, and paycheck roulette. The badge is not shiny; it is worn, tattered, and singed, more a well-earned badge of honor than a showpiece. But we got it. Here are some of the tools we both used along the way that helped us earn this elusive prize. **Kristi Nelson**

1. Enthusiasm and Belief - Knowing what Randy and I know now, neither one of us could have ever expected to survive the tumultuous, careening ride of our life together. Enthusiasm and belief in the vision is critical not just for the entrepreneur but for both partners. It sets a positive tone for the entire family.

2. Trust - Mutual trust is a necessity. I had to trust that my partner would, in some tiny corner of his churning, entrepreneurial brain, remember he had a family. And he had to trust that I would take care of the family when he didn't remember he had one. Saying family comes first is not the same as putting the family first.

The Decision Series™

3. Tolerance - Unceasing, chart-topping levels of tolerance. Let me share something … this journey never ends. As partner to an entrepreneur, you may think it will end at some point. You may think you can see the finish line, with the sale of the company, the hiring of a CFO, or the startup's wild success or crushing failure. But wait—as you get closer, you can see that it's not a finish line at all, but the starting line of a new race! You haven't completed that race at all, you've just unwittingly signed up for a new one! And this happens again … and again … and AGAIN.

4. Independence - You will be alone. A lot. Even if your partner is physically present, he or she will be mentally absent a good portion of the time. I have learned to deal with this. I don't like it all the time, but I accept it, and when the kids were still living at home, my acceptance helped them find theirs.

5. Directness - When my husband veered too far of course with respect to his work/life balance, I threw the warning flag. Yes, THE flag, and it was thrown not lightly, but with vigor. Sometimes I threw it with "I can't take any more of this shit" vigor. I let him know he was in a danger zone, that was affecting his marriage and family. It was my job to clearly let him know he had strayed into this zone. It was his job to fix it.

6. Pride in Your Partner - Over the many years of being married and building a family together, I have never ceased to admire Randy. I am always, always, proud of him. Even when I viewed his business as a challenging competitor for his time, I was proud of him.

> I let him know he was in a danger zone, that was affecting his marriage and family. It was my job to clearly let him know he had strayed into this zone. It was his job to fix it.

The Decision Series™

TOOL: WARREN BUFFETT EXERCISE

Write down your top 25 goals for both your life and career.
These can be both personal and professional.

1.
2.
3.
4.
5.
6.
7.
8.
9.
10.
11.
12.
13.
14.
15.
16.
17.
18.
19.
20.
21.
22.
23.
24.
25.

The Decision Series™

TOOL: WARREN BUFFETT EXERCISE

Choose your TOP 5 from your list of your TOP 25
goals for both your life and your career.

1.

2.

3.

4.

5.

The Decision Series™

TOOL: NONNEGOTIABLE TOOL
FOR ENTREPRENEURS

Warren Buffet Top 5 Goals List

1.
2.
3.
4.
5.

What would your *Ten-Year older version* of yourself tell you to start, stop and keep doing?

START	STOP	KEEP

What does success look like in your business and life three years from today?

Non-Negotiables (Blended Life) Next 12 Months

TOOL: N-MSC-T BUSINESS MODEL

Productive
Work/Life
Blending

NON - NEGOTIABLES (BLENDED LIFE)

- • • •
- • • •
- • • •

↓ ALIGNED

MUST DO (ROCKS) (YES!!)

1.
2.
3.
4.
5.

BUILDING ORGANIZATION VALUE

SHOULD DO (PULL) (MAYBE??)	COULD DO (PUSH) (NO!!)
• •	• •
• •	• •
• •	• •
• •	• •
• •	• •

BUILDING CUSTOMER VALUE

↑ ALIGNED

DAILY/WEEKLY/MONTHLY TO DO's

- • • • •
- • • • •
- • • • •

"Busy" Work Focus

The Decision Series™

TOOL: N-MSC-T PERSONAL LIFE MODEL

Productive
Work/life
Blending

NON - NEGOTIABLES (BLENDED LIFE)

- •
- •
- •

↓ ALIGNED

MUST DO (ROCKS) (YES!!)

1.
2.
3.
4.
5.

BUILDING ORGANIZATION VALUE

WHAT DO YOU NEED TO STOP DOING IN YOUR PERSONAL LIFE?	*WHAT DO YOU NEED TO SAY NO IN YOUR PERSONAL LIFE?*

WORK/LIFE BLENDING VALUE

↑ ALIGNED

DAILY/WEEKLY/MONTHLY TO DO's (LANES)

"Busy" Work Focus

The Decision Series™

RANDYH
NELSON

PRACTICE AREA 2—LEADERSHIP DEVELOPMENT AND QUALIFICATION/SELF-AWARENESS

Three focus areas: the leader, the leadership team, and emerging leaders. The qualification system is unique, built around the successful military system of "qual cards." This system gets the company leaders to "rethink delegation" by verifying that potential leaders are qualified, rather than simply promoting them.

Tools/PDFs

1. The Qual Card

2. The Qual Card Development Tool

3. The ME Bridge Tool

4. The Self-Awareness Decision Tool

5. Core Values / Performance Tool

6. The Five Challenges (formerly Pillars) of the Decision Series

7. Leadership Quiz (Randyhnelson.com website)

8. QE/IE/ME Definitions

TOOL: THE QUAL CARD

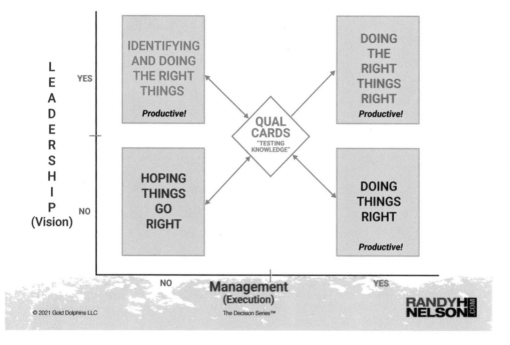

TOOL: "QUAL CARD" DEVELOPMENT

Company Name: _____

Division: _____

Job Title: _____

Step One – **Identify**
What qual cards do you need to create? Utilize the Self-Awareness Decision Tool (Qualify Others blocks) to help you decide!

1. _____

2. _____

3. _____

Step Two – **Develop**
List the general knowledge requirements for each qual card. Each knowledge requirement will be followed by a signature block and date. Develop an overall list of knowledge requirements. Be careful not to make the qual card so long and onerous that few will want to complete it. The next step allows you to ask more in-depth questions around the general knowledge requirements to ensure that the person has a strong grasp on each of them.

Step Three – **Verify**
This is another critical success factor for the qual card. The person who desires to get qualified must take the initiative to seek out the "expert" in each knowledge requirement and ask them for a "check-out". At this point the expert will ask questions to ensure that the person truly has the general knowledge required to get their qual card "signed off" for that specific line item on the qual card.

Step Four – **Qualify**
Once all the blocks of the qual card are completed, there will be a final oral interview by the leader/overall expert as a final check-out prior to signing off on the person being qualified. By being able to identify the knowledge requirements first, then verify that the person has a firm grasp of them, and then finally qualifying them, the qual card process will build speed and trust in the critically important delegation process necessary to grow organizations to reach their full potential.

TOOL: THE ME BRIDGE

Entrepreneur	Desire to Cross Yes/No		Audit-Ready/Qualified Yes/No	Maximized Entrepreneur
Saying Yes		ᴧᴧᴧᴧᴧᴧᴧ		...and Saying NO
Entrepreneur		ᴧᴧᴧᴧᴧᴧᴧ		and QE/IE/ME
In a hurry		ᴧᴧᴧᴧᴧᴧᴧ		or not always in a hurry?
Negotiables		ᴧᴧᴧᴧᴧᴧᴧ		and non-negotiables
Reactive decisions		ᴧᴧᴧᴧᴧᴧᴧ		or proactive decisions?
Do what you love to do		ᴧᴧᴧᴧᴧᴧᴧ		and love the people you work with
Self Confident		ᴧᴧᴧᴧᴧᴧᴧ		and ...ME Level Self-Awareness
Do everything		ᴧᴧᴧᴧᴧᴧᴧ		or Work in your genius/excellence?
Speed up		ᴧᴧᴧᴧᴧᴧᴧ		or learn to slow down to speed up?
Work long hours		ᴧᴧᴧᴧᴧᴧᴧ		and/or work smart hours
Work with brute force		ᴧᴧᴧᴧᴧᴧᴧ		or work with finesse/priorities?
Perfection		ᴧᴧᴧᴧᴧᴧᴧ		or Progress?
Quantity mindset		ᴧᴧᴧᴧᴧᴧᴧ		or quality and quantity mindset?
Bore-E-Gaged		ᴧᴧᴧᴧᴧᴧᴧ		or Qual-E-Gaged?
Successful		ᴧᴧᴧᴧᴧᴧᴧ		and Full-Potential
Growing the company		ᴧᴧᴧᴧᴧᴧᴧ		and taking more time truly off
Ego		ᴧᴧᴧᴧᴧᴧᴧ		and Humility
Little to no strategy		ᴧᴧᴧᴧᴧᴧᴧ		or Strategic rocks fully in place?

The Decision Series™

Entrepreneur	Desire to Cross Yes/No		Audit-Ready/Qualified Yes/No	Maximized Entrepreneur
Setbacks		ᴧᴧᴧᴧᴧᴧᴧ		and Learnings
Learning		ᴧᴧᴧᴧᴧᴧᴧ		or learning and implementing?
Want focus		ᴧᴧᴧᴧᴧᴧᴧ		and need focus
Delegate		ᴧᴧᴧᴧᴧᴧᴧ		and verify with qual cards
Push		ᴧᴧᴧᴧᴧᴧᴧ		and Pull mentalities
Checking blocks		ᴧᴧᴧᴧᴧᴧᴧ		or maximizing focus?
SC model		ᴧᴧᴧᴧᴧᴧᴧ		or N-MSC-T Model?
?????? Model		ᴧᴧᴧᴧᴧᴧᴧ		or Full-Potential Growth Model?
??????? Mindset		ᴧᴧᴧᴧᴧᴧᴧ		or Audit-Ready Mindset?
Work Hard		ᴧᴧᴧᴧᴧᴧᴧ		and Work different
30-60 minutes-quick		ᴧᴧᴧᴧᴧᴧᴧ		or 2 hours focused?
Risk		ᴧᴧᴧᴧᴧᴧᴧ		and/or Controlled risk
Know all the answers		ᴧᴧᴧᴧᴧᴧᴧ		or ask all the right questions?
Make all decisions		ᴧᴧᴧᴧᴧᴧᴧ		or develop qualified leaders?
Internal focus		ᴧᴧᴧᴧᴧᴧᴧ		and customer awareness
Rushed thinking		ᴧᴧᴧᴧᴧᴧᴧ		or think days/hours?

The Decision Series™

You have seen my list above; now add a customized section just for you, with the words that describe your trip across your own ME Bridge.

Currently	Desire to Cross Yes/No	Audit Ready/ Qualified Yes/No	Future Time Frame

TOOL: SELF-AWARENESS DECISIONS

NAME/DATE		Baseline - "The Truth and the Trends"		

		1	2	3
You have been fired	Your successor has been wildly successful over the past 12 months. What did they do that (1) you didn't want to do, (2) you didn't know what to do, and (3) you didn't know how to do it?			

Assessments/Date Completed		"The growth of a company is limited by the growth of its leaders" "Double your personal capacity in the next 12 months" "The fatal flaw of a leader is their lack of self-awareness"			
Culture Index					

Kolbe A		Fact Finder	Follow Through	Quick Start	Implementor

CliftonStrengths 34	1	2	3	4	5
Top 5 Strengths					
	30	31	32	33	34
Bottom 5 Strengths					

Self-Awareness (Top 3 in Each)		1	2	3
Know Thyself	**What** are your greatest strengths/ your areas of Genius/Excellence? *Don't include strengths that you are just competent at (Genius/Excellence/ Competence/Incompetence)*			
Accept Thyself	**What** are your greatest weaknesses - that if you don't improve upon or delegate to others - the company will underperform? *Which strengths are also weaknesses?*			
Improve Thyself	**What** specifically do you need to commit to improving in the next 12 months to double your personal capacity?			
Accept Others	**What** do you need to delegate in order to set the organization up to reach its full potential? *BY WHEN?*			
Qualify Others	**What** Qual Card (s) do you need to create in order to *delegate and verify?* *BY WHEN?*			
Comple- ment Thyself	**Who** do you need to complement yourself with so that the organization is set up to reach its full potential? *BY WHEN?*			

The Decision Series™

RANDYH NELSON.COM

TOOL: CORE VALUES / PERFORMANCE

TOOL: THE FIVE CHALLENGES (FORMERLY PILLARS) OF THE DECISION SERIES

1. **To grow your leadership skills as fast as your company (companies) (portolio) is growing. Why?**
"The growth of a company is limited by the growth of its leaders".

2. **To grow your self-awareness. Why?**
"The lack of self-awareness is the fatal flow of a leader".

3. **To double your personal capacity every two to three years. Why?**
"To always be qualifying for your next role...for what is coming next".

4. **To become more intentional and to set your non-negotables. Why?**
"To live a life with work/life blending as a focus, with no regrets and no alibis".

5. **To grow your financial leadership skills, mining for gold and diamonds. Why?**
"To help you make better, diamond level calculated decisions, faster and with more confidence".

TOOL: LEADERSHIP QUIZ

Located on the www.randyhnelson.com website.

TOOL: QE/IE/ME DEFINITIONS

Qualified Entrepreneur (QE)
- becomes fully self-aware that they don't know what they don't know, and that it's better to achieve a status of "I know what I don't know." This self-knowledge makes it clear how the entrepreneur's shortcomings may be affecting his/her company…and usually results in a commitment to a lifelong learning process.
- becomes fully self-aware that, for the business to succeed long term, a transition must occur from the business being about "me" as its entrepreneur/CEO to being about the overall needs of the company.
- commits to undertaking the preparation necessary for making the Second Decision. This is a conscious choice to acquire a more disciplined approach to management and leadership—or to bring that discipline to the company in another way. The QE knows that it's less important how his/her role is shaped for the next three years, than that the company excels and succeeds.

Intentional Entrepreneur (IE)
- becomes fully self-aware of the alibis they are using to justify the decisions they make in business and life.
- becomes fully self-aware of the areas of their nonbusiness life where future regrets may be forming.
- commits to undertaking the preparation necessary for making the Third Decision. This is a conscious, considered decision to set some non-negotiables in their nonbusiness lives for the next 12 months.

Maximized Entrepreneur (ME)
- becomes fully ready to embrace their drive towards full potential, for both themselves and their companies.
- becomes fully ready to achieve true entrepreneurial leadership with both strategic and tactical alignment—through a new or enhanced application of discipline, both in their professional and personal lives.
- commits to undertaking the preparation necessary for making The Fourth Decision. This is a conscious choice to proactively shift their mindset and actions for a lifetime career as an ME.

The Decision Series™

PRACTICE AREA 3—BASELINE EVERYTHING: FINANCIALS, LEADERSHIP ASSESSMENTS, THE COMPANY, ETC.

Goal: By combining data/metrics with intuition and "gut feel," the leader can make better-calculated decisions faster and with more confidence.

Tools/PDFs/Chapters

1. The Gold-Diamond Mine PDF

2. The Truth and Trends Tool

3. The Self-Awareness Decision Tool

4. Leadership assessments

5. Cash, *The Second Decision*, chapter 7

6. COGS, *The Second Decision*, chapter 8

7. *Reset, The Second Decision*, chapter 13

TOOL: THE GOLD-DIAMOND MINE

MAKE BETTER, CALCULATED DECISIONS FASTER, AND WITH MORE CONFIDENCE

TOOL: THE TRUTH AND THE TRENDS™

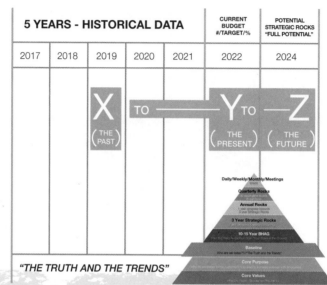

5 YEARS - HISTORICAL DATA					CURRENT BUDGET #/TARGET/%	POTENTIAL STRATEGIC ROCKS "FULL POTENTIAL"
2017	2018	2019	2020	2021	2022	2024

Make better, calculated decisions faster, and with more confidence.

X (THE PAST) TO ——— Y TO Z
(THE PRESENT) (THE FUTURE)

DATA
=
REVENUE
—
EXPENSES
—
METRICS
#'s/ %'s
—

Daily/Weekly/Monthly/Meetings
Quarterly Rocks
Annual Rocks
3 Year Strategic Rocks
10-15 Year BHAG
Baseline
Core Purpose
Core Values

"THE TRUTH AND THE TRENDS"

The Decision Series™

TOOL: SELF-AWARENESS DECISIONS

NAME/DATE	Baseline - "The Truth and the Trends"		

		1	2	3
You have been fired	Your successor has been wildly successful over the past 12 months. What did they do that (1) you didn't want to do, (2) you didn't know what to do, and (3) you didn't know how to do it?			

Assessments/Date Completed	"The growth of a company is limited by the growth of its leaders" "Double your personal capacity in the next 12 months" "The fatal flaw of a leader is their lack of self-awareness"			
Culture Index				

		Fact Finder	Follow Through	Quick Start	Implementor
Kolbe A					

CliftonStrengths 34	1	2	3	4	5
Top 5 Strengths					
	30	31	32	33	34
Bottom 5 Strengths					

Self-Awareness (Top 3 in Each)		1	2	3
Know Thyself	*What* are your greatest strengths/ your areas of Genius/Excellence? *Don't include strengths that you are just competent at (Genius/Excellence/ Competence/Incompetence)*			
Accept Thyself	*What* are your greatest weaknesses - that if you don't improve upon or delegate to others - the company will underperform? *Which strengths are also weaknesses?*			
Improve Thyself	*What* specifically do you need to commit to improving in the next 12 months to double your personal capacity?			
Accept Others	*What* do you need to delegate in order to set the organization up to reach its full potential? *BY WHEN?*			
Qualify Others	*What* Qual Card (s) do you need to create in order to *delegate and verify*? *BY WHEN?*			
Comple-ment Thyself	*Who* do you need to complement yourself with so that the organization is set up to reach its full potential? *BY WHEN?*			

TOOL: LEADERSHIP ASSESSMENTS

These will be customized for every organization.

READ THESE CHAPTERS IN
THE SECOND DECISION

Cash—Chapter 7
Cogs—Chapter 8
Reset—Chapter 13

PRACTICE AREA 4—DECISION-MAKING
ORGANIZATIONAL MODELS

Saying yes to every idea you have is entrepreneurial. Learning to say no to many of your ideas to focus on the right ideas is transformational. In fact, it is so important that I have added three new tools to this section for you: the Must Do, Should Do, and Could Do tools. The Should Do and Could Do can now be broken into three different sections— Vendor, Partner, and Strategic Partner. This ensures that all of your "pulls" are not treated the same. The Must Do adds a new section, where you need to decide, if you have too many must do's, to either delegate them to somebody else or to defer them to a later time frame.

> Saying yes to every idea you have is entrepreneurial. Learning to say no to many of your ideas to focus on the right ideas is transformational.

Goal: Use the CLDS to ensure that you'll say no proactively, both in life and business, and set priorities that align with achieving full-potential growth.

Tools/PDFs

1. N-MSC-T—Business Model Tool

2. N-MSC-T—Personal Model Tool

3. Must Do—new tool—Vendor/Partner/Strategic Partner

4. Should Do—new tool—Vendor/Partner/Strategic Partner

5. Could Do—new tool—Vendor/Partner/Strategic Partner

6. Self-Awareness Decision Tool

TOOL: N-MSC-T BUSINESS MODEL

Productive Work/Life Blending

NON - NEGOTIABLES (BLENDED LIFE)

-
-
-

ALIGNED

MUST DO (ROCKS) (YES!!)

1.
2.
3.
4.
5.

BUILDING ORGANIZATION VALUE

SHOULD DO (PULL) (MAYBE??)

-
-
-
-
-

BUILDING CUSTOMER VALUE

COULD DO (PUSH) (NO!!)

-
-
-
-
-

ALIGNED

DAILY/WEEKLY/MONTHLY TO DO's

-
-
-

"Busy" Work Focus

TOOL: N-MSC-T PERSONAL LIFE MODEL

Productive
Work/life
Blending

NON - NEGOTIABLES (BLENDED LIFE)

- •
- •
- •

- •
- •
- •

- •
- •
- •

↓ ALIGNED

MUST DO (ROCKS) (YES!!)

1.
2.
3.
4.
5.

BUILDING ORGANIZATION VALUE

WHAT DO YOU NEED TO *STOP DOING* IN YOUR PERSONAL LIFE?	WHAT DO YOU NEED TO SAY NO IN YOUR PERSONAL LIFE?
• • • • • • • • • •	• • • • • • • • • •

WORK/LIFE BLENDING VALUE

↑ ALIGNED

DAILY/WEEKLY/MONTHLY TO DO's (LANES)

- •
- •
- •

- •
- •
- •

- •
- •
- •

- •
- •
- •

"Busy" Work Focus

RANDYH
NELSON

TOOL: MUST DO—ROCKS

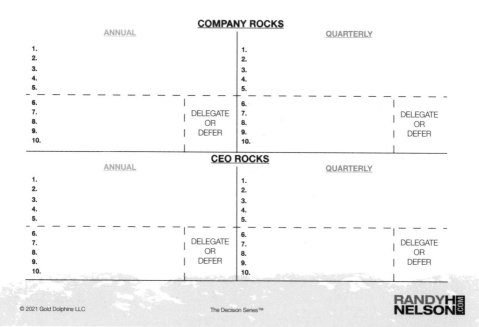

COMPANY ROCKS

ANNUAL			QUARTERLY	
1.		1.		
2.		2.		
3.		3.		
4.		4.		
5.		5.		
6.		6.		
7.	DELEGATE	7.	DELEGATE	
8.	OR	8.	OR	
9.	DEFER	9.	DEFER	
10.		10.		

CEO ROCKS

ANNUAL			QUARTERLY	
1.		1.		
2.		2.		
3.		3.		
4.		4.		
5.		5.		
6.		6.		
7.	DELEGATE	7.	DELEGATE	
8.	OR	8.	OR	
9.	DEFER	9.	DEFER	
10.		10.		

The Decision Series™   RANDYH NELSON.COM

TOOL: SHOULD DO—PULL

STRATEGIC PARTNER

1.
2.
3.
4.
5.

PARTNER

1.
2.
3.
4.
5.

VENDOR

1.
2.
3.
4.
5.

"THE GREATEST INEQUITY IS THE EQUAL TREATMENT OF UNEQUALS"

The Decision Series™   RANDYH NELSON.COM

TOOL: COULD DO—PUSH

STRATEGIC PARTNER

1.
2.
3.
4.
5.

PARTNER	VENDOR
1.	1.
2.	2.
3.	3.
4.	4.
5.	5.

"THE GREATEST INEQUITY IS THE EQUAL TREATMENT OF UNEQUALS"

The Decision Series™

TOOL: SELF-AWARENESS DECISIONS

NAME/DATE	Baseline - "The Truth and the Trends"		
	1	**2**	**3**
You have been fired — Your successor has been wildly successful over the past 12 months. What did they do that (1) you didn't want to do, (2) you didn't know what to do, and (3) you didn't know how to do it?			

Assessments/Date Completed

"The growth of a company is limited by the growth of its leaders"
"Double your personal capacity in the next 12 months"
"The fatal flaw of a leader is their lack of self-awareness"

Culture Index				
	Fact Finder	Follow Through	Quick Start	Implementor
Kolbe A				

CliftonStrengths 34	1	2	3	4	5
Top 5 Strengths					
	30	31	32	33	34
Bottom 5 Strengths					

Self-Awareness (Top 3 in Each)	1	2	3
Know Thyself — *What* are your greatest strengths/ your areas of Genius/Excellence? *Don't include strengths that you are just competent at (Genius/Excellence/ Competence/Incompetence)*			
Accept Thyself — *What* are your greatest weaknesses - that if you don't improve upon or delegate to others - the company will underperform? *Which strengths are also weaknesses?*			
Improve Thyself — *What* specifically do you need to commit to improving in the next 12 months to double your personal capacity?			
Accept Others — *What* do you need to delegate in order to set the organization up to reach its full potential? *BY WHEN?*			
Qualify Others — *What* Qual Card (s) do you need to create in order to *delegate and verify?* *BY WHEN?*			
Complement Thyself — *Who* do you need to complement yourself with so that the organization is set up to reach its full potential? *BY WHEN?*			

© 2021 Gold Dolphins LLC

The Decision Series™

RANDYH NELSON.COM

PRACTICE AREA 5—BUSINESS GROWTH/GOALS

Core Values, Core Purpose, Baseline, BHAG, Three-Year Strategic Rocks, Annual Rocks, Quarterly Rocks, Daily/Weekly/Monthly focus.

Goal: The aim here is to place financial and strategic goal-setting in its proper place—after other forms of baselining have occurred.

Tools/PDFs

1. Top Reasons for Great Performance Audit Tool

2. Top Reasons for Underperformance Audit Tool

3. The Productive Growth Pyramid Audit Tool

4. The Busy Growth Pyramid

5. The Full Potential Growth Model PDF

6. The Numbers Growth Model

7. The Undisciplined Entrepreneurial Growth Model

8. The Subjective Strategy Growth Model

9. The Revenue Lever Strategy Tool

10. The Customer Diamond Bridge PDF

11. The Entrepreneurial Qual Card from *The Second Decision*, appendix B

12. The *Maximized* Entrepreneurial Qual Card (see appendix A)

13. Vision and Execution Checklist from *The Second Decision*, page 72

14. Greiner Curve from *The Second Decision*

TOOL: TOP REASONS FOR GREAT PERFORMANCE AUDIT

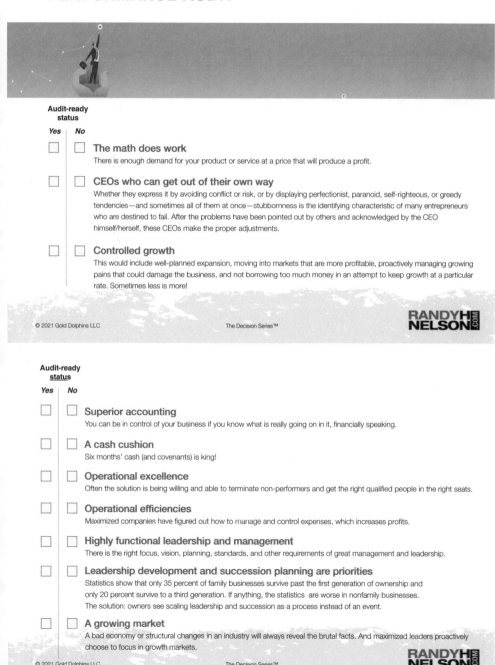

Audit-ready status

Yes | No

☐ | ☐ **The math does work**
There is enough demand for your product or service at a price that will produce a profit.

☐ | ☐ **CEOs who can get out of their own way**
Whether they express it by avoiding conflict or risk, or by displaying perfectionist, paranoid, self-righteous, or greedy tendencies—and sometimes all of them at once—stubbornness is the identifying characteristic of many entrepreneurs who are destined to fail. After the problems have been pointed out by others and acknowledged by the CEO himself/herself, these CEOs make the proper adjustments.

☐ | ☐ **Controlled growth**
This would include well-planned expansion, moving into markets that are more profitable, proactively managing growing pains that could damage the business, and not borrowing too much money in an attempt to keep growth at a particular rate. Sometimes less is more!

   The Decision Series™   RANDYH NELSON.COM

Audit-ready status

Yes | No

☐ | ☐ **Superior accounting**
You can be in control of your business if you know what is really going on in it, financially speaking.

☐ | ☐ **A cash cushion**
Six months' cash (and covenants) is king!

☐ | ☐ **Operational excellence**
Often the solution is being willing and able to terminate non-performers and get the right qualified people in the right seats.

☐ | ☐ **Operational efficiencies**
Maximized companies have figured out how to manage and control expenses, which increases profits.

☐ | ☐ **Highly functional leadership and management**
There is the right focus, vision, planning, standards, and other requirements of great management and leadership.

☐ | ☐ **Leadership development and succession planning are priorities**
Statistics show that only 35 percent of family businesses survive past the first generation of ownership and only 20 percent survive to a third generation. If anything, the statistics are worse in nonfamily businesses. The solution: owners see scaling leadership and succession as a process instead of an event.

☐ | ☐ **A growing market**
A bad economy or structural changes in an industry will always reveal the brutal facts. And maximized leaders proactively choose to focus in growth markets.

   The Decision Series™   RANDYH NELSON.COM

TOOL: TOP REASONS FOR UNDERPERFORMANCE AUDIT

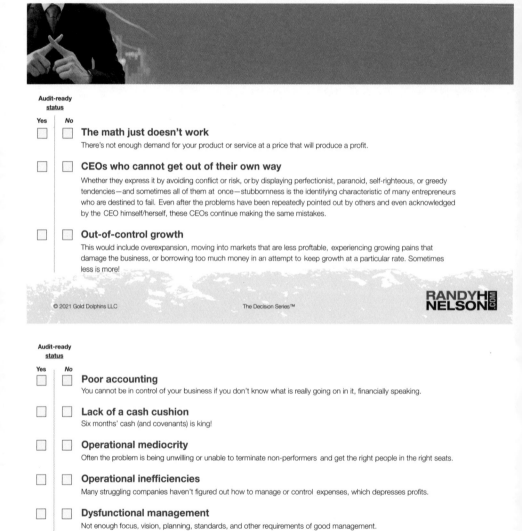

Audit-ready status

Yes	No	

The math just doesn't work

There's not enough demand for your product or service at a price that will produce a profit.

CEOs who cannot get out of their own way

Whether they express it by avoiding conflict or risk, or by displaying perfectionist, paranoid, self-righteous, or greedy tendencies—and sometimes all of them at once—stubbornness is the identifying characteristic of many entrepreneurs who are destined to fail. Even after the problems have been repeatedly pointed out by others and even acknowledged by the CEO himself/herself, these CEOs continue making the same mistakes.

Out-of-control growth

This would include overexpansion, moving into markets that are less profitable, experiencing growing pains that damage the business, or borrowing too much money in an attempt to keep growth at a particular rate. Sometimes less is more!

The Decision Series™

Audit-ready status

Poor accounting

You cannot be in control of your business if you don't know what is really going on in it, financially speaking.

Lack of a cash cushion

Six months' cash (and covenants) is king!

Operational mediocrity

Often the problem is being unwilling or unable to terminate non-performers and get the right people in the right seats.

Operational inefficiencies

Many struggling companies haven't figured out how to manage or control expenses, which depresses profits.

Dysfunctional management

Not enough focus, vision, planning, standards, and other requirements of good management.

The lack of a succession plan

Statistics show that only 35 percent of family businesses survive past the first generation of ownership and only 20 percent survive to a third generation. If anything, the statistics are worse in nonfamily businesses. Part of the problem: owners see succession as an event instead of a process.

A declining market

A bad economy or structural changes in an industry will always reveal managerial skill - or lack of it.

The Decision Series™

TOOL: THE PRODUCTIVE GROWTH PYRAMID

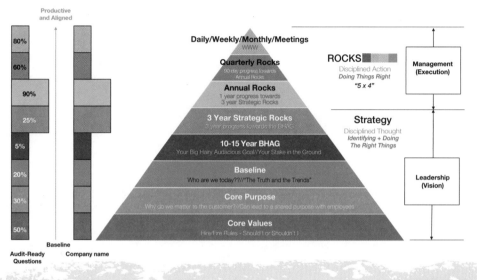

TOOL: THE BUSY GROWTH PYRAMID

TOOL: THE FULL POTENTIAL GROWTH MODEL

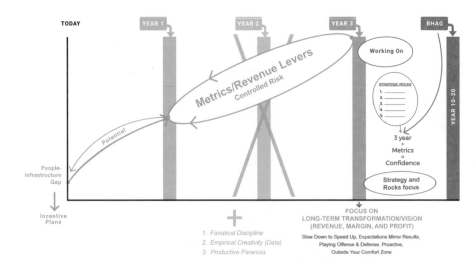

TOOL: THE NUMBERS GROWTH MODEL

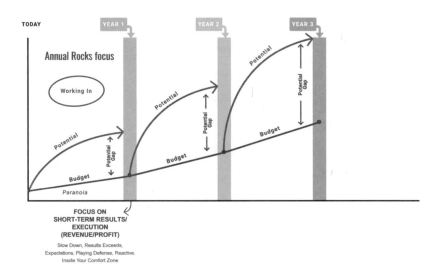

TOOL: THE UNDISCIPLINED ENTREPRENEURIAL GROWTH MODEL

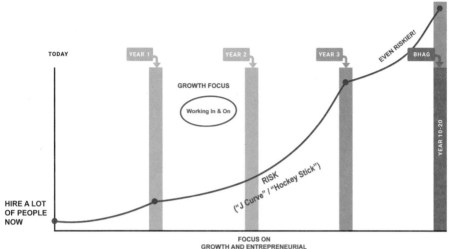

THE SUBJECTIVE STRATEGY GROWTH MODEL

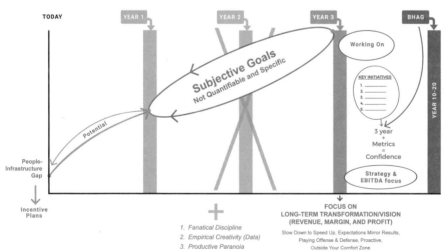

TOOL: THE REVENUE LEVER STRATEGY

THE TRUTH AND THE TRENDS	CURRENT BUDGET	REVENUE LEVER EXERCISE	STRATEGIC ROCKS
"Who are we Today"	*Set X ──→Y Growth Goal*	*"Where should we be in Three Years"*	*"Where will we be in Three Years"*
Baseline All of Your Levers	Review Actions Vs. Goal Monthly	Develop Full - Potential Growth of Each Lever... With 100% Focus	Select Levers that will be your Strategic Rocks... your "Stakes in the Ground"

$$X \longrightarrow Y \longrightarrow Z$$

Make Better, Calculated Decisions Faster, and with more Confidence

The Decision Series™

TOOL: THE CUSTOMER DIAMOND BRIDGE

Know Thy Customer - Complement Thy Customer - Improve Thy Customer

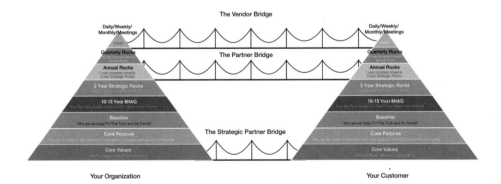

The Decision Series™

456

THE ENTREPRENEURIAL QUAL CARD FROM *THE SECOND DECISION*, APPENDIX B

The Entrepreneurial Qual Card in appendix B of *The Second Decision*.

THE *MAXIMIZED* ENTREPRENEURIAL QUAL CARD (SEE APPENDIX A)

TOOL: VISION AND EXECUTION CHECKLIST FROM *THE SECOND DECISION*, PAGE 72

Audit ready status (Check the one that applies)	CEO Plan	CEO Value (And Why?)	Performance Rating	Where Are You?	Next Grading Period - Board of Directors (BOD)	Employee Response
☐	Three-year/ One-year and Quarterly plan	Discplined Thought and Action	A	2 steps ahead- *The Full-Potential Model*	Promote	Excited/ passionate
☐	Specific One-year/ Quarterly plan	Disciplined Action	B	1 step ahead – *The Numbers Model*	Train and promote	"I'm in, but I want to see more."
☐	General One-Year/ Quarterly plan	CEO is sitting in his/her comfort zone	C	On the same step -*The Subjective Strategy Model or Entrepreneurial Model*	Train	On the bubble
☐	A quarterly plan is all we can manage."	"I'm too busy!"	D	1 step behind	Counsel— train	"Why am I listening to you?"
☐	Today's plan may or may not be in place	Banking on hope and hope alone.	F	2 steps behind	Progressive discipline	Active on the Job Boards this afternoon

The Decision Series™

GREINER CURVE FROM *THE SECOND DECISION*

All kinds of organizations—from design shops to manufacturers, construction companies to professional service firms—experience these. Each growth phase is made up of a period of relatively stable growth, followed by a "crisis" when major organizational change is needed if the company is to continue growing. Picture the phase that your organization is in, and use that position to guide you in your self-assessment moving forward. The Greiner Curve, developed by Larry E. Greiner, allows you to see what is coming next for you as its leader, but realize that each company may go through the stages differently.

PHASE 1

GROWTH THROUGH CREATIVITY

Here, the entrepreneurs who founded the firm are busy creating products and opening up markets. There aren't many staff, so informal communication works fine, and rewards for long hours are probably through profit share or stock options. However, as more staff join, production expands and capital is injected, there's a need for more formal communication.

*This phase ends with a **Leadership Crisis**, where professional management is needed. The founders may change their style and take on this role, but often someone new will be brought in.*

PHASE 2

GROWTH THROUGH DIRECTION

Growth continues in an environment of more formal communications, budgets and focus on separate activities like marketing and production. Incentive schemes replace stock as a financial reward.

However, there comes a point when the products and processes become so numerous that there are not enough hours in the day for one person to manage them all, and he or she can't possibly know as much about all these products or services as those lower down the hierarchy.

*This phase ends with **Autonomy Crisis**: New structures based on delegation are called for.*

PHASE 3

GROWTH THROUGH DIRECTION

With mid-level managers freed up to react fast to opportunities for new products or in new markets, the organization continues to grow, with top management just monitoring and dealing with the big issues (perhaps starting to look at merger or acquisition opportunities). Many businesses flounder at this stage, as the manager whose directive approach solved the problems at the end of Phase 1 finds it hard to let go, yet the mid-level managers struggle with their new roles as leaders.

*This phase ends with a **Control Crisis**: A much more sophisticated head office function is required, and the separate parts of the business need to work together.*

PHASE 4

GROWTH THROUGH COORDINATION AND MONITORING

Growth continues with the previously isolated business units re-organized into product groups or service practices. Investment finance is allocated centrally and managed according to Return on Investment (ROI) and not just profits. Incentives are shared through company-wide profit share schemes aligned to corporate goals. Eventually, though, work becomes submerged under increasing amounts of bureaucracy, and growth may become stifled.

*This phase ends on a **Red-Tape Crisis**: A new culture and structure must be introduced.*

PHASE 5

GROWTH THROUGH COLLABORATION

The formal controls of phases 2-4 are replaced by professional good sense as staff group and re-group flexibly in teams to deliver projects in a matrix structure supported by sophisticated information systems and team-based financial rewards.

*This phase ends with a crisis of **Internal Growth**: Further growth can only come by developing partnerships with complementary organizations.*

PHASE 6

GROWTH THROUGH EXTRA-ORGANIZATIONAL SOLUTIONS

Greiner's recently added sixth phase suggests that growth may continue through merger, outsourcing, networks and other solutions involving other companies.

Growth rates will vary between and even within phases. The duration of each phase depends almost totally on the rate of growth of the market in which the organization operates. The longer a phase lasts, though, the harder it will be to implement a transition.

The Decision Series™

You now have everything you need—from across the chapters of this book as well as from the other two books in the Decision Series—to self-qualify as a *maximized* entrepreneur. Having begun your reading here as a highly successful and experienced business builder and life blender, you have now done the work necessary to bring to life the action word for this Fourth Decision experience: "**align**." You've aligned (or realigned) everything that makes your entrepreneurial life so rewarding and fulfilling. This includes your role selection going forward, your choices regarding a potential exit, your resolve to see your company or companies reach full potential, and your desire to create and establish new entrepreneurial leaders within your organization(s). Most of all, you have undertaken this with a determination to align everything with the personal life intentions you've set, evaluated, and set again.

Yes, this is a graduation—but only in terms of a commencement, a new beginning. Celebrate! Then move forward to consider your own, individualized "What's Next?!"

> Having begun your reading here as a highly successful and experienced business builder and life blender, you have now done the work necessary to bring to life the action word for this Fourth Decision experience: "**align**." You've aligned (or realigned) everything that makes your entrepreneurial life so rewarding and fulfilling.

Let's allow Sir Edmund Hillary, the first person to summit Mt. Everest, to have the last word:

"It's not the mountain we conquer, but ourselves."

Well said, Sir Edmund!

I wish you the very best in your ME journeys.

Randy

The Maximized Entrepreneurial Qual Card—What's Next?!

Learn. Think. Decide. Implement.

Initials

Review the maximized entrepreneur's qualifications list and put a check mark next to all that apply to your career.

- Significant *successful* experience   _____

- Energy   _____

- Curiosity   _____

- Self-knowledge   _____

- An innate drive toward self-improvement

- A focus widened beyond "entrepreneur" and toward "entrepreneurial leadership"   _____

- A bias toward creative discipline   _____

- A sense of limits or preferred parameters   _____

- A commitment to an entrepreneurial "calling" (Introduction)   _____

Commit to making the Fourth Decision, adopting a mindset that allows you to begin thinking ahead to the next five to twenty-five years. *Maximized* entrepreneurs learn to continually evaluate the gap between their current skills and their full potential, and then develop the forward-going techniques necessary to hold themselves accountable for closing the gap. (Introduction)

_____

Commit to moving forward as an ME, ready to learn new ways of combining entrepreneurial leadership and discipline. (Introduction)

_____

Commit to the Five Challenges (Pillars) of the Decision Series—growing your self-awareness, growing your leadership skills, doubling your personal capacity, setting or resetting your nonnegotiables, and enhancing your financial leadership skills. (Introduction)

_____

The ME commits to growing his or her self-awareness by taking at least three assessments, such as Kolbe A, CliftonStrengths Finder, Culture Index, Enneagram, Leadership Circle, DiSC, Myers-Briggs, and PRF. In order to be qualified, the assessments have to be reviewed by a professional who is trained in the assessment, and then the ME reviews the results with a coach, a peer group, etc. (Chapter 1)

_____

The ME defines and explains the ME Equation, detailing how full potential is reached through all the different components of the equation. (Chapter 1)

_____

The ME completes the Self-Awareness Decision
Tool, filling out all blocks completely—repeating
this on at least an annual basis, and explaining
in detail the answers to all blocks in the tool.
(Chapter 1)

_____

The ME commits to doubling his or her personal
capacity every two to three years. This "improve
thyself" task should be undertaken only after
completing the baselining in number 1 and
number 3 of this chapter's qual card and reaching
the strengths and weaknesses awareness that is
required to "accept thyself." (Chapter 1)

_____

The ME commits to the Unconscious Competence level as the standard for the remainder of
his or her ME career, both for himself/herself and
for the organization. (Chapter 1)

_____

The ME reads or rereads their notes from *The
Second Decision* and *The Third Decision* books,
prior to moving on in this book, to get maximum
value from *The Fourth Decision*. The ME
discusses in depth *The Second Decision* and *The
Third Decision* notes during the checkout—with a
coach, peer group, etc. (Chapter 1)

_____

The ME commits to and can fully explain the
"*and*" philosophy, giving at least ten examples of
how the "*and*" applies in his or her entrepreneurial
career. (Chapter 1)

_____

Explain the differences between fluid and crystallized intelligence, applying it in a practical way to your entrepreneurial career between ages thirty-five and fifty-one and fifty-one and sixty-eight. (Chapter 2)

_____

Explain the four Hindu stages of life in detail and apply them to your own life. (Chapter 2)

_____

Explain in detail your understanding of the U-curve (or U-bend) of happiness, considering how it applies to your life, both now and in the future. (Chapter 2)

_____

Plot your own life on the ME Entrepreneurial Life Stages chart, noting your child-raising years, their high-activity years, the recessions you've experienced, etc. Identify both known and potential regrets and alibis that may stem from these phases, as well as potential future regrets based on nonnegotiables you haven't set yet. (Chapter 2)

_____

Set goals and nonnegotiables around your physical and mental health for the next twelve months and also for the foreseeable future. (Chapter 2)

_____

Describe in detail the two phases of the ME Life Stages in this chapter as they apply to you, during your thirty-five to fifty-one and fifty-one to sixty-eight age ranges. Also capture your own thoughts on a potential or actual midlife crisis and the changes you anticipate making or have already made. (Chapter 2)

_____

Discuss your current Core Purpose—Why do you matter as an entrepreneur, and how has this changed (or will this change) across your various entrepreneurial life stages? (Chapter 3)

    _____

Identify the four stages of exit for an entrepreneur. Discuss in detail any experiences in your own career with these stages and your lessons learned. What advice would you give other entrepreneurs? (Chapter 3)

    _____

As part of your checkout, discuss the results of the (minimum three) assessments you have taken during your career. Combine your explanations with an update to the Self-Awareness Decision Tool if you have recently taken new assessments. (Chapter 3)

    _____

Write down the advice you would give a decade-younger version of yourself or an entrepreneurial audience. Explain in detail how the advice applies to you today—in the form of a start, stop, and keep-doing list. (Chapter 3)

    _____

Identify and explain which role(s) you would consider for your future. Which roles would you rule out? (Chapter 3)

    _____

Finalize your customized version of the Entrepreneurial Life Stages chart, writing down lessons learned and plans developed for your future. (Chapter 3)

    _____

Discuss why you were born. What does this tell you about your personal "What's Next?!" (Chapter 3)

    _____

Answer the five ME prep questions in the bullets below:

- Do you want to be in (majority) control, or are you willing to give up control and remain a minority owner?

  _____

- Do you want to build businesses for just yourself, and/or build to support or create for other entrepreneurial CEOs?

  _____

- Day to day, do you want to play an active role, or are you okay with a passive role?

  _____

- Do you want to increase the blend of your life and business at this point in your career, or are you okay with the blend you have now—which may be tilted toward business?

  _____

- Is remaining visible and "relevant" important to you?

  _____

(Chapter 4)   _____

Grade your organization on the due diligence checklist, 1–10, with 1 not prepared at all, and 10 being fully prepared. What are your next steps, if any, after thinking about your current status? (Chapter 4)   _____

Explain the different ME roles you can play in a postexit future and identify your preliminary role choice moving forward, taking into account your vision of what constitutes a perfect day. (Chapter 4)   _____

What are your unique and exceptional strengths and abilities, and what are your areas of genius? (Chapter 4)

_____

Describe your current thinking and planning around your own version of 5 + 5 = 10. When do you think each part of the equation will occur in your career, taking into account the content of *The Fourth Decision* thus far? (Chapter 4)

_____

What is your current Core Purpose? If this chapter has changed or revealed your new Core Purpose, explain the change. Given that, what might be your future Core Purpose at the end of your ME transition phase? (Chapter 4)

_____

Describe in detail what you could learn as an intrapreneur, if you had the right "learning mindset" in place. (Chapter 4)

_____

Discuss the three cardinal rules for MEs:

- Don't assume that your employees know what to do just because you hired them and gave them freedom to do their job.
- Don't give your employees complete freedom to do their jobs without setting goals for them and making it clear what you expect them to do (job description, goals, metrics, etc.).
- Don't assume your employees are qualified just because you trained them and gave them a job description with metrics. Hold them accountable for being qualified. Training without including some Navy-style qualification strategies just adds to the risk in the organization and, as we will discuss in future chapters, there is a lot to be said about *controlled risk* versus *pure risk*. (Chapter 5)

_____

Complete the Self-Awareness Decision Tool and explain all of your answers in detail. (Chapter 5) _____

Explain in detail the difference between an entrepreneur who is Bor-E-Gaged and a *maximized* entrepreneur who is Qual-E-Gaged. How are they the same? How are they different? (Chapter 5) _____

Develop the CEO Qual Card for your organization(s). (Chapter 5) _____

Develop a general Leadership Development Qual Card for your organization. (Chapter 5) _____

Develop a specific Leadership Development Qual Card for a hire you intend to make. (Chapter 5) _____

Develop the Senior Leader (outside hire) Qual Card for your organization. (Chapter 5) _____

The ME commits to a baselining approach—the Truth and Trends—to all aspects of his or her business, ensuring that all company metrics/data/KPIs for the past five years are measured as a baseline and compared with both a current budget target and a strategic target three years out. (Chapter 6) _____

The ME commits to becoming a fully productive organization utilizing the Audit-Ready Decision Tool independently or alongside other operating and leadership systems currently in use. (Chapter 6) _____

The ME completes the Audit-Ready Decision Tool on a quarterly basis, filling in the audit-ready numbers for each of the blocks of the Productive Growth Pyramid. Using the baseline data gathered, the ME uses the Audit-Ready Decision Tool to set specific targets and establish action steps needed for improvement in all blocks shown in the model. (Chapter 6) _____

The ME completes the Vision and Execution
Checklist in parallel with the Audit-Ready Decision
Tool, setting specific targets for improvement for
the next quarter. (Chapter 6)   _____

The ME develops a customized qual card for the
organization, building the Productive and Busy
Growth Pyramids into the current operating system
to verify alignment with leadership on the overall
company business model. (Chapter 6)   _____

The ME commits to the philosophy of the
"ands," and to consistently improving his or her
self-awareness through the philosophy of *know
thyself, improve thyself, and complement thyself*,
as discussed earlier in this book. (Chapter 6)

Describe in detail the three main business growth
models introduced in this chapter, along with the
fourth, which helps identify where even installing
the right model can fall short. (Chapter 7)   _____

Identify which model most resembles your
company's current approach to strategy. Identify
"What's Next?!" (Chapter 7)   _____

With an audit-ready mindset and methodology,
identify the ways in which your current model sets
your organization up for falling short of reaching
full potential. Identify "What's Next?!" (Chapter 7)

Commit to the Full Potential Growth Model and
work the action steps necessary to transition to
this model. Develop the ongoing execution plan
that is consistent with the Audit-Ready Decision
Tool (and your quarterly rhythm) to update
progress. (Chapter 7)   _____

Develop a customized qual card for your organization to qualify leaders on the Revenue Lever Strategy Tool to increase the number of leaders capable of setting strategy within the organization. (Chapter 8)

_____

Identify all of the revenue levers for your organization(s), categorizing them in ways that make sense for careful apples-to-apples analysis and comparison. (Chapter 8)

_____

Utilizing the Truth and Trends Tool, baseline your data/metrics for all revenue levers. (Chapter 8)

_____

Conduct the exercise using the Revenue Lever Strategy Tool on each category of customer, and then each customer, asking "Where should we be in three years?" (Chapter 8)

_____

Discuss in detail how you set your Three-Year Strategic Rocks utilizing the Revenue Lever Strategy Tool. (Chapter 8)

Describe the SC, MSC, and Revised MSC Models in detail. (Chapter 9)

_____

Describe the N-MSC-T Model in detail. (Chapter 9)

Describe the changes necessary to move the organization from the SC, MSC, and Revised MSC Model to the N-MSC-T Model. (Chapter 9)

_____

Implement the meeting routine to decide when changes will be reviewed with the N-MSC-T Model. (Chapter 9)

_____

Explain how you will accomplish the following:
You will learn to just say no—in your business and in your life! (Chapter 9)

_____

Explain how you will accomplish the following:
You will position yourself to truly being present when you are present—in your business and in your life! (Chapter 9)

_____

Fill out the N-MSC-T Model for your business life and review it with your coach, peer, etc. (Chapter 9)

_____

Fill out the N-MSC-T Model for your personal life and review it with your coach, peer, perhaps your family as well! (Chapter 9)

_____

Discuss in detail the purpose of crossing the Diamond Bridge to your customer's Productive Growth Pyramid. Ask yourself "What's Next?!" to move your customer relationships toward higher-level win/win relationships (Vendor, Partner, and Strategic Partner). (Chapter 10)

_____

Segment your customers into Vendor, Partner, and Strategic Partner relationships. (Chapter 10)

_____

Complete a SWOTT analysis (explain your strengths, weaknesses, opportunities, threats and trends) with regard to each current customer, focusing on conversations, connections, capabilities, and capacity. Start with Strategic Partner first, then Partner, then Vendor. (Chapter 10)

_____

Discuss in detail your Defendable Differentiators. (Chapter 10)

_____

Explain where your organization is set up for potential failure because of its lack of differentiation. (Chapter 10)

_____

Discuss in detail the Diamond Review System and the use of "What's Next?!" to implement the Diamond Full Potential Tool in your organization. Define Diamond Value Potential, the Diamond Gap, the annual AE forecast, and the Ninety-Day Diamond Forecast. (Chapter 10)

_____

Develop a Diamond Review Process for your organization, to include the steps necessary to forecast company annual Diamond potential, and Ninety-Day Forecasts for individual AEs and the company. (Chapter 10)

_____

Develop a Diamond plan for new salespeople (AEs). (Chapter 10)

_____

Complete the ME Bridge exercise and determine (1) in which tools you desire to be qualified, (2) in which tools you are already qualified at an audit-ready level, and (3) the career time frame in which you intend to get qualified. (Chapter 11)

_____

Complete the Nonnegotiables Decision Tool exercise, including both parts of the Warren Buffett question, the start/stop/keep "What would your decade-older self advise?" question, and the question "What does success look like three years from now?" Repeat on an annual basis, or sooner if there are significant changes in your business and life. (Chapter 11)

_____

Complete the Intentional Entrepreneur Checklist. Repeat on an annual basis, or sooner if significant changes occur in your business and life. (Chapter 11)

_____

Decide on your blended nonnegotiables and reconsider them on an annual basis, or sooner if significant change dictates. (Chapter 11)

_____

Determine what your *reset* button looks like, identifying the specific changes you will make to ensure you savor the ME journey that you have mapped out. Reconsider on an annual basis, or sooner if significant change dictates. (Chapter 11)

_____

About the Decision Center

From founder to CEO, most successful entrepreneurial business leaders have journeyed alone. Upon reaching a career crossroads of some sort, they may find themselves at a point where it's no longer clear what to do next. They realize they can't go on without help.

Leading with ego got them where they are. But the challenges of leadership can't be solved the same way. At this critical decision point, these entrepreneurs must choose one of three paths: (1) continue as a "serial" entrepreneur, walking away to create additional ventures; (2) remain in the key leadership role of their organization; or (3) transition into a supporting role and appoint someone to lead in their stead.

Our Common Challenge

Because we are entrepreneurs ourselves, we understand that knowing which path to take requires a healthy dose of objectivity and self-awareness and, importantly, thoughtful pause. This is often a major shift in thinking for growth-focused entrepreneurs who are used to measuring success through forward momentum. They must set ego aside and slow down—acknowledging their shortcomings and giving total trust to their teams. Only then can they activate their fullest potential—and make the transformation from entrepreneur to *entrepreneurial leader*. And saying *yes* to every idea is entrepreneurial; saying *no* is transformational.

This mindset shift is massive but critical to long-term success—personally, professionally, and for the whole organization.

This shift, this tipping point, is what we call the Leadership Decision. At the Decision Center, we help our clients make better-calculated decisions faster and with more confidence to unlock and *maximize* their inner entrepreneurial leader. We get the entrepreneur right … first … throughout every stage of their entrepreneurial career.

Our Common Enemy

The single most powerful negative force preventing our target audiences' needs from being met—their entrepreneurial *ego*.

The Decision Center's Unique Value Proposition

Other groups, consultants, and methodologies teach you how to do your job. Our methods empower you to decide *what kind of entrepreneur you want to be.*

We apply brutal honesty, accountability, and a unique qualification process that challenges clients at every step to balance data with intuition, empowering them to answer the question "What's next?!" This common sense process allows them to transform as individuals, qualify their teams, and scale leadership across the organization.

Our "Elevator Pitch"

The Decision Center is a robust resource hub and physical learning center.

It's for entrepreneurs, leaders, and emerging leaders (e.g., teams) who embrace accountability, discipline, and qualification.

We teach you to rethink delegation—through verification and qualification.

We stand ready to help entrepreneurs, intrapreneurs, and those who think like them—anyone who needs an objective framework with which to facilitate honest self-development and productive decision-making. We're here for those who wish to grow themselves, empower their team, and scale their organization for reaching full potential while also finding their ideal blend of work and life. Our sights are set on people who seek vision and a perspective with which to develop a structure for making better-calculated decisions faster.

> We teach you to rethink delegation—through verification and qualification.

The simplest, most powerful idea that we want people to associate with our brand—what we are really selling—is **clarity.**

Through our **Clarity Leadership Decision System** (CLDS), we help people objectively choose the best path forward—using a variety of proprietary tools that can be used as standalones or, if desired, paired with existing strategic management systems. The following values and associated beliefs serve as guidelines for setting our team's shared expectations and holding others accountable to these purposes.

Core Values and Beliefs

Be passionate about growth—we love to find entrepreneurial leaders who embrace coaching and learning and empower them to grow.

Keep a whiteboard mentality—always two steps ahead, helping challenge clients to think, *What's before that?!* and *What's next?!*

Lead with "and"—take a hands-on, in-the-ring approach. Help clients both envision Mt. Everest *and* develop the detailed summit plan.

Challenge respectfully—we first listen to understand. Then we ask the right questions to guide a client toward deeper thought, reflection, and decision, in every meeting.

Maximize objective creativity—combine data and intuition to make Diamond Level decisions.

Grow self-awareness, always—know and accept thyself. Improve thyself. Accept and qualify others. Complement thyself. None of this can be done without facing the brutal truth, whatever it may be.

Always be qualifying—we work on doubling our personal capacity every two to three years as well as passionately pursuing the Five Challenges of the Decision Series on a daily basis.

ACKNOWLEDGMENTS

My family—Thank you for sharing your lives with Kristi and me ... we love our time together and fully realize that time can fly by very quickly, as we watch our grandkids get older and taller and Papa Ry gets older and smaller!

Avery—Thanks for continuing to inspire me to "make today, and every day, a good day."

My friends—Thanks for the laughter and the true friendship ... I love our time together as well, especially on the golf course!

Bill Buxton and Vistage 488—Thanks for making me a better leader and person; I would not be where I am today without your guidance, coaching, and tough love. You are inspiring leaders ... I learn from you every meeting.

EO (Entrepreneurs Organization) Entourage Forum—Thanks for your continued friendship, support, entrepreneurial brilliance and creativity, and for your direct and candid feedback—always.

EO Raleigh-Durham—Thanks for the opportunity for me to pay it forward to the next generation of entrepreneurs ... keep creating and building the great companies of tomorrow!

Bunker Labs—Thanks to Dean Bundschu, Todd Connor, and Nick Bradfield for your amazing support of the military entrepreneur, a group near and dear to my heart.

Lori Simnor—Thanks for your amazing financial support and friendship over the past three decades!

Jackie Prillaman—Thanks for your career-long accounting support throughout all the growth challenges our businesses have gone through.

Tom Nelson/Hodgson Russ—Thanks for all the spot-on legal support through the years, especially as the number and complexity of my businesses grew.

Rajan Bagga and Ajay Anand—Thanks for your invaluable marketing creativity and genius—I cannot say enough about your support in the development of my tools in *The Fourth Decision* that will now be shared with the entrepreneurial and leadership worlds.

Mikki Williams—Thanks for teaching me how to speak professionally … you continue to inspire me every time I get on a stage.

Miami University NROTC and Lou Pollock—I would not be where I am in my life without you, period.

Verne Harnish, Dan Sullivan, and Jim Collins—I learned from the very best and am now doing my best to pay my lessons learned forward to the next generation of entrepreneurial leaders everywhere … thank you for teaching and inspiring me. Looking forward to collaborating in the future!